INTRODUCTION TO BELGIAN LABOUR LAW

INTRODUCTION TO BELGIAN LABOUR LAW

P. Humblet
M. Rigaux

intersentia
Cambridge – Antwerp – Portland

Intersentia Ltd
Sheraton House | Castle Park
Cambridge | CB3 0AX | United Kingdom
Tel.: +44 1223 370 170 | Fax: +44 1223 370 169
Email: mail@intersentia.co.uk
www.intersentia.com | www.intersentia.co.uk

Distribution for the UK and Ireland:
NBN International
Airport Business Centre, 10 Thornbury Road
Plymouth, PL6 7PP
United Kingdom
Tel: +44 1752 202 301 | Fax: +44 1752 202 331
Email: orders@nbninternational.com

Distribution for Europe and all other countries:
Intersentia Publishing nv
Groenstraat 31
2640 Mortsel
Belgium
Tel.: +32 3 680 15 50 | Fax: +32 3 658 71 21
Email: mail@intersentia.be

Distribution for the USA and Canada:
International Specialized Book Services
920 NE 58th Ave Suite 300
Portland, OR 97213
USA
Tel.: +1 800 944 6190 (toll free) | Fax: +1 503 280 8832
Email: info@isbs.com

ISBN 978-1-78068-409-3
D/2016/7849/124
NUR 825

British Library Cataloguing in Publication Data. A catalogue record for this book is available from the British Library.

PREFACE

This book gives an overall picture of the principles of Belgian labour law, i.e. employment law as well as industrial relations law. It is intended for all those who want to get acquainted with Belgian labour law: foreign law firms, entrepreneurs who want to invest in Belgium, etc. That is the reason why this book focuses on topics that are relevant in practice.

Foreign readers who are interested in specific aspects we refer to the footnotes and to the concise bibliography at the end of this book; they may also contact us by email: patrick.humblet@ugent.be.

Belgian case law and doctrine are mainly published in Dutch and French. The odds are that the reader is not fluent in the first of these languages. Therefore we chose to limit the bibliographical material to the sources written in French.

Finally, the authors wish to express their gratitude to Elizabeth MacDonald, Sofie Moentjens and (especially) Erika Peeters for the translation.

Patrick HUMBLET
Ghent University

Marc RIGAUX
University of Antwerp

CONTENTS

LIST OF ABBREVIATIONS

(including Dutch, French and English where applicable)

ABVV	Algemeen Belgisch Vakverbond	FGTB	Fédération Générale du Travail de Belgique		Belgian General Federation of Labour (social democratic)
ACLVB	Algemene Centrale der liberale vakbonden	CGSLB	Centrale Générale des Syndicats Libéraux de Belgique		Federation of Liberal Trade Unions
ACOD	Algemene Centrale der Openbare Diensten	CGSP	Centrale Générale des Services Publics		General Public Sector Union (social democratic)
ACV	Algemeen Christelijk Vakverbond	CSC	Confédération des Syndicats Chrétiens		Confederation of Christian Trade Unions
		ADIC	Assocation chrétienne des dirigeants et cadres		
ARAB	Algemeen reglement voor de arbeidsbescherming	RGPT	Règlement général pour la protection du travail		General rules on employment safety
Arbeidsrechtbank		Tribunal du travail			Labour Court
BGESR	Brusselse Gewestelijke en Sociale Raad	CBRS	Conseil Bruxellois Régional et Social		Brussels Regional and Social Council
BS	Belgisch Staatsblad	MB	Moniteur belge		Belgian Official Journal
		Bull.	Bulletin des arrêts de la Cour de Cassation		
Cass.	Hof van Cassatie		Cour de cassation		Court of Cassation
				CEEP	European Centre of Employers and Enterprises providing Public Services
		CESRW	Conseil Economique et Social de la Région Wallonne		Walloon Economic and Social Council

CPBW	Comité voor Preventie en Bescherming op het werk	CPPT	Comité pour la prévention et la protection au travail	Health and Safety Committee	
CRB	Centrale Raad voor het Bedrijfsleven	CCE	Conseil Central de l'Economie	National Economic Council	
ESH	Europees Sociaal Handvest	CSE	Charte sociale européenne	ESC	European Social Charter
Hoge Raad voor Preventie en Bescherming op het Werk		Conseil supérieur pour la prévention et la protection au travail		High Council for Workplace Safety	
				ICFTU	International Confederation of Free Trade Unions
		JT	Journal des tribunaux		
		JTT	Journal des tribunaux du travail		
NAR	Nationale Arbeids-raad	CNT	Conseil National du Travail	National Labour Council	
NCK	Nationale Confe-deratie van het Kaderpersoneel	CNC	Confédération Nationale des Cadres	National Confederation of Managers	
OR	Ondernemingsraad	CE	Conseil d'Entreprise	Works Council	
		Ors.	Orientations		
		Pas.	Pasicrisie belge		
Parl.St.	Parlementaire stukken	Doc. Parl.	Documents parlementaires	Parliamentary Proceedings	
Pb.	Publicatieblad	JO	Journal Officiel	OJ	Official Journal
PBO	Publiekrechtelijke bedrijfsorganisatie		Organisation de l'économie en droit public	Public law industrial regula-tory body	
R.A.C.E.	Arresten van de Raad van State	Recueil des arrêts du Conseil d'Etat		Decisions of the Council of State	
		RCJB	Revue critique de jurisprudence belge		
		Rev.Dr.Ulg.	Revue de la Faculté de droit de Liège		
		Rev.Trav.	Revue du travail		
		RGAR	Revue générale des assurances et des responsabili-tés		

RSVZ	Rijksinstituut voor de Sociale Verzekeringen der Zelfstandigen	INASTI	Institut national d'assurances sociales pour travailleurs indépendants		National Institute for the Social Security of the Self-Employed
RSZ	Rijksdienst voor Sociale Zekerheid	ONSS	Office National de Sécurité Sociale		National Office for Social Security
SERV	Sociaal Economische Raad voor Vlaanderen				Flanders' Social and Economic Council
Soc. Kron.	Sociaalrechtelijke Kronieken	Chron. D.S.	Chroniques de droit social		
TSR	Tijdschrift voor Sociaal Recht	Revue de Droit Social			
		UCM	Union des classes moyennes		
				UEAPME	European Association of Craft, Small and Medium-sized Enterprises
				UNICE	Union of Industrial and Employers' Confederations of Europe
UNIZO	Unie van Zelfstandige Ondernemers				
		UWE	Union Wallonne des Entreprises		Walloon Business Federation
VA	Vakbonds-afvaardiging	DS	Délégation Syndicale		Union delegation
VBO	Verbond van Belgische Ondernemingen	FEB	Fédération des entreprises de Belgique		Belgian Federation of Enterprises
VESOC	Vlaams Economisch en Sociaal Overlegcomité				Flanders' Economic and Social Consultative Committee
VOKA	Vlaams netwerk van ondernemingen				
VSOA	Vrij Syndicaat Openbaar Ambt	SLFP	Syndicat Libre de la Fonction Publique		Public Sector Workers' Union

PART I
EMPLOYMENT LAW

I

THE CONTRACT OF EMPLOYMENT[1]

CHAPTER 1

DEFINING THE CONTRACT OF EMPLOYMENT

The contract of employment is an agreement in which an employee undertakes to work for wages under the authority of an employer.

The Employment Contract Act[2] regulates the employment contracts for blue-collar workers, white-collar workers, sales representatives, servants, students and home workers.[3] It also applies to workers employed by the government insofar as their position is not laid down by specific legislation.

1 Vannes, V., *Le contrat de travail : aspects théoriques et pratiques*, Brussels, Bruylant, 2011, 1252 p.; Jamoulle, M., *Le contrat de travail*, I, Liège, Law Faculty, 1982, 419 pp. and II, 1986, 545 pp.

2 Law of 3 July 1978 regarding contracts of employment, *BS/MB* 22 August 1978, hereinafter referred to as Employment Contract Act.

3 Article 1 Employment Contract Act.

CHAPTER 2
SUBORDINATION[4]

SECTION 1. MEANING

A prerequisite for the existence of an employment contract is an employee carrying out work for remuneration under someone's authority, i.e. in subordination: the employer has the right to give orders and the employee has to obey. The way in which the authority is expressed and/or the extent to which it is used is of less importance for the existence of an employment contract. It suffices that the employer has the right to exert authority in order to decide that there is indeed a contract of employment. It is precisely this power relationship that distinguishes work carried out within the framework of an employment contract and work done outside such a framework. The two other elements – work and wages – are also present in the case of self-employed activities. Here, too, we are dealing with work that is remunerated in some way. So it is the relationship of subordination that determines the scope of employment contract law. However, to a large extent this criterion is also the basis for the applicable social security scheme. Article 1 of the Social Security Act[5] stipulates that this law applies to employees and employers bound by an employment contract. Accordingly, through the reference to the employment contract the relationship of subordination is also used for the application of the social security legislation for employees. On the other hand, the existence of an employment contract rules out the application of the social security legislation for self-employed persons and this as a result of the fact that pursuant to the legislation regarding the social status for self-employed persons this system only applies 'in the absence of an employment contract'. In principle, this means that the employment status determines the social security status and not *vice versa*. Only if the social security qualification deviates explicitly from the qualification under labour law, will this qualification take precedence. However, in that case it remains limited to the application of the social security regulations.

---

4 Vannes, V. (ed.), *Le lien de subordination dans le contrat de travail*, Brussels, Bruylant, 2005, 216 p.; Jamoulle, M., 'La notion de subordination', in *Seize leçons sur le droit du travail*, Liège, Collection Scientifique de la Faculté de Droit de Liège, 1994, pp. 109–136.

5 Law of 27 June 1969 providing for a review of the Decree-law of 28 December 1944 concerning the social security of workers.

SECTION 2. EVIDENCE

The person invoking the existence of a relationship of subordination must produce proof of this. However, the legislator created presumptions as a result of which the burden of proof is reversed, e.g. for the benefit of sales representatives and students. They are considered to be bound to an employer by means of an employment contract unless the opposite is proven.

A rebuttable presumption was introduced for the benefit of pharmacists by Article 3*quater* of the Employment Contract Act. Pharmacists employed in a pharmacy accessible to the public are presumed to be bound by an employment contract for white-collar workers to the natural or legal person, owner or tenant of the pharmacy.

Article 5*bis* of the Employment Contract Act establishes an irrefutable presumption as a result of which additional activities carried out in the implementation of a contracting agreement are considered to be carried out on the basis of an employment contract when the person performing these services and the person for whom he/she performs them are bound by an employment contract for the performance of similar activities.

SECTION 3. ELEMENTS OF ASSESSMENT

Until the ruling by the Court of Cassation of 23 December 2002[6] judges mainly used the 'method of indicia'. When judging a conflict concerning the existence or non-existence of a subordinate relation they went looking for elements that were considered typical of working within the framework of a contract of employment. For instance, the duty of the person concerned to report his/her absence and/or the fact that the working hours were set by the one commissioning the job rather pointed to subordination.

However, it is not uncommon that parties agree to have work done by means of a contracting agreement (i.e. without any mentioning of authority) and that this qualification is contested later.

The Employment Relations Act of 27 December 2006[7] – which took effect on 1 January 2007 – tries to refine and clarify the notion of authority on the basis of general and, if need be, specific criteria.

---

6 *JTT* 2003, 271.

7 Title XIII Programme Law of 27 December 2006, *BS/MB* 28 December 2006, hereinafter called Employment Relations Act.

SECTION 4. OTHER SIMILAR AGREEMENTS

One can make one's labour available without concluding an employment contract. Mandates, partnership agreements and contracting are examples of this. In all of these cases the worker is not subjected to the authority of a third party although he/she will have to follow certain guidelines when carrying out his/her activities.

A person can also work under authority without receiving any remuneration. Since 2005 these 'volunteers' have been protected.[8] The arrangement includes, *inter alia*, provisions with regard to liability, insurance and the (fixed) allowance for expenses.

SECTION 5. FALSE SELF-EMPLOYMENT[9]

Persons who in theory only have the self-employed status, either chosen or obtained, whereas the reality of their employment situation shows that they carry out work for an employer in the same way as employees, are referred to as 'false self-employed persons' in the literature. Feigning self-employment is almost always linked to motives of a financial and economic nature. If the court finds that the qualification of collaboration on a self-employed basis is wrong, it will re-qualify the agreement as an employment contract. This kind of new qualification has significant financial consequences for the employer because he will have to pay overdue social security contributions with retroactive effect (although within the limitation period of three years). Apart from this the supplier who has been re-qualified as 'employee' can claim the benefits established by the mandatory provisions of the Employment Contract Act, for instance claiming – also within the limits of the limitation period – overdue wages, holiday allowances, end-of-year bonuses and, if need be, compensation in lieu of notice.

§ 1. THE EMPLOYMENT RELATIONS ACT[10]

Although in the past a lot of initiatives had already been taken to fight false self-employment we had to wait until 2007 for a law tackling this issue: the Employment Relations Act.

---

8 Law of 3 July 2005 regarding the rights of volunteers, *BS/MB* 29 August 2005.

9 G. Willems, *La fausse indépendance*, Waterloo, Kluwer, 2009, 138 pp.

10 P. Verdonck (ed.), *La nouvelle loi sur les relations de travail*, Louvain-la-Neuve, Anthemis, 2007, 171 pp.

A. Principles

As long as public policy (*ordre public*), public decency and mandatory laws are not breached parties are free to choose the nature of their employment relationship, provided that the effective implementation of the agreement corresponds to the nature of their employment relationship. Precedence must be given to the qualification as demonstrated by the actual performance if this excludes the legal qualification chosen by the parties.

If the practice of the employment relationship has sufficient elements which, assessed in accordance with the provisions of this law and its implementing orders, are incompatible with the qualification the parties accorded to their employment relation, a re-qualification will take place and the corresponding system of social security will be applied. The elements referred to will be assessed on the basis of general and, possibly, specific criteria. The general criteria are laid down in the law itself whereas the specific criteria are laid down by Royal Decree after an advisory procedure in which the social partners play a major role.

The general criteria allowing assessment of the existence or the absence of authority are:

- the will of the parties;
- freedom to organise the working time;
- freedom to organise the work; and
- the possibility to exert hierarchical control.

Obligations which are inherent to the pursuance of one's profession and which are imposed by or by virtue of a law are not taken into consideration to assess the nature of an employment relationship.

On their own, the following elements are not sufficient to qualify the employment relationship adequately:

- title of the agreement;
- registration with a social security agency;
- registration with the Crossroad Bank for Social Security (a central database registering all enterprises);
- registration with the VAT administration; and
- the manner in which the earnings are reported to the fiscal administration.

The fact that these elements by themselves are not decisive for the qualification of the employment relationship does not mean that in combination with other elements they can be an indication of the will of the parties. This has been explicitly confirmed in the relevant case law.

After an advisory procedure the Crown can make a list of specific criteria typical of a sector, one or more occupations or one or more categories of occupations.

This list with specific criteria can include the following elements of a socio-economic and legal nature:

- responsibility for, and power of, decision-making regarding the financial means to keep the enterprise profitable;
- fixed and/or guaranteed remuneration;
- personal and substantial investment in the enterprise with private means and personal and substantial participation in the losses and profits of the enterprise;
- the possibility to hire personnel or arrange replacements;
- manifesting oneself as an enterprise *vis-à-vis* the co-contractor or third parties;
- working in privately owned spaces and/or with privately owned equipment.

This list is by no means exhaustive, nor is it binding for establishing specific criteria.

B. The Administrative Committee responsible for the regulation of the employment relationship

In the context of this law an 'Administrative Committee responsible for the regulation of the employment relationship' has been set up.

The chambers of this committee have the duty to take decisions on the qualification of a specific labour relationship (the so-called social ruling) and this is part of the pursuit of more legal certainty. The intention is to prevent disputes by laying down the investigation of power relations – which allegedly takes place 'afterwards' in legal proceedings – in an administrative procedure which takes place in advance. The decisions are binding on the institutions represented in the administrative chamber, i.e. the National Office for Social Security (RSZ/ONSS) and the National Institute for the Social Security of the Self-employed (RSVZ/INASTI). The parties of the employment relationship can lodge an appeal against these decisions with the labour courts by registered letter within the month following the notification of these decisions.

C. Rebuttable presumption of an employment contract

For the building industry, security firms and the sector of goods and persons transport nine criteria have been listed. If the analysis of the employment relationship shows that more than half of these criteria are met, there is a rebuttable presumption of an employment contract.

CHAPTER 3
A WRITTEN DOCUMENT

An employment contract is a consensual agreement which can be concluded orally and for which no written proof is required. However, in some cases the law requires that prior to recruitment a document is made up. Sometimes this requirement refers to the whole of the agreement. Written documents are necessary for: employment contracts for a fixed period or for a specified task,[11] part-time employment contracts,[12] replacement contracts,[13] employment contracts for home workers,[14] employment contracts for students,[15] employment contracts for temporary work and temporary agency work,[16] and employment contracts for tele-work.[17] The law also requires certain stipulations of the contract to be laid down in writing: the competition clause and the Delcredere clause for sales representatives. These clauses do not necessarily need to be written down at the time of recruitment.[18]

---

[11] Article 9 Employment Contract Act.

[12] Article 11*bis* Employment Contract Act.

[13] Article 11*ter* Employment Contract Act.

[14] Article 119.4 Employment Contract Act.

[15] Article 123 Employment Contract Act.

[16] Articles 4 and 8 Employment Agency Act.

[17] Article 4 Collective Agreement no. 85 concluded in the National Labour Council of 9 November 2005.

[18] Articles 65, 86, 104 and 107 Employment Contract Act.

II

CONCLUDING THE CONTRACT

CHAPTER 1

RECRUITMENT

Recruitment is free. The employer's freedom of recruitment stems from the freedom of enterprise which is legitimised by the private ownership of the means of production. However, the freedom of recruitment is not absolute. It is subject to general rules of law and to specific regulations.

SECTION 1. OBLIGATION TO RECRUIT CERTAIN CATEGORIES OF WORKERS

As a result of their weak(er) position in the labour market it is hard for certain workers to enter employment on their own. This is mainly the case for people with a physical or economic handicap. In order to prevent these categories of workers from being excluded the legislator has issued a number of measures to promote or to impose recruitment of these persons.

For instance, private sector employers employing over 50 employees must recruit workers pro rata of 3% of their personnel. Moreover, all employers in the private sector together and, this irrespective of their number of employees, must recruit new employees pro rata of 1% of the total personnel. The type of persons eligible for these extra jobs may vary. At present they are jobseekers under the age of 26. In the past persons from other age categories also qualified. Apart from this, labour law contains a few other situations in which employers are obliged to recruit.

SECTION 2. PROHIBITION OF DISCRIMINATION

§ 1. THIRTY YEARS OF DISCRIMINATION LEGISLATION

The first prohibition of discrimination in the national legislation referred to discrimination on the basis of sex.

Equal treatment of men and women is a fundamental right which had already been formulated in Article 119 EC Treaty (now 157) in the form of the obligation to remunerate men and women equally for equal work. The ban on sex discrimination was further elaborated in various Directives. The principles in question were transposed into Belgian law in the Law of 4 August 1978, which was amended by the Law of 7 May 1999[19] (the Equal Treatment Men and Women Act).

Later on discrimination of (potential) employees was also prohibited on the grounds of race,[20] age[21] as well as because of them working part-time[22] or with a fixed-term employment contract.[23] By means of Article 2*bis* Collective Agreement No. 38[24] it was forbidden for an employer to make a distinction between applicants on the basis of a whole series of reasons, such as past illnesses.

By the Anti-Discrimination Act of 25 February 2003,[25] Directive 2000/43/EC of 29 June 2000 and Directive 2000/78/EC of 27 November 2000 were implemented.

In October 2004 the Constitutional Court[26] repealed part of the Anti-Discrimination Act because its provisions were not in keeping with the constitutional principle of equality.

§ 2. THE NEW ANTI-DISCRIMINATION LEGISLATION

In the course of 2005–2006 the legislation was revised and replaced by three laws, each regulating one aspect:

- the law combating specific forms of discrimination: prohibition of discrimination on grounds of age,[27] sexual orientation, civil status, birth,

---

19 *BS/MB* 19 June 1999.

20 Law of 12 April 1994, *BS/MB* 14 May 1994.

21 Articles 2 through 11 Law of 13 February 1998, *BS/MB* 9 February 1998. Note that only discrimination regarding recruitment was prohibited.

22 Law of 5 March 2002, *BS/MB* 13 March 2002. This law is an implementation of Directive 97/81/EC.

23 Law of 5 June 2002, *BS/MB* 26 June 2002. This law is an implementation of Directive 1999/70/EC.

24 Collective Agreement of 6 December 1983 regarding recruitment and selection of employees.

25 Law of 25 February 2003 to combat discrimination and to amend the Law of 15 February 1993 with a view to establishing an Interfederal Centre for Equal Opportunities, *BS/MB* 17 March 2003, err. *BS/MB*13 May 2003.

26 Constitutional Court 6 October 2004, No. 157/2004.

27 Law of 10 May 2007 combating specific forms of discrimination, *BS/MB* 30 May 2007.

wealth, religious or other beliefs, present or future state of health, disability, physical or genetic feature or social origin;
- the law combating discrimination between men and women;[28]
- the law punishing certain acts inspired by racism and xenophobia;[29] prohibition of discrimination on grounds of nationality, so-called race, descent, national or ethnic origin.

A common feature of the new legislation is that, as a rule, direct and/or indirect distinction and direct and/or indirect discrimination are prohibited as well as orders to discriminate and intimidate:

- *direct distinction*: when a person is treated less favourably than another in a comparable situation on the basis of one of the protected criteria;
- *indirect distinction*: when an apparently neutral provision, criterion or manner of conduct may put persons to whom a protected criterion applies, at a disadvantage compared to other persons;
- *direct discrimination*: direct distinction on the basis of a protected criterion which cannot be justified;
- *indirect discrimination*: indirect distinction on the basis of a protected criterion which cannot be justified.

A direct/indirect distinction on the basis of a protected criterion amounts to direct/indirect discrimination unless the distinction is justified by a legitimate aim and the means for achieving that aim are appropriate and necessary. As far as sex discrimination is concerned, direct discrimination is not allowed unless the distinction is based on an essential and determining occupational requirement. In that case the exception must be included in a Royal Decree.

Affirmative action is not considered as discrimination.

Making reasonable adaptations with a view to the employment of disabled persons is not considered discriminatory either. On the contrary, the employer is even obliged to do this unless it is impossible.

The legislation provides for civil and criminal sanctions. However, in labour relations the focus is on civil sanctions.

When the victim of alleged discrimination, the Interfederal Centre for Equal Opportunities (UNIA), the Institute for Equality of Men and Women (in the event of sex discrimination) or another organised interest group puts forward facts leading to a presumption of discrimination, the burden of proof that there is no discrimination lies with the defendant. The proof may be given, *inter alia*, by

28 Law of 10 May 2007 combating the discrimination between men and women, *BS/MB* 30 May 2007.

29 Added to the Law of 10 May 2007, *BS/MB* 30 May 2007.

means of statistic facts or a practical test carried out by a bailiff. The terms must be established by the Crown.

The Anti-Discrimination Act provides for a prohibitory injunction, as a result of which the alleged victim can address the president of the competent court with the request to order cessation of the discriminatory practice under forfeiture of a penalty. An employee who has filed a complaint or has taken legal action is protected by the law against dismissal and against a unilateral change of the employment conditions for 12 months after the complaint has been filed or – in the event of a legal action – for three months after the final judgment.

§ 3. RECENT DEVELOPMENTS

The issue of discrimination keeps evolving. Some examples to illustrate this.

In a ruling of 2 April 2009[30] the Constitutional Court nullified a number of Articles of the Law of 10 May 2007 combating specific forms of discrimination insofar as these do not aim at trade union affiliation within the 'protected criteria'.

Another example refers to the wage based determination. A lot of collective agreements (for white-collar workers) include wage scales according to age: the social partners agreed to increase the pay according to the age of the person concerned. This is no longer possible. Discriminatory collective agreements will no longer be declared generally binding by the Crown.

The case law of the European Court of Justice in *Feryn*[31] also caused some commotion. An installer of up-and-over doors had stated in the press that he did not recruit persons from ethnic minority groups because they tend to put off older customers. The Interfederal Centre for Equal Opportunities started proceedings, which finally resulted in a reference for a preliminary ruling by the Court of Justice. The Court decided that the fact that an employer openly declares that he is not going to recruit workers of a certain ethnic origin or race constitutes direct discrimination since statements of this kind could be a serious reason for some applicants not to apply and therefore could hinder their access to the labour market.

After the ruling employers openly dissociated themselves from the practice of their colleague. In the National Labour Council Collective Agreement No. 38 was adapted by Collective Agreement 38*sexies* followed by the conclusion of Collective Agreement No. 95 of 10 October 2008.[32] The aim of the latter is to promote compliance with the principle of equal treatment during all stages of the employment relationship, i.e. during recruitment, employment and dismissal.

---

30 Constitutional Court 2 April 2009, No 64/2009.

31 ECJ 10 July 2008, Case C-54/07 *Centrum voor gelijkheid van kansen en racismebestrijding v. Feryn* [2008].

32 Made generally binding by way of the Royal Decree of 11 January 2009, *BS/MB* 4 February 2009.

The significance of Collective Agreement No. 95 is limited. Indeed the three other anti-discrimination acts that have a wider scope.

SECTION 3. THE EMPLOYER'S OBLIGATIONS *VIS-À-VIS* THE APPLICANT

By means of Collective Agreement No. 38 of 6 December 1983[33] standards and rules of conduct for selection and recruitment were established. This collective labour agreement obliges the employer to comply with certain rules *vis-à-vis* the prospective employee.

The employer owes the applicant the following five duties. He:

- is not allowed to treat the applicants in a discriminatory way;
- is obliged to bear the costs of assessments and inquiries organised as part of the selection procedure he has commissioned;
- shall provide applicants who are subject to unemployment control with a certificate if the latter request this. This certificate must mention time, date and place of the selection procedure in which the applicant participated and, if so desired, also the reason why the applicant was not recruited;
- is obliged to keep the documents accompanying the application at the applicant's disposal for a reasonable period, obviously only when the applicant has been rejected;
- is not allowed to demand the applicant to present sealed and certified copies of diplomas, certificates or other documents. However, the employer is entitled to ask for a properly readable copy of the original document. If there is any doubt, the employer may ask the applicant to submit the original document.

Apart from the above described duties the signatory parties of the collective agreement undertook to respect certain 'rules of conduct' with regard to recruitment and selection. This is a moral commitment only and not legally enforceable.

- The first recommendation refers to the vacancy itself. This must contain sufficient information, such as the nature of the job, the qualifications necessary to fulfil it, the place where the job will have to be done, the possible intention of constituting a reserve for future recruitment and the way in which to apply for the job.

---

33 *BS/MB* 28 July 1984.

- The applicant should be able to comply with the job requirements. When an applicant has not been selected the employer must inform him/her of this decision within a reasonable period.
- During the recruitment and selection procedures questions regarding the applicant's private life are only allowed insofar as they are directly relevant to the nature of the job and the conditions for the pursuit of these activities.
- As a rule employers are requested to treat the information they receive with due confidentiality.
- The employer is also obliged to finish the selection procedure within a reasonable period.
- Furthermore, employers are requested to see to it that practical tests do not take longer than the time required to test the candidate's competence.
- Employers are also urged to keep application costs as low as possible.
- Finally, the collective agreement calls on the employers to refrain from fictitious vacancies whose only purpose is publicity.

The applicant is requested to participate in the selection procedure in good faith. He/she is also expected to give the employer the necessary information about his or her professional experience and education, as far as this is relevant to the nature of the job and conditions for the pursuit of the activities in question. He/she shall not spread the confidential information he/she has been given in the context of the recruitment and selection procedures.

By Collective Agreement No. 38*sexies* the prohibition of discrimination is linked to a code of conduct.

SECTION 4. MEDICAL EXAMINATION

§ 1. HEALTH ASSESSMENT

The company doctor shall examine[34] the workers who are recruited to be employed in amongst others:

- a safety position;
- activities with a specific risk.

He shall take a decision regarding the employee's suitability and inform the employee of this before the worker is effectively employed in the function or activity in question.

[34] Article 26 Royal Decree Health Surveillance Employees.

§ 2. MEDICAL TESTS

Medical tests and examinations may only aim at discovering the present (not future) suitability of the (prospective) employee for a vacancy.[35] Any test or medical examination aimed at obtaining medical information about the (prospective) employee's or civil servant's state of health or genealogy information is prohibited. Predictive genetic examinations or AIDS tests are also prohibited. In certain cases deviations are possible. However, each deviation must be established by a Royal Decree and the responsible Minister is obliged to ask the advisory bio-ethics committee for advice.

Biological tests and medical examinations can only be asked for or carried out by the company doctor.

SECTION 5. REPORTING RECRUITMENT

The employer must notify the National Office for Social Security – by means of email – of the beginning and end of the employment.[36] Initially, immediate registration only existed for certain sectors, but now it is obligatory, both in the private and in the public sectors. The generalisation of the DIMONA[37] registration makes it possible to simplify a number of obligations with regard to the so-called social documents.

35 The Law of 28 January 2003 concerning the medical examinations carried out in the context of labour relations, *BS/MB* 9 April 2003.

36 Royal Decree 5 November 2002 concerning the immediate registration of employment, *BS/MB* 20 November 2002.

37 Abbreviation of '*Déclaration IMmédiate – ONmiddellijke Aangifte*' (immediate notification), (www.socialsecurity.be/site_nl/Applics/dimona/index.htm).

CHAPTER 2

PRINCIPLES OF CONTRACT LAW IN THE CONTEXT OF THE EMPLOYMENT CONTRACT

SECTION 1. AUTONOMY OF WILL

Parties are entirely free to give a contract the content they want. In principle this also applies to the individual contract of employment.

However, whereas in the past the individual employment relationship was almost completely regulated by the parties, it is now the subject of extensive and specific regulations in legislation, collective labour agreements and work rules.

SECTION 2. CONSENSUALISM

Consensualism presupposes that prior to the conclusion of the agreement mere consent by the parties suffices. In the context of the employment contract this principle is given another content. Consensualism does not play a role in fixed-term employment contracts, replacement contracts etc. In all these cases the law imposes certain formal requirements. The aim of these formal requirements is not only to make it easier to produce evidence, but also to protect the employee.

SECTION 3. THE BINDING EFFECT OF THE CONTRACT

The principle of the binding effect of the contract (Article 1134 Civil Code) also applies to employment contract law. Once the contract has been concluded neither of the parties may make any changes.

SECTION 4. IMPLEMENTATION OF THE AGREEMENT *BONA FIDE*

The employment contract is expected to be implemented in good faith.

CHAPTER 3
CONDITIONS OF VALIDITY

SECTION 1. COMPETENCE

§ 1. MINORS[38]

A minor – i.e. anyone who has not reached the age of 18 – lacks the legal capacity to conclude a contract of employment on his/her own. He/she must obtain the explicit or tacit permission from his/her father, mother or guardian. Failing this permission or in the event of refusal, the juvenile court may grant authority at the request of the public prosecutor or a relative. A father, mother or guardian will be heard or summoned prior to this.

§ 2. MARRIED PERSONS

Article 216 of the Civil Code gives each spouse the right to exert a profession without the approval of the other spouse.

However, if a spouse is of the opinion that this causes serious damage to his/her moral or material interests or to those of minor children he/she has the right to appeal to the Court of First Instance, and in urgent cases to the President of this court.

The court may make the professional activity dependent on a preliminary change of the marriage settlement of the spouses, for instance, when the chosen activity is financially risky for a partner.

§ 3. GUARDIANSHIP

An adult who, because of his/her health is incapable, either fully or partially, whether or not temporarily, of defending his/her interests without assistance or other protective measures, can be placed under protection, if and to the extent the protection of his/her interests requires this. This means that in certain cases after a decision by the Justice of the Peace a person can only conclude an employment

[38] Articles 43 *et seq.* Employment Contract Act.

contract after authorisation or assistance by a guardian and this under penalty of nullity.[39]

SECTION 2. VALID CONSENT

Error, deceit and violence may affect the validity of the permission. In such cases the general principles of contract law are applied.

§ 1. ERROR

Error may be invoked to ask for the annulment of the contract. In labour law matters error with regard to the cause of the agreement or the nature of the job hardly ever occurs except for errors concerning the capacities of the persons recruited.

Nonetheless, the judge will not be inclined to accept error invoked by the employer since the latter has enough means at his disposal to test the capacities and qualifications of the persons before proceeding to recruitment.

§ 2. VIOLENCE

Violence is more common in the form of moral coercion than in the form of physical violence.

It is not likely that a contract of employment will be concluded under moral coercion. Rather, defect of consent will present itself as a result of termination of the employment contract.

§ 3. DECEIT

An employer can dispute the validity of his consent if the person recruited committed deceit, for instance, when the latter purposely deceived the employer with regard to his/her capacities at the time of his/her application.

From the above it may not be concluded that the employee must reveal his/her past to the employer of his/her own volition. The employer himself must ask for this. Analogously the employer cannot invoke the poor professional qualities of the employee as deceit since the employer is capable of testing this prior to recruitment.

---

39 Articles 491 and 492/2 Civil Code.

However, this does mean that employees have to bear the consequences of their own deceit when they pretend or claim to possess certain diplomas, certificates or qualifications, provided that the possession thereof is a decisive factor in the recruitment.

The same applies when employees deceive the employer with regard to their personal situation, such as fulfilment of military obligations.

For the deceit on the part of the employee to be such that it would affect the employer's consent the element lied about must have been a decisive factor in the recruitment decisions.

The deceived party has the choice between two means of action: either to terminate the agreement on the basis of just cause, or to ask the judge to annul the agreement. Whatever way the employer chooses, he will have to act as soon as possible after having been informed of the deceit.

The annulment of the agreement only has *ex nunc* consequences, in other words from now and for the future, not for the past. As a result, as far as the period prior to the annulment is concerned, the employer will have to comply with the obligations imposed on him by social legislation, including industrial accident legislation.

SECTION 3. OBJECT AND CAUSE

Article 1131 of the Civil Code states that 'an agreement which has been concluded without cause or for a false or unlawful cause can have no consequences'. This provision also applies to employment contracts. What exactly should be understood by permissible object or permissible cause is a question of fact. The cause of the contract refers to the decisive motive for establishing it, whereas the object refers to the content of the contractual agreements.

The contract by which a worker commits himself/herself for life, for instance, will lack a lawful object because this is contrary to an explicit prohibition, namely Article 7 Employment Contract Act.

In a number of cases this rule has been mitigated in the context of individual employment contracts. It is not possible to invoke nullity with regard to younger employees.[40]

[40] Labour Act of 16 March 1971, *BS/MB* 30 March 1971.

Furthermore, nullity of the contract cannot be invoked[41] with regard to the employee's rights that follow from the application of the Employment Contract Act when the work is carried out:

- by virtue of a contract that is invalid because it is contrary to the provisions governing the regulation of labour relations, e.g. an employment contract concluded with a foreigner illegally residing in Belgium;
- by gambling hall personnel.

As a result of this decision employees whose contract is invalid are still entitled to the benefits provided for by labour law legislation.

41 *Ibid.*

CHAPTER 4
FORMAL REQUIREMENTS

With regard to a number (of terms) of employment contracts the legislator has imposed certain formal requirements. As a rule these refer to the requirement of a document or obligatory statements within this document. They are not so much intended to facilitate the furnishing of proof but rather aim at a better protection of employees. The sanctions applied clearly demonstrate this. In the event of non-compliance with the formal requirements these sanctions often prescribe a legal situation which is more favourable to the employee than that in which he/she would have found himself/herself if the formal requirement had been respected.

SECTION 1. PRINCIPLES

An open-ended employment contract does not necessarily need to be laid down in writing. If the opposite has not been explicitly recorded in writing, every contract of employment is supposed to be for an unlimited period.

Conversely, all other employment contracts must be laid down in writing, such as the fixed-term employment contract,[42, 43] a contract for a specified task,[44] or a contract for a replacement.[45]

The same applies to – despite the unlimited period – student contracts[46] and contracts for part-time employment.[47]

All written employment contracts must be drawn up in duplicate and signed, at the latest, at the moment of commencement of the employment.

---

42 Article 9 Employment Contract Act.

43 Failing the legally required document a fixed-term employment contract is conversed into an open-ended contract.

44 Article 9 Employment Contract Act.

45 Article 11*ter* Employment Contract Act.

46 Article 123 Employment Contract Act.

47 Article 11*bis* Employment Contract Act.

SECTION 2. ELECTRONIC SIGNATURE[48]

An electronically signed employment contract is put on a par with a signed employment contract on paper, provided that it is archived with a records department.

48 Article 3*bis* Employment Contract Act.

CHAPTER 5
TYPES OF EMPLOYMENT CONTRACTS

Employment contracts can be subdivided on the basis of three criteria:

- the period for which the agreement is concluded;
- the specification of the work to be carried out;
- the nature of the work or the qualification of the person who has to carry it out.

Furthermore, there are also replacement contracts and employment contracts for part-time work.

SECTION 1. PERIOD FOR WHICH THE EMPLOYMENT CONTRACT IS CONCLUDED

§ 1. GENERAL

Depending on the period for which the employment contract was concluded a distinction can be made between contracts for a fixed period and employment contracts for an indefinite period.[49]

In the context of an open-ended employment contract no time limit is set. In principle both parties can terminate the agreement subject to the legal provisions.

The essence of a fixed-term employment contract is that the parties lay down the length of the agreement beforehand. The contract automatically ends on the expiry date, i.e. the date or the day specified by the parties at the moment the contract was concluded. In principle, neither the employee nor the employer may unilaterally terminate a fixed-term employment contract before the term has expired.

In implementation of Directive 1999/70/EC fixed-term contract workers may not be treated less favourably than comparable permanent workers.[50]

[49] Article 7 Employment Contract Act.

[50] Law of 5 June 2002 concerning the non-discrimination principle for employees with a fixed-term employment contract, *BS/MB* 26 June 2002.

§ 2. CONSECUTIVE FIXED-TERM EMPLOYMENT CONTRACTS

Employment contract law provides more guarantees in terms of job security to open-ended contracts than to fixed-term contracts. For instance, the provisions with regard to suspension and termination of the contract are, as a rule, more favourable to employees with open-ended contracts. As a result, in the past employers sometimes resorted to a practice which consisted of concluding consecutive fixed-term contracts, instead of concluding one open-ended contract.

The legislator has tried to remedy this shortcoming by adding a provision in this respect to the Employment Contract Act, more specifically, Article 10 Employment Contract Act.

When parties have concluded several consecutive fixed-term employment contracts without there having been an interruption caused by the employee, they are considered to have concluded an open-ended contract; except when the employer proves that these contracts were justified because of the nature of the job or because of another legitimate reason.

In other words, this provision contains a rebuttable presumption that several fixed-term employment contracts actually amount to an open-ended contract. However, there are two cases in which the presumption is not applicable, i.e.:

- when the interruption(s) can be attributed to the employee himself/herself;
- insofar as the employer proves that the conclusion of several fixed-term contracts can be justified by the nature of the job (e.g. extension of seasonal work in a tourist attraction as a result of good weather conditions) or any other legitimate reason (e.g. bad economic situation, an enterprise in financial difficulties).

By the Law of 30 March 1994 on social provisions Article 10*bis* was added to the Employment Contract Act. This Article establishes two exceptions to the principle that consecutive fixed-term employment contracts are presumed to have been concluded for an indefinite period. First of all, the provision allows the conclusion of four consecutive contracts, and this under a double condition. On the one hand the length of each of the agreements may not be less than three months, and on the other hand the total length of the consecutive contracts may not exceed two years. The second exception allows – provided that prior permission has been given by a government official – consecutive fixed-term contracts to be concluded for a minimum duration of six months each, provided that the total duration of the consecutive contracts does not exceed three years.

SECTION 2. SPECIFICATION OF THE WORK TO BE CARRIED OUT

Upon concluding an employment contract a worker may commit himself/herself to perform a specified task.[51]

The distinction between an open-ended employment contract and one for a specified task is that in the latter case the employee knows when the agreement will end in principle, i.e. at the moment the work has been completed, even though no specific time can be set.

For there to be an employment contract for a specified task, the work in question must be determined as far as its object and extent are concerned so that the parties can estimate the expected length of the agreement at the moment they commit themselves.

The prohibition of concluding several consecutive employment contracts of the same nature also applies to contracts for a specified task.[52]

SECTION 3. NATURE OF THE JOB

Depending on the nature of the work to be done different types of employment contracts can be distinguished. The two most important types are the employment contract for labourers or blue-collar workers and the employment contract for white-collar workers.

The employment contract for blue-collar workers is an agreement in which the employee – the labourer – commits himself to perform predominantly manual labour for wages under the authority of an employer.[53]

The employment contract for white-collar workers presupposes that the employee mainly performs intellectual work.[54]

The law does not specify which professions or activities must be considered as manual labour or intellectual work. Whether or not an employee carries out manual labour or intellectual work is an issue that the judge will have to assess autonomously. Usually, precedence is given to the principle of autonomy of will. This means that the judge lets himself be guided by the qualification that the parties gave to the agreement, except in the event of mistake, fraud or the existence of stipulations that are incompatible with the given qualification.

A lot of lawyers regard the difference in treatment between blue-collar and white-collar workers as discriminatory. After having been confronted with a question regarding the disparity of the different terms of notice, the Constitutional Court stated in its ruling No. 56/93 of 8 July 1993 that in the case submitted there

[51] Article 7 Employment Contract Act.
[52] Article 10 Employment Contract Act.
[53] Article 2 Employment Contract Act.
[54] Article 3 Employment Contract Act.

was no question of conflict with Articles 10 and 11 of the Constitution, but the Court also gave the legislator a clear hint that the distinction should gradually be lifted. Indeed, little by little steps were taken to remove the distinction.

In its judgment of 7 July 2011 (No. 125/2011) the Court stated that a number of Articles of the Employment Contract Act were in conflict with Articles 10 and 11 of the Constitution, and that the legislator was expected to make arrangements to amend this situation by 8 July 2013 at the latest (= 20 years after the first judgment).

On Friday 5 July 2013 the social partners reached a compromise on a uniform status. This was transposed into the Law of 26 December 2013 on the introduction of a uniform status of blue-collar workers and white-collar workers. The new regulation amounts to a genuine revolution of which the main point is the new law governing dismissal which entered into force on 1 January 2014. However, on some levels the distinction continues to exist, but there is a real chance that this will be removed in the years to come.

SECTION 4. THE REPLACEMENT CONTRACT[55, 56]

§ 1. PRINCIPLE

An employer may use a replacement worker when the employment contract of another employee has been suspended for certain reasons, other than shortage of work because of economic necessity, bad weather, strike or lock-out. Such a replacement can be appropriate in the absence of an employee who is unable to work for a long time, is on pregnancy or maternity leave, takes a career break, or in the event of temporary work, etc.

§ 2. FORMAL REQUIREMENTS

A replacement contract must always be made in writing, for each employee separately, and at the latest, at the moment the employment commences. In the absence of a document the employment agreement is considered to be concluded for an unlimited period.

---

55 Article 11*ter* Employment Contract Act.

56 Crabeels, E., 'Le contrat de remplacement: une vraie fausse bonne solution' in Claeys & Engels, *Arbeidsovereenkomstenwet na 30 jaar... anders bekeken*, Brussels, Larcier, 2008, pp. 51–61; Bartholome, J., 'Quelques réflexions sur le contrat de remplacement', *Rev.Dr.ULg.* 2008, pp. 67–79; Verbrugge, F., 'Le contrat de travail de remplacement: ses limites et contraintes', *Ors.* 2005/8, pp. 19–36; Beauthier, G. en Wantiez, C., 'Le contrat de remplacement', *JTT* 1987, pp. 261-265.

Aside from the regular statements the contract must also mention:

- the reason for the replacement;
- the identity of the replaced employee;
- the conditions of the recruitment.

Conditions for recruitment are: the remuneration, the working hours, the probation clause if any, duration of the replacement, and the term of notice when the parties wish to be able to use the possibility of shortened periods of notice.

§ 3. TERMS

A. *Principle*

A replacement contract can either be concluded for a fixed period or for an unlimited period.

B. *Limitation in time*

The length of a replacement contract may not exceed two years unless such a contract has been concluded to replace an employee who takes a career break.

Non-observance of these provisions with regard to the maximum duration results in application of the rules of the open-ended employment contract. This means, *inter alia*, that it is not (no longer) possible to stipulate shortened periods of notice.

C. *Consecutive replacement contracts*

At the moment a replacement contract is concluded the exact duration of absence of the employee to be replaced is not always known. For that reason the law allows the parties to conclude consecutive replacement contracts.

In this situation too, the above described restriction in time has to be taken into account. The total length of the various replacement contracts, without there having been a disruption caused by the replacement himself/herself, may never exceed two years, except to replace a worker on a career break.

This restriction only applies to consecutive replacement contracts concluded between the same parties. It goes without saying that it does not apply to consecutive replacement contracts concluded by the same employer with different replacement workers.

For that matter, the restriction does apply when consecutive replacement contracts are concluded between the same parties but for different reasons. Consequently, the maximum duration of two years also applies in the case of replacements which have a different cause or are intended to replace other employees.

Only when the replacement worker is to be blamed for interruptions, does this principle not apply.

§ 4. TERMINATION

The fixed-term replacement contract ends automatically and without notice when the term has expired.

A. *Open-ended replacement contract*

1. General

If a replacement contract has been concluded for an unlimited period, a distinction has to be made depending on whether dismissal/resignation occurs prior to the end of the replacement or with a view to its ending.

2. Prior to the end of the replacement

In the event of a unilateral termination of the replacement contract for another reason than the end of the replacement the normal rules with regard to dismissal/resignation must be complied with.

3. Return of the replaced employee

When the contract is terminated at the end of the replacement, in other words, at the moment in which the replaced employee resumes his/her job, the Employment Contract Act provides for the possibility of entering shortened periods of notice in the contract. Deviations from the legal provisions regarding the time when the period of notice starts are also allowed. However, in that case notice has to be given under the same terms as for an open-ended employment contract.

Parties may even agree that the replacement contract ends automatically without notice or compensation upon the return of the replaced person. If a stipulation of this kind has been included in the replacement contract, it goes without saying that there are no formalities to be complied with.

However, this deviation from the general principles must be interpreted strictly, and only takes effect when the replaced employee performs his original duties again. Even so, this means that the regular rules of dismissal must be respected if:

- the replaced employee does not return;

- the latter is back at work in a function other than his/her initial one. In this case the emphasis is on the content of his/her duties.

SECTION 5. PART-TIME WORK

§ 1. WHAT IS PART-TIME WORK?

Article 2 Law of 5 March 2002[57] defines a part-time employee as a person whose normal time of working, calculated at a weekly basis or as an average over a working period of maximum a year, is less than that of a full-time employee in a similar situation.

Part-time work differs from other incidental, temporary or seasonal work. It should also not be confused with other flexible agreements such as an on-call contract.

§ 2. FORMAL REQUIREMENTS[58]

An employment contract for part-time work must be laid down in writing for each employee individually, at the latest, on the date on which the worker starts the work agreed to in the contract.

The document must include the agreed part-time work arrangement (for instance, 18 hours a week) and a (reference to) – a possibly flexible – work schedule.

In the absence of a document or when the work arrangement and schedule are not mentioned, the employee may choose the arrangement that suits him/her the most amongst those:

- either provided for in the work rules;
- or, which, in the absence thereof, is apparent from a social record whose keeping is required by Royal Decree No. 5 of 23 October 1978.

§ 3. PROTECTION OF THE PART-TIME EMPLOYEE

Besides the fact that an employment contract for part-time work has to be formulated in writing and must also contain the work schedules and work arrangements, the legislature has built in a number of extra protection measures.

---

57 *BS/MB* 13 March 2002.

58 Article 11*bis* Employment Contract Act.

A. *Minimum weekly employment*

The weekly working time of a part-time employee may not be less than one third of the weekly working time of a full-timer who belongs to the same category of company workers. In the absence of a point of reference the working hours applicable in the same branch are to be taken into account.

Under certain conditions the Crown may allow a deviation from the limit of one third in the industrial sectors, industrial categories, branches of enterprise, categories of workers or jobs to which this limit cannot be applied.[59]

A similar deviation may also be laid down in a collective labour agreement. If the collective agreement is concluded outside the competent joint committee, it must be approved by this joint committee.

When the employment contract for part-time work stipulates working hours below the above described rule of one third, the wages due are nonetheless on the basis of the legal minimum limits.

B. *Minimum daily employment*

The duration of a working period may not be shorter than three hours. This duration can be changed by the Crown or by a collective labour agreement.[60]

C. *Work organisation*

The work can be organised in three different ways:

a. according to a fixed roster: a copy of the employment contract or an excerpt thereof with a roster including the employee's identity as well as his/her signature and that of his/her employer must be kept at a place where the work rules can be consulted;[61]
b. according to a rotating scheme provided for in the work rules: when, at any time, it can be established when the rotation starts, this is considered to be a fixed work roster. In other cases we are dealing with a flexible work schedule;[62]
c. according to a flexible roster: the daily rosters must be made known to the persons concerned by posters at least five days beforehand. The announcement must be made for each employee separately.[63]

---

59 In this context see the Royal Decree of 21 December 1992, *BS/MB* 30 December 1992.
60 Article 21 Employment Contract Act. See in this context Royal Decree 18 June 1990, *BS/MB* 30 June 1990.
61 Article 157 Programme Law 22 December 1989, *BS/MB* 30 December 1989.
62 Article 158 Programme Law 22 December 1989, *BS/MB* 30 December 1989.
63 Article 159 Programme Law 22 December 1989, *BS/MB* 30 December 1989.

The announcement must be made for a year, to be counted from the day the roster is no longer in force.

In the absence of the above described obligatory announcement of the rosters, the employer can be subjected to sanctions and the employee will be rebuttably presumed to have worked full time.[64] For that matter, this presumption does not necessarily imply an advantage for the employee. The legal presumption has been created for the benefit of the inspectorate and the institutions.

D. *The employer's duty to keep records*

The employer must keep a record of all roster deviations. At the proposal of a joint committee, industries may opt for a different control mechanism. Employers who have a suitable time registration device or register may be exempted from this obligation. In order to induce employers to comply with the law rather severe penalties are included in the law.

E. *Too much flexibility is not financially attractive to the employer*

So as to avoid the employee from suffering financially through the use of flexible rosters, a certain continuity in the payment of wages is provided for. Each pay day the employer is expected to pay the normal wages for the agreed weekly working hours, even when the employee has worked less.

Deviations from the working time are also financially punished.

F. *Part-time work as an exception*

A part-time employee can submit a written request to his/her employer to obtain a full-time job or another (extra) job, as a result of which he/she will get a new employment arrangement with more weekly working hours. In concrete terms this means that someone working 25 hours a week is eligible for a full-time job as well as for any job whose working hours exceed 25 hours a week.

Moreover, he/she can also ask to combine a job of less than 25 hours a week with the job he/she already has.

---

64 Article 171 Programme Law 22 December 1989, as amended by Law 26 July 1996. See also Article 22*ter* Social Security Act.

G. *Prohibition of discrimination*

In implementation of Directive 97/81/EC part-time workers may not be treated less favourably than full-time employees in a similar situation merely on the basis that they are part-timers, unless the difference in treatment is objectively justified.[65]

[65] Article 4 Law 5 March 2002 concerning the principle of non-discrimination for part-time workers, *BS/MB* 13 March 2002.

CHAPTER 6
THE CONTENT OF THE CONTRACT

The parties may include certain arrangements in the employment contract. Some clauses are explicitly regulated by the legislator, other ones are explicitly forbidden.

SECTION 1. PROHIBITED CLAUSES

§ 1. AVOIDANCE CLAUSES

Clauses stating that marriage, motherhood or reaching the legal or conventional retirement age terminate the contract are invalid.[66]

Also invalid are clauses that give the employer the right to terminate the employment contract without notice or before the term has expired when the employee's wages are garnished because of a credit agreement established by the Law of 12 June 1991 regarding consumer credit.[67]

§ 2. THE MODIFICATION CLAUSE

Sometimes parties agree that the employer has the right to change the terms of the contract unilaterally. Executive staff members, for instance, may agree to be employed 'anywhere in the world'. Such a clause is null and void.[68] With this the legislator wanted to avoid employees from being at the mercy of the entrepreneur. However, parties may agree to employment in a limited number of locations. This is not a case of unilateral modification of the contract. At the time the contract is concluded the employee already knows where he/she may end up.

[66] Article 36 Employment Contract Act.
[67] Article 36*bis* Employment Contract Act.
[68] Article 25 Employment Contract Act.

SECTION 2. CONDITIONS LAID DOWN IN THE EMPLOYMENT CONTRACT ACT

§ 1. PROBATION CLAUSE

A probation clause is a clause in the contract of employment enabling the employer to assess the employee's suitability or enabling the employee to assess the suitability of the job. On 1 January 2014 this clause was removed from law except for a few categories of workers.

§ 2. GUARANTEE DEPOSIT[69]

An employee can only be asked to provide a guarantee deposit under the provisions laid down in a collective labour agreement. If no collective agreement has been concluded at enterprise level or at the level of the joint (sub-)committee, the provisions of Collective Agreement No. 41 apply. To prevent the employer from capitalising these deposits there are very strict rules.[70]

§ 3. ARBITRATION CLAUSE

See *infra*.

§ 4. COMPETITION CLAUSE

See *infra*.

§ 5. THE *DELCREDERE* CLAUSE

See *infra*.

§ 6. THE TRAINING CLAUSE

See *infra*.

---

[69] Articles 23 and 23*bis* Employment Contract Act.

[70] *Ibid.*

SECTION 3. CLAUSES NOT REGULATED BY THE LEGISLATOR

Article 6 Employment Contract Act determines that clauses that are contrary to the provision of this law and its implementing orders are invalid insofar as these are intended to curtail the employee's rights or to aggravate his/her obligations. As a result, a job applicant cannot renounce his/her legal rights. If he/she were to do this anyway, the questionable passage in the contract would be invalid and could not be invoked against the employee.

Examples of clauses whose validity was examined by the labour tribunals in the past:

- the exclusivity clause: the employee commits himself/herself to work solely for the employer and, for instance, not to work as a self-employed person in his/her free time;
- the residence clause: the employee must have his/her address within a certain distance from the enterprise.

III
EMPLOYMENT

CHAPTER 1
RIGHTS AND DUTIES

Employers and employees have certain rights and duties. These may stem from the individual employment contract, work rules, collective labour agreements and the law.

Therefore it is impossible to discuss all the rights and duties of the parties in this context. We will restrict ourselves to the most important ones, more specifically, those included in the Employment Contract Act.

SECTION 1. THE EMPLOYER'S DUTIES

§ 1. GENERAL

The employer shall:[71]

- show respect and regard for his employee;
- observe and make the observation of propriety and decency a priority This obligation is not only imposed by Article 6 Employment Contract Act but also by the provisions of chapter V*bis* of the law concerning the well-being of employees, which includes a number of provisions with regard to improper behaviour such as sexual harassment;
- allow the employee to work in the manner, place and time agreed, in particular when the circumstances require this and except for contrary provisions in the agreement, by providing the necessary assistance, equipment and materials. The employer may not employ the employee contrary to that which has been agreed in the employment contract. Nevertheless, the employer may adapt the working conditions with some flexibility;

71 Articles 16 and 20 Employment Contract Act.

- see to it with due diligence that the work is done in proper circumstances with regard for the employee's health and safety, and that in the event of an accident, first aid is available. To this end a first-aid kit must be at the personnel's disposal;
- pay the wages in the agreed manner, time and place. Actually, the parties' freedom to regulate the manner in which the wages are fixed and paid is very limited. The Wage Protection Act[72] regulates the various aspects of this obligation;
- accommodate the employee properly as well as provide him/her with healthy and sufficient food insofar as the employer has undertaken to provide him/her with board and lodging;
- give the employee enough time to observe his/her religious obligations as well as the civil duties ensuing from the law;
- pay proper attention to the reception of the new employee, and in particular, of young employees;
- take care with due diligence of the equipment belonging to the employee as well as to the personal objects which the employee must entrust to the employer. Under no condition may the employer refuse to return the equipment or the personal objects to the employee;
- hand the employee who asks for this a certificate at the end of the contract;
- refund the guarantee deposit under the conditions provided by the law.

§ 2. OBLIGATIONS WITH REGARD TO EXPATS

If the employee has to work in another country for longer than one month, the employer must hand the employee a document before his/her departure.[73] This document must contain the following particulars:

- the duration of the work abroad;
- the currency in which the wages will be paid;
- the benefits, if any, linked to the assignment abroad;
- as the occasion arises, the conditions of the employee's return to his/her own country.

§ 3. PAYMENT OF WAGES

Article 20, 3° Employment Contract Act determines that the employer must pay the wages in the manner, time and place agreed. From the employee's point of

[72] Law of 12 April 1965, *BS/MB* 30 April 1965.
[73] Article 20*bis* Employment Contract Act.

view, this is the most important obligation. The legislator protected this right of the employee first and foremost by means of the Wage Protection Act. This law includes rules with regard to the payment of wages, the measurement of work, the interest due, rules with regard to deductions, wage garnishment, wage transfer, etc. The Wage Protection Act is also very important for another reason: it contains a concept of wage which is referred to in several laws.

A. *Definition of wage*

Article 2 Wage Protection Act defines wages as the money and benefits expressed in terms of money to which the employee is entitled as a result of his/her employment contract and which are to be paid by the employer. Gratuities and service charges to which the employee is entitled are also part of the wages. However, not considered to be wages are: holiday allowances, supplements of fees due as a result of industrial accidents or occupational diseases and all other supplements paid on top of the payments accorded pursuant to the various branches of social security.

B. *Protection at various levels*

Wage protection has many aspects.

- *The way in which the wages are paid*[74]
  This must take place by giro transfer.
  Wages in kind[75]
- The wages may only be partly paid in kind, in principle one fifth of the total gross income, when this manner of payment is customary or desirable because of the nature of the branch of industry in question or because of the occupation concerned.
- *Moment of payment*[76]
  Wages must be paid at regular intervals. For blue-collar workers this must be at least twice a month with an interval of 16 days at the most. For white-collar workers it should be at least every month.
  When the employment contract ends the wages still due must be paid without delay and, more specifically, at the latest on the first pay day following the date on which the employment contract ends.[77]

---

74 Article 5, § 1 Wage Protection Act.
75 Article 6 Wage Protection Act.
76 Article 9 Wage Protection Act.
77 Article 11 Wage Protection Act.

- *The quittance*[78]
  The quittance handed over by the employee on termination of employment is only a receipt and does not imply a renunciation of rights. However, this does not prevent him/her from explicitly renouncing his/her rights when the quittance is handed over.
- *The interests*[79]
  Legally interest is due on the basis of the gross income.
- *The wage specification*[80]
  With every definite payment the employee must receive a specification.
- *Wage deductions*[81]
  The only amounts allowed to be deducted from wages are:
  1. advance tax payment, the employee's social security contributions and his/her contribution for additional social security benefits;
  2. fines imposed under the work rules;
  3. indemnity due under Article 18 Employment Contract Act;
  4. advances paid by the employer;
  5. the guarantee deposited with regard to the employee's observance of obligations by the employee.

  The total of the amounts withheld may not exceed one fifth of the wage due after deduction of the advance tax payments and the legal and additional social security benefits. This limitation does not apply when the employee has committed a deliberate error or when he/she has voluntarily terminated his/her employment contract before payment of the damages he/she owes.
- *Wage transfer and wage garnishment*
  The monthly net amount is only subject to garnishment and transfer to a limited extent:[82]
  - under € 1,091: nihil;
  - between € 1,091 and € 1,171: 20%;
  - between € 1,171 and € 1,293: 30%;
  - between € 1,293 and € 1,414: 40%;
  - over € 1,414: 100%.

  These income limits are increased by € 67 for each dependent child.
  The limits no longer apply when the transfer or garnishment is done on account of non-observance of maintenance obligations.[83]
  The Wage Protection Act also contains rules with regard to the procedure to be followed in case of wage transfer.[84]

---

[78] Article 12 Wage Protection Act and Article 42 Employment Contract Act.
[79] Article 10 Wage Protection Act.
[80] Article 15 Wage Protection Act.
[81] Article 23 Wage Protection Act.
[82] Figures from 1 January 2016. The amounts mentioned are indexed annually. See Article 1409 Judicial Code.
[83] Article 1412 Judicial Code.
[84] Article 27 through 35 Wage Protection Act.

- *Precedence*
  The employee's wage claims take precedence over all movables of the employer. In a number of cases – e.g. termination compensations – this precedence is restricted to a certain amount.

C. *The amount*

In Belgium minimum wages are determined by collective labour agreements, more specifically, sectoral collective agreements although collective agreements at enterprise level, or individual employment contracts may provide for higher wages.

Despite sectoral diversity, there are general norms that apply to all private sector employers. These can be found in Collective Agreement No. 43 of the National Labour Council.[85] For employees under 21 years of age there are separate rules imposed by Collective Agreement No. 50.[86]

§ 4. WORKING TIME LIMITS

A. *Survey*

The first law limiting working hours dates from 1921. Nowadays the maximum number of working hours is chiefly regulated by the Labour Act. In the last few years the legislator's attention has been shifting toward a more flexible regulation of working hours, be it that this is subject to certain conditions. For instance, the Working Time Act of 7 March 1987 and Collective Agreement No. 42[87] of the National Labour Council offer the possibility of deviating from a number of legal rules by means of negotiated agreements. With this flexibilisation the legislator aims at improving the output of companies, and consequently at creating more employment.

For night work there are also special rules. For this kind of work the legislator has provided a number of supporting social measures. Furthermore, the social partners have agreed on a number of advisory measures with regard to night work, such as the employer's obligation to pay a specific financial compensation.[88]

---

85 Collective Agreement No. 43 of 2 May 1988, amended several times.

86 Declared generally binding by the Royal Decree of 17 December 1991, *BS/MB* 10 January 1992.

87 Collective Agreement No. 42 of 2 June 1987 concerning the introduction of new labour regulations in enterprises.

88 Law of 17 February 1997 concerning night work; Collective Agreement No. 46 of 23 March 1990 concerning the advisory measures for shift work that includes night work, as well as other forms of night work; Collective Agreement No. 49 of 21 May 1991 concerning the guarantee of a specific financial compensation in the case of night work.

B. *Scope*

The legislation concerning working time has a broad personal scope. It applies to all persons who, whether or not they are working under an employment contract, carry out work under the authority of another person.

Certain groups of employees or persons who work under authority are excluded from the application of the working time regulation, e.g. employees who have an executive function or fulfil a position of trust,[89] persons working in a family business, etc.

C. *Concept of 'working time'*

The law defines working time as the time in which staff are at the disposal of the employer, so not only the time in which work is carried out effectively.

Moreover, in certain cases the legislator explicitly considers the time in which personnel are not at the disposal of the employer as working time, *inter alia*:

- the meeting time spent by the members of the Works Council and the Committee for Prevention and Protection at Work;
- the time in which the union delegates act in this capacity;
- time spent on educational leave;
- the time spent to act as witnesses during social elections;
- etc.

For specific sectors the Crown may further specify the notion of working time. This concerns a restriction of the notion of working time, i.e. although the employee is at the employer's disposal there is no question of working time. Such restrictions have been laid down for transport companies and security firms.

D. *Limits*

1. Fixed hours of work

The working time may not exceed 8 hours a day and 38 hours a week.[90, 91] In a five-day week the daily limit is 9 hours. The legal working time can be reduced by means of a collective agreement or by Royal Decree. The working hours regulation is rather complex and contains a number of special arrangements for, amongst

[89] Royal Decree 10 February 1965, *BS/MB* 12 February 1965.

[90] Article 19 Employment Contract Act as amended by Article 2 Law of 10 August 2001 concerning the conciliation between employment and quality of life, *BS/MB* 15 September 2001.

[91] At the time this text was written it was not yet clear whether or not this regulation would be replaced by a 45-hours limit per week combined with a 38-hours limit on an annual basis.

others, shift work, continuous shift work, night work, etc. In addition, there is the possibility of introducing flexible arrangements. However, this is only possible if certain strict conditions are fulfilled (*inter alia*, intervention by the employee organisations). As a rule the employer can ask his workers to do overtime up to a certain maximum. The advantage of this is that peak times can be taken care of without additional recruitment.

E. *Overtime*[92]

Overtime can be defined as work that is done in transgression of the legal working time limits or in transgression of the replacing working time limits (usually established by means of a collective agreement).

As for the right to extra pay, overtime is defined more restrictively as work exceeding 9 hours a day or 40 hours a week or exceeding the lower limits established by collective agreement. Certain cases of permissible overtime on the other hand are not considered as overtime, entitling an employee to extra pay. Overtime is strictly regulated and only permitted in certain cases. Moreover, in most cases the employer has to follow a (consultation) procedure. Overtime is allowed, *inter alia*, in the event of:

- extraordinary increase in the workload;
- urgent or unforeseeable work;
- taking stock and preparing the accounts;
- preliminary work or finishing up;
- an accident.

In principle, overtime entitles the worker to a bonus (extra pay) of 50% of the ordinary wage. The increase is 100% for overtime on Sundays or a public holiday. Sometimes the extra pay is higher under a collective agreement. As mentioned before, certain forms of overtime do not entail the right to extra pay. This is the case in the event of:

- flexible working time schedules;
- shift work;
- continuous shift work;
- new employment regulation;
- a Royal Decree for branches of industry where the working time limits cannot be applied.

[92] Article 29 Labour Act.

Employees working part-time are entitled to extra pay for their extra time starting from the 13th extra hour a month.[93]

Extra pay may be replaced by extra days off. This must be provided for by collective agreement. Moreover, every hour entitling a person to an extra pay of 50% must be replaced by at least half an hour of rest, and any overtime with a bonus of 100% by at least one hour.

F. Enforcement

Breaches of labour legislation can be prosecuted as offences.

§ 5. LANGUAGE LEGISLATION

Through the decentralisation of powers by several constitutional revisions, the linguistic communities obtained the authority to regulate the language used in the social contacts between employer and employee.[94] This transfer of competences led to the establishment of two decrees, namely the Dutch Language Decree of 19 July 1973[95] and the French Language Decree of 30 June 1982.[96] Each decree only has effect in the corresponding Dutch or French speaking region, with the exception of the municipalities with linguistic facilities, the bilingual area Brussels-Capital and the German speaking region. In those areas the older federal language law of 18 July 1966[97] concerning administrative matters applies, also with regard to labour relations. Although the communities are authorised to regulate the use of language in individual and collective labour relations as well as in the pre-contractual legal relationship between an employer and an applicant, they are not authorised to do so with regard to the language used for vacancies.[98]

Employers who have a place of business in the Dutch language region must use Dutch in social contacts, regardless of the place where the employees are employed. However, if the composition of the staff justifies this it is allowed to add a translation in one or several languages to the documents drawn up in Dutch at the joint request of the employee representatives of the works councils, the trade union delegation or a delegate of a representative trade union organisation (the one acting in the absence of the other).

93 Royal Decree June 1990 with a view to the equalization of some of the work done by part-timers doing overtime.
94 Article 129 § 1, 3° Constitution.
95 *BS/MB* 6 September 1973.
96 *BS/MB* 27 August 1982.
97 *BS/MB* 2 August 1966.
98 Constitutional Court 9 November 1995, No. 106/2007.

Documents or acts in violation of the Dutch Language Decree are invalid *ex officio*. The lifting of the nullity by a replacement in Dutch only takes effect for the future, i.e. from the day of the replacement. The sanction of nullity may not harm the employee, nor the rights of third parties.

Penalties guarantee the observance of the Dutch Language Decree.

Employers who have a place of business in the French language region must use French in their social contacts with their employees. However, parties are free to use another chosen language in addition.

Acts and documents in violation of the French Language Decree are invalid *ex officio*. The lifting of the nullity only takes effect at the moment a version in accordance with the French Language Decree is made available to the parties. The French Language Decree is not subject to penalties.

Employers who have a place of business in Brussels-Capital, in a municipality with linguistic facilities or in the German language region must use the language of the area in their social contacts with the staff. However, as regards the employer with a company in the bilingual area of Brussels-Capital, it should be noted that they have to use Dutch for Dutch speaking employees and French for French speaking staff. Without prejudice to these obligations the companies may add a translation into one or more languages if the composition of the staff justifies this.

When the acts or documents are contrary to the prescribed language rules they must be replaced by acts or documents in the correct language.

The way in which the observance of the language legislation is controlled is rather laborious. In Flanders this is handled by the department Inspectorate Employment of the Flemish Ministry of Employment. In Brussels and the municipalities with language facilities the control is consigned to civil servants of the Belgian Federal Public Service for Employment, Labour and Social Dialogue. For Belgium as a whole, the Permanent Committee for Language Surveillance (VCT/CPCL) is the competent body.

People who think that their rights have been violated can file a complaint. A civil servant of the Committee may then ask the labour tribunals for an annulment of documents and acts contrary to the Flemish Language Decree.

In 2011 the European Court of Justice was confronted with the question whether or not this legislation hindered the free movement of workers.[99] A Dutch citizen had concluded an employment contract pursuant to Belgian law, but the document was written in English. When the employee was dismissed, he requested nullity of the employment contract. The Court submitted a preliminary question. With this the referring judge wanted to be informed 'whether Article 45 TFEU should be interpreted in such a way that this provision is contrary to the

[99] Case C-202/11 *Anton Las v. PSA Antwerp NV*, [2013].

regulation established by a federated entity of a Member State, (...) which obliges all employers whose established place of business is situated on the territory of this entity to conclude employment contracts with a cross-border dimension solely in the official language unity under penalty of nullity'. In its judgment of 16 April the Court ruled that the Treaty provision on free movement of workers has to be understood to mean that this provision is contrary to the regulation obliging all employers with a place of business on the territory of a language region of a Member State to conclude employment contracts with a cross-border dimension solely in the official language of that regions under penalty of nullity. As a result, the Flemish Language Decree was amended by decree on 14 March 2014. In addition to some cosmetic changes, provisions regarding individual employment contracts with a cross-border dimension were included in this decree.

A. *The individual employment contract*

For an individual employment contract an additional legally valid version can be made up in one of the following languages as long as this language is understood by all parties involved:.

1° an official language of the European Union;
2° an official language of one of the Member States of the European Economic Area that are not members of the European Union.

However, this is only possible if the employee:

1° resides on the territory of one of the other Member States of the European Union or one of the Member States of the European Economic Area;
2° resides on Belgian territory and uses the right to free movement of workers or the freedom of establishment;
3° falls under the scope of the free movement of workers on the basis of an international or supranational treaty.

B. *Communication*

If the personnel composition justifies this and at the joint request of members of the works council or, failing a works council, at the joint request of union representatives, or failing both, at the request of a delegate of a representative trade union, the employer is obliged to add a translation into one or more languages to the communications, certificates, attestations and forms for the personnel.

However, this regulation only applies for one year and has to be made in writing, under penalty of nullity. The employers have to submit this to the civil servants in charge of the supervision of the implementation of this decree within one month.

If there is a discrepancy between the Dutch version and the other versions of a document, the Dutch version prevails.

C. *Application*

Employers are entitled to demand multilingualism from applicants and test this knowledge during the selection procedure.

§ 6. WORK RULES

Most of the work rules can be found in the Work Rules Act.[100] However, this is not a coordinated law so that the obligation to include certain provisions becomes apparent from other texts. For instance, the employer must add a copy of Collective Agreement No. 25 to the work rules on the basis of an agreement between the social partners.[101]

The scope of the law is very broad and even includes the public sector.

A. *Content*

The work rules contain a number of compulsory and optional statements. The compulsory ones refer to, *inter alia*, the work rosters, measurement and control of the work done, payment of wages, supervisory personnel, discipline, etc. For instance, sanctions (among which are fines) can be included in the work rules.

B. *Binding aspect*

The work rules are binding on the employer and the employees in question. However, this aspect is supplemental because it can be deviated from by a written individual employment contract.

Work rules are only binding on an individual employee when the employer has handed him/her a copy of these rules, even if the employee has become acquainted with them in a different way.

C. *Formulating/changing*

In enterprises with a works council the work rules are formulated and changed by the works council itself, which in this respect has decision-making power. If there is no works council the employer has to inform the employees of any draft of rules

[100] Law 8 April 1965 establishing work rules, *BS/MB* 5 May 1965.
[101] Article 8 Collective Agreement No. 25 of 15 October 1975.

or changes. Within 15 days the latter can then write down their comments in a register set up for this purpose through a personnel or union delegation.

In the event of disagreement within the works council or between the employer and employees when there is no works council, a civil servant of the social inspectorate is the first one that will try to reconcile the opinions within 30 days. If no resolution is achieved, the dispute will be brought before the joint committee. The joint committee will have to decide by a majority of 75% of the votes of each of the parties within the joint committee.

SECTION 2. THE EMPLOYEE'S DUTIES

- The employee too has certain obligations: the employee owes the employer respect and regard;
- during the implementation of the employment contract the employee shall observe propriety and decency;
- the employee is obliged to perform his/her job meticulously, honestly and precisely in the place, time and manner agreed;
- during the agreement as well as after its termination the employee shall refrain from:
  - disclosing factory secrets, business secrets or secrets with regard to personal or confidential matters which he/she may get acquainted with during his/her job;
  - performing acts of unfair competition or participating in such actions;
  - anything that may harm either his/her own safety or that of his/her colleagues, his/her employer or third parties;
- the employee shall return the equipment and unused materials entrusted to him/her to the employer in proper condition.

One of the passages of the Employment Contract Act, namely Article 17, 2°, needs some further explanation. This Article states that the employee is obliged to act in accordance with the orders and instructions given to him/her by his/her employer, the latter's agents or appointees with a view to the implementation of the contract. This could be interpreted as the employer being completely free to exercise his authority and the employee being obliged to follow any order. This is not the case. By concluding the employment contract the employee does accept the employer's authority, but this authority is subject to restrictions. For instance, the employer is entitled to check on the employee but he may not violate the latter's privacy.

The limits of the exercise of authority were not laid down explicitly by the legislator, so this is a source of many disputes.[102] Some aspects of this right of

[102] See P. Humblet, *De gezagsuitoefening door de werkgever*, Antwerp, Kluwer Rechtswetenschappen, 1994, 420 pp..

control are so controversial that explicit rules are laid down by agreement. Certain surveillance techniques, for instance, are explicitly regulated.

- camera surveillance: Collective Agreement No. 68;[103]
- control of the use of email and internet: Collective Agreement No. 81;[104]
- exit control: Collective Agreement No. 89.[105]

103 Collective Agreement No. 68 of 16 June 1998, declared generally binding by the Royal Decree of 20 December 1998, *BS/MB* 2 October 1998.

104 Collective Agreement No. 81 of 26 April 2002, declared generally binding by the Royal Decree of 12 June 2002, *BS/MB* 29 June 2002.

105 Collective Agreement No. 89 of 30 January 2007, declared generally binding by the Royal Decree of 25 April 2007, *BS/MB* 11 May 2007.

CHAPTER 2

LIABILITY[106]

SECTION 1. THE (EXTRA-)CONTRACTUAL LIABILITY OF THE EMPLOYEE *VIS-À-VIS* THE EMPLOYER

§ 1. CONTRACTUAL LIABILITY

Article 18 Employment Contract Act states in its first and second paragraphs that the employee is liable to the employer and a third party for gross errors, deceit and minor errors occurring frequently rather than occasionally. In the third paragraph of the same provision the principle is upheld that deviations from the legal liability rule are invalid except when these occur by means of a generally binding collective agreement. However, this kind of deviation may only relate to the employee-employer relationship.

The last paragraph of Article 18 Employment Contract Act states that the compensations and damages to be paid by the employee to the employer as a result of an agreement with the employer or as a result of a judicial decision may only be deducted from the wages by the employer in accordance with the terms of the Wage Protection Act.[107]

The first requirement for the application of the liability restriction is that this concerns employees. So the rule only relates to the liability of the employee in respect of the employer, and not the other way round.

The employee's liability is only limited when he/she commits an error in the implementation of the employment contract, i.e. insofar as he/she finds himself/herself under the authority of the employer. Article 18 Employment Contract Act cannot be applied when the court holds that the facts show that the employee did not find himself/herself under the authority of an employer at the

---

106 Lagasse, F., en Milde, M., 'La responsabilité du travailleur', *Ors.* 1993, pp. 61–67; Fagnart, J.L., 'La responsabilité dans la relation de travail' in *Le contrat de travail dix ans après la loi du 3 juillet 1978*, Brussels, Story-Scientia, 1989, pp. 163–184; Hoer., H., 'L'article 18 de la loi du 3 juillet 1978 relative aux contrats de travail et la responsabilité civile suivant les articles 1382 et 1384 du Code civil', *JTT* 1983, pp. 239–242; Dalcq, R., 'Le législateur contre le droit: à propos de l'article 18 de la loi du 13 juillet 1978', *RGAR* 1979, no. 10.040.

107 Article 23 Wage Protection Act.

time the mistake was made. In the latter case the liability is judged on the basis of the principles of ordinary law.

Gross error, deceit, frequently occurring minor error: the legislator has limited the employee's liability to gross error, deceit or intentional error and the frequently occurring minor error.

Intentional error is usually defined as a fault committed to cause damage. According to a different view an intentional error is the conscious and intentional non-observance of a contractual obligation or a non-contractual generally applicable norm. Common to both views is the presence of an intentional element.

Gross error differs from intentional error in that in the case of the former the intentional element – bad faith – is lacking. Distinguishing between gross error and minor error is (more) difficult. In general, one could say that for an error to be gross it has to be worse than an ordinary error. According to some, the more serious element would lie in the foreseeable and/or unavoidable character of the damage. Others define gross error as the breach of an essential contractual provision.

Finally, the legislator also maintains the employee's liability for the *minor error* which occurs as a rule rather than occasionally. It was the legislator's aim to punish erroneous habits of employees. Despite the fact that an employee only commits small errors, the frequency and multiplicity raise the question of the employee's liability. For there to be a question of frequently occurring minor errors, it is not necessary that these errors are identical

Damage to the employer or to the enterprise: to hold the employee liable it is necessary that the error he/she has damaged the employer. This covers both damage to the enterprise and the person of the employer himself.

The damages to be paid by the employee are added to the employer's property.

Wage deduction: from the last paragraph of Article 18 Employment Contract Act it follows that the employer, under the strict conditions prescribed by Article 23 Wage Protection Act, is allowed to obtain his damages by set-off.

§ 2. CONCURRENCE OF CONTRACTUAL AND EXTRA-CONTRACTUAL LIABILITY

It is generally accepted that claims between contracting parties have their basis in the contract itself. A claim because of extra-contractual liability between parties is only possible if the error the person is charged with constitutes a breach, not of the contractual obligation, but of an obligation which has been imposed on everyone, and if this error has caused damage other than that due to bad implementation of the contract. This is in particular the case when the infringement of the contract is also subject to criminal prosecution.

§ 3. LIABILITY FOR FAULTY WORKMANSHIP

In accordance with Article 19 Employment Contract Act the employee is no longer liable for faulty workmanship as soon as the employer has taken delivery of the piece of work. Taking delivery is synonymous with approving, accepting or agreeing. Whether or not there has been a delivery is a question of fact.

The employee's liability for work not yet taken delivery of is judged on the basis of the principles and criteria of Article 18 Employment Contract Act.

In accordance with Article 19 Employment Contract Act the employee is not liable either for the accidental loss of an object or for the damage or wear that are the result of regular use. This, too, is a rule that has to be interpreted by the trial courts.

SECTION 2. THE EXTRA-CONTRACTUAL LIABILITY *VIS-À-VIS* THIRD PARTIES

Within the framework of the implementation of the employment contract the employee is only liable *vis-à-vis* third parties for gross errors, intentional errors and frequently occurring minor errors. This extra-contractual liability is a special application of the liability principles included in Articles 1382 and 1383 Civil Code. Article 18 Employment Contract Act does not detract from Article 1384, 3 Civil Code, which states that the master is liable for his employees. Therefore, a third party who is the victim of a fault on the part of an employee in the implementation of the employment contract may claim compensation from either the employee or the employer.

When the third party addresses the employee directly he shall, as far as this employee is concerned, have to prove the existence of gross error, intentional error or a frequently occurring minor error. This last situation particularly may lead to practical problems in terms of providing evidence.

When the third party invokes Article 1384, 3 Civil Code or the contractual liability for auxiliary personnel, it suffices for him to prove the existence of an error by the employee (even the slightest one) for the employer to be held liable. Supposing that the second option is chosen and the employer is ordered to pay compensation, the employer can only recover the compensation from the employee if he can prove that the employee committed a gross error, an intentional error or a frequently occurring minor error.

So, the combined application of Article 18 Employment Contract Act and Article 1384, 3 Civil Code leads to the employee's immunity from liability for all errors committed against third parties that do not involve gross errors, intentional errors or frequently occurring minor errors. This immunity does not detract from the liability of the employer by virtue of Article 1384, 3 Civil Code.

CHAPTER 3
SUSPENSION OF THE EMPLOYMENT CONTRACT

SECTION 1. GENERAL[108]

§ 1. TYPES

The grounds for suspension can be grouped according to their legal origin or on the basis of whether or not a guaranteed wage is due.

A. *Origin*

The first type consists of the grounds for suspension regulated by the employment contract legislation.

The second series has its origin in the application of the principles of general contract law on the employment contract.

In the context of civil law two kinds of suspension are acknowledged: the suspension of the contract that can be put down to the erroneous conduct of one of the contracting parties, and the suspensions for which an extraneous cause or circumstances beyond one of the parties' control can be blamed.

The third type refers to the conventional grounds for suspension. There is nothing to prevent the parties from agreeing that some or other event will suspend the employment contract. For instance, the employer may agree that the employment contract is suspended to allow the employee to travel around the world.

Finally, there are certain grounds for suspension that cannot be put in any of the previous categories. This is, for instance, the case in the event of a strike and lock-out, which are qualified by jurisprudence as a ground for suspension of the employment contract.

---

108 Nyssen, B., 'La suspension de l'exécution du contrat' in C. Wantiez (ed.), *Contrats de travail: 20e anniversaire de la loi du 3 juillet 1978*, Brussels, Editions du Jeune Barreau de Bruxelles, 1998, pp. 107–130; Sevrain, A. en Funck, H., 'La suspension de l'exécution du contrat de travail' in *Le contrat de travail dix ans après la loi du 3 juillet 1978*, Brussels, Story-Scientia, pp. 185–214.

B. *Guaranteed wages*

It is also possible to subdivide the grounds for suspension of the employment contract depending or whether or not they lead to the payment of guaranteed wages.

The Employment Contract Act distinguishes between three forms of interruption of employment with guaranteed wages, namely the grounds for suspension with preservation of guaranteed daily, weekly and monthly wages.

The Employment Contract Act also regulates a number of cases of suspension without linking these to any allowances.

§ 2. SETTING

The establishment of legal grounds for suspension must be seen in the context of the legislator's pursuit of more job and socio-economic security for employees. The legislator does this by prescribing that in a number of cases, even though no work is undertaken, wages must be paid and by restricting the employer's right of dismissal, to a greater or lesser extent, during a certain number of periods of suspension.

The suspension of the implementation of the employment contract does not have as a consequence that all obligations of the parties are suspended. The employee concerned remains part of the staff. As a result his/her seniority still increases during the time of suspension. This has implications for the payment of certain seniority-related allowances, such as compensation in lieu of notice and a number of special dismissal compensations.

In principle the contract is not extended by the suspension. Naturally, this is not the case for open-ended employment contracts. However, the suspension will not lead to an extension of the fixed-term contract or a contract for a specified task. The only case in which the suspension may cause an extension is the employment contract with a probation clause.

SECTION 2. TEMPORARY *FORCE MAJEURE*[109, 110]

Force majeure can lead to suspension – and not to termination as one would expect – of the employment contract.

[109] Article 26 Employment Contract Act.

[110] Jourdan, M., 'La force majeure et le contrat de travail (première approche)' in E. Vogel-Polsky (ed.), *Permanence du droit civil en droit du travail*, Brussels, ed. de l'ULB, 1983, pp. 19–43.

Facts such as bankruptcy or temporary or permanent closure of the enterprise because of the application of the regulation on the protection of the environment are considered to be cases of temporary *force majeure*.

The employee may claim unemployment benefits.

SECTION 3. GUARANTEED DAILY WAGES[111, 112]

§ 1. DELAY AND ABSENCE

The employee who has set off for work as usual and arrives late or not at all is entitled to a guaranteed daily wage on the condition that the delay or the impossibility to reach the workplace is a consequence of something that took place on his/her way to work and is entirely unrelated to the employee himself/herself.

These conditions must be fulfilled separately each day.

If a strike of public transport has been going on for several days, the employer is not obliged to pay the daily wage. After all, the employee who is aware of the strike and still sets off for the train, tram or bus stop, does not leave for work in a normal manner. Moreover, the cause does not arise on his/her way to work, but was already present before he/she left for work.

Examples of situations that are not predictable and for which a guaranteed daily wage is due are: bad weather conditions (snow, fog, black ice), train delay, a collision in which the employee himself/herself is involved, or for which he/she has to act as a witness, etc.

Not qualified are: delay or absence due to negligence or lack of precautions on the part of the employee, such as getting up too late, fuel trouble, etc.

§ 2. INTERRUPTED WORKING DAY

An employee is entitled to a guaranteed daily wage if he/she is capable to work, and because of circumstances, independent of his/her will, is not able to start or continue his/her work. However, in the latter case no guaranteed pay will be due when the abovementioned circumstance is a strike.

---

111 Article 27 Employment Contract Act.

112 Raepsaet, F., 'Les heures perdues tout de même gagnées' in Claeys and Engels, *De Arbeidsovereenkomstenwet na 30 jaar... anders bekeken*, Brussels Larcier, 2008, pp. 125–134; Jacqmain, J., 'Heures perdues: via dolorosa', *Chron. D.S.* 1988, 293–295; Jacqmain, J., 'Les heures perdues', *JTT* 1984, pp. 157–164.

§ 3. ELECTIONS

An employee who does not fulfil the conditions to vote by proxy is entitled to his/her full daily wage for the time he/she needs to participate in the elections held on Belgian territory.

SECTION 4. ANNUAL HOLIDAYS[113, 114]

§ 1. INTRODUCTION

The implementation of the employment contract is suspended during the days on which the company is closed because of the annual holiday period and during the days on which the individual employee goes on holiday.

For blue-collar workers the regulation concerning the annual holiday period is part of the social security system; for white-collar workers this is part of employment contract law. For manual workers the holiday allowance is, in principle, financed by the employer's social security contributions and paid by a holiday fund of which the employer is a member, or by the National Agency for Annual Holidays (RJV/ONVA). The holiday allowance for white-collar workers is paid directly by the employer.

The holiday scheme is twofold. On the one hand it consists of the Annual Holidays Act and the Royal Decree of 30 March 1967, and of national Collective Agreement No. 63 often supplemented by sectoral collective agreements, on the other.

§ 2. DURATION OF THE ANNUAL HOLIDAYS

The duration of the annual holidays to which the employee is entitled in a certain year is proportionate to the effective working days or days of work interruption ranking on a par with working days (e.g. days of incapacity for work or annual holidays) in the previous calendar year, which is referred to as the holiday reference year.[115] The number of days considered equal is limited.

A full holiday period for 12 months of labour or days considered equal in the holiday reference year amounts to 24 days in a six-day working week, and to 20 days in a five-day working week, i.e. four weeks. In the case of fewer working

113 Article 28, 1° Employment Contract Act.

114 Morsa, M., 'La réglementation en matière des vacances annuelles du secteur privé à la lumière de la jurisprudence récente de la Cour de justice des Communautés européennes, partie (II): la période 2009–2012', *JTT* 2012, pp. 129–134; Dellisse, M., 'Vacances annuelles des employés. Questions pratiques', *Ors.* 2009/5, pp. 16–25.

115 Article 2 Annual Holidays Act.

days or days considered equal in the reference year, the holiday period is shortened proportionately, on the understanding that for manual workers the right to a certain number of holidays is established on the basis of the number of effective working days or equal days in the reference year; and for white-collar workers on the basis of 2 days a month in the holiday reference year (in a six-day week).[116]

There is an exception to the rule that the right to annual holidays depends on the number of effective working days or equal days, namely for young employees, i.e. persons who have not reached the age of 25 years on 31 December of the holiday reference year, who have completed their studies, apprenticeship or training in the course of the reference year, and after this completion have worked at least one month in the course of the holiday reference year.

Besides the ordinary number of holidays, they are entitled to extra holidays.

By means of Article 54 of the Law concerning the so-called Generation Pact,[117] a similar regulation was introduced for employees who are 50 years old on 31 December of the holiday reference year, and who resume work after a period of inactivity as a result of which they have no right or incomplete rights to an annual holiday. These employees now qualify for so-called 'senior holidays'.

§ 3. ADDITIONAL HOLIDAYS

Until recently Belgium was the only country in the European Union where employees were not entitled to holidays in the year that they started working or resumed working. This meant that school-leavers who started working immediately after finishing school had to wait a year after their graduation before they were entitled to annual holidays. The same applied to the long-term unemployed who had not worked in the reference year. However, this state of affairs is a breach of Article 7 of Directive 2003/88/EC1 on a number of aspects of the organisation of working time. Therefore, the European Commission declared Belgium in default. Through the Royal Decree of 19 June 2012[118] the government put things right by establishing the so-called 'additional holidays'. School-leavers who started working on 1 July 2016 are entitled to 10 holidays in 2016 (12 days in a six-day system).

§ 4. HOLIDAY ALLOWANCE

For blue-collar workers the holiday allowance is 15.38% of the wages of the holiday reference year used as the basis for the calculation of the social security

[116] Article 3 Annual Holidays Act; Article 35 Implementing Order for manual workers; Article 60 Implementing Order concerning white-collar workers.

[117] Law of 23 December 2005, *BS/MB* 30 December 2005.

[118] *BS/MB* 28 June 2012.

contributions, if necessary, increased with the fictitious wage for the days put on a par with the effective working days.[119]

The holiday allowance white-collar workers are paid by their employers consist of two parts:

- the normal wages in accordance with the number of holidays;
- a monthly bonus for the working days or equal days in the holiday reference year equalling 1/12 of 92% of the gross earnings of the month in which the holidays start.

The first part of the holiday allowance is called 'single holiday allowance'; and the second part, 'double holiday allowance'. Both for blue-collar and white-collar workers the holiday legislation means that the four holiday weeks are paid doubly.

For white-collar workers there is a special regulation in the event of dismissal, resignation or other methods of termination of the employment contract. In this case the employer must pay the holiday allowance in advance. The employer pays 15.34% of the salary of the current year and 15.34% of the salary of the holiday reference year if the holidays have not been taken.

After their ordinary number of holidays has been exhausted, young employees and employees entitled to senior holidays may be eligible for extra holiday allowances. These allowances are regarded as unemployment benefits.

§ 5. DATES OF THE HOLIDAYS

To determine the dates of the holiday period the law set up a system going from the collective level to the individual employment contract.[120]

a) The joint committees may take a decision regarding the dates of the holidays and the way these are spread. This decision can be declared generally binding by Royal Decree.
b) In the absence of a decision by the joint committee, the works council can take a decision regarding the collective holiday period.
c) In the absence of a decision by the works council, an internal company decision may be taken between the employer on the one hand and the trade union delegation on the other, or in the absence of the latter, by the employees themselves.
d) Should it not be possible to take a decision on this matter at any of the various levels, then the dates of the holidays have to be determined by an individual agreement between employer and employee. This means that the employee is

119 Article 9 Annual Holidays Act; Article 14 Implementing Order.
120 Article 8 Annual Holidays Act; Article 63 Holidays Order.

not allowed to determine the period of his/her holidays unilaterally. Disputes in this respect must be settled by the labour tribunals.

§ 6. HOLIDAYS AND ILLNESS

If a person becomes ill before his/her holidays, the holidays will not take effect. He/she will then be able to take these days off at a later date. However, when someone becomes ill during his/her holiday period, things are different. The holidays are lost. However, in its judgment of 21 June 2012 (*Anged v. Fasga*)[121] the European Court of Justice ruled that this rule is in conflict with Article 7 (1) of Directive 2003/88/EC. An employee falling ill during his/her holiday period is entitled to take these days at a later date. So, it is very likely that in this matter too a legislative initiative will be required.

SECTION 5. SHORT LEAVE OF ABSENCE[122]

The employee is entitled to be absent whilst retaining his/her normal wages for family reasons, for fulfilling civil duties or assignments, and when he/she has to appear in court.

A limited list of events or duties that give rise to these rights are the subject of the Royal Decree of 28 August 1963.[123] The provisions concerned are regarded as minimum rules. This implies that they can always be deviated from by convention, at least insofar as these arrangements are more favourable.

As far as the application of the regulation regarding the short leave of absence is concerned, the person legally living together with the employee is placed on the same footing as the employee's wife or husband.[124] Legal cohabitation should be regarded rather strictly as the situation in which two persons have given a statement of legal cohabitation by submitting a document to the registrar.[125]

121 Case C-78/11 [2012].
122 Article 30 Employment Contract Act.
123 *BS/MB* 11 September 1963.
124 Article 4*bis* Royal Decree 28 August 1963. See also Collective Agreement No. 74, 17 November 1999, declared generally binding by Royal Decree 7 February 2000 (*BS/MB* 24 February 2000).
125 See Articles 1475 and 1476 Civil Code, as included in Article 2 Law of 23 November 1998 establishing legal cohabitation (*BS/MB* 1 December 1999).

§ 1. REASON AND DURATION OF ABSENCE

A. *The employee's wedding*

Two days, to be spent by the employee in the week in which the event takes place, or in the week following it. This arrangement applies to every marriage, not only the first one. When the civil wedding and the religious wedding are not concluded on the same day, the employee has to choose when to take his/her leave.

B. *Marriage of certain family members of the employee or his/her spouse.*

The wedding day itself.

Eligible are: the marriage of an employee's or his/her spouse's child, brother, sisters, brother-in-law, sister-in-law, father, mother, father-in-law, stepfather, mother-in-law, stepmother or grandchild.

In these cases, too, one will have to choose between the civil and religious wedding.

C. *Ordination or convent entry of certain family members of the employee*

The day of the ceremony.

These are the relatives concerned: children of the employee or his/her spouse, brothers, sisters, brothers-in-law or sisters-in-law.

D. *Birth of an employee's child*

Since 1 July 2002[126] each employee has the right to be absent from work for ten days because of the birth of a child. It suffices that the paternal parentage is established. He may make this leave as he wishes in the course of a period of 30 days from the date of delivery.

During the first three days of absence the father retains his normal wages at the expense of the employer. The following seven days the employee receives an allowance from the compulsory insurance fund for medical care and allowances. Put in more concrete terms, this means that the employee is entitled to 82% of his wages, however with the usual upper sick pay limit. To this end the person in question has to submit a request to the health insurance fund or the Auxiliary Fund for Sickness and Disability Insurance (HZIV/CAAMI) and hand in the necessary documents.

---

[126] See Article 346, 4 Law 10 August 2001 concerning the conciliation of employment and quality of life, (*BS/MB* September 2001; err., *BS/MB* 9 October 2001). The condition is that the delivery took place after 1 July 2001 (see Article 31, § 1 Law of 10 August 2001).

In 2011, the right to leave of absence was extended to the co-parent. This concerns, among others, the partner with whom the child's mother lives together but who is not a blood-relative of the child.

This form of paid absence should not be confused with the paternity leave when, as a result of the child's birth, the mother has to stay in the hospital or dies.

E. Death of certain family members of the employee or his/her spouse

The number of days varies according to the degree of kinship. Also taken into account is the fact of whether or not the deceased lived under the same roof as the employee.

The death of the spouse, a child of the employee or his/her spouse, the employee's father, mother, father-in-law, stepfather, mother-in-law or stepmother, entitles the employee to three days of absence, to be chosen by the employee in the period beginning on the day of death and ending on the day of the funeral.

Upon the death of a brother, sister, brother-in-law, sister-in-law, (great)grandfather, (great)grandmother, (great)grandchild, son-in-law or daughter-in-law living with the employee, the person concerned is entitled to his/her normal wages during two days between the death and the funeral. This also applies in the case of the death of a brother-in-law, sister-in-law, grandfather and grandmother of the spouse. If the abovementioned family members do not live with the employee, only the day of the funeral is regarded as a short leave of absence.

This arrangement no longer applies when the person concerned is divorced from the spouse because of whom the kinship was established.

F. Confirmation of a child of the employee or his/her spouse

Day of the ceremony.

When this day coincides with a Sunday, a holiday or a normal day of inactivity, the employee is entitled to be absent on the working day immediately preceding or following the day of the ceremony.

G. Non-Confessional Youth Celebration of a child of the employee or his/her spouse

The day of the celebration itself.

The rules are the same as those for the Confirmation.

H. Serving on a jury, summons as a witness for the court or personal appearance at the request of the labour tribunal

When an employee has to serve on a jury, is summoned as a witness for the court or is demanded by the labour tribunal to appear in person, he/she is entitled to full pay during his/her absence for the time required, up to a maximum of five days.

These provisions must be interpreted strictly. Personal appearances before other courts or voluntary appearances before the labour tribunal do not qualify.

The general rules regarding legal fees in criminal cases include a special arrangement to the advantage of the jurors at the Assize Courts. An employer who has continued to pay his employee-juror full wages after the fifth day may recover these from the department for court fees at the Federal Public Service of Justice. For each extra day the employee has to spend in court or to attend the debates as a (replacement) juror, the employer shall be accorded compensation equal to the daily gross pay, increased with the employer's contributions for social security and the holiday allowance and end of year bonus referring to these. Supralegal payments, however, are not taken into consideration. The daily compensation corresponds to eight times the gross hourly wage or 1/20 of the monthly salary, depending on whether the wages the employer pays are expressed in hourly wages or monthly wages.

I. Duties during elections

Assessors in a chief polling station or any other polling station for parliamentary, provincial and municipal elections: the time required.

Assessors in any of the chief polling stations during the election of the European Parliament: the time required, up to a maximum of five days.

Assessors in a chief office for the counting of votes during parliamentary, provincial and municipal elections: the time required, limited to five days.

§ 2. PART-TIME WORK

Just like full-time employees, part-time employees are entitled to take a leave of absence while retaining full pay insofar as this leave of absence coincides with the days and periods in which they would have worked normally. Here, the legislator does not apply the rule of proportionality. It rather maintains the starting point that pay is only due if the employee would have had to work on the day of the leave of absence.

§ 3. TERMS

Not only is the employee allowed to be absent, but he/she also receives guaranteed wages. The normal pay is calculated in accordance with the Public Holiday Act.

However, in order to qualify the employee must satisfy a number of conditions:

- he/she must inform the employer in advance. If this is not possible, he/she must do this as soon as possible;
- he/she must use his/her leave of absence for the matter for which it has been granted, although without having to prove this. If so desired the employer has the right to demonstrate that the employee misused his/her leave of absence.

During the period of absence the employee is only entitled to the normal wages for the days of inactivity for which he/she could have claimed wages if he/she had been able to work. If the employee does not lose wages because of his/her absence the employer is not obliged to compensate him/her.

SECTION 6. PUBLIC HOLIDAYS

§ 1. LEGAL HOLIDAYS

Legal holidays are not considered a ground for suspension by the Employment Contract Act, whereas the general principle of the Public Holidays Act[127] is that the employee may not be employed during ten legal annual holidays.

These are the ten public holidays in question:

- New Year's Day (1 January);
- Easter Monday;
- Labour Day (1 May);
- Ascension Day;
- Whit Monday;
- National Holiday (21 July);
- Assumption Day (15 August);
- All Saints' Day (1 November);
- Armistice Day (11 November);
- Christmas Day (25 December).

§ 2. SUBSTITUTE DAYS

When a legal holiday falls on a Sunday or another day on which no work has to be done, it is replaced by a normal day of activity.

[127] Law of 4 January 1974 concerning the public holidays (*BS/MB* 31 January 1974). The further implementation of this law is the subject of Royal Decree 18 April 1974 (*BS/MB* 24 April 1974).

§ 3. COMPENSATORY DAYS OFF

Under certain conditions the employee may be put to work on a legal holiday. In that case the worker in question is entitled to time off in lieu.

§ 4. GUARANTEED WAGES

The employee is entitled to wages for each legal holiday or substitute day during which he/she was not employed, as well as for every day taken in lieu.

SECTION 7. SICKNESS OR INJURY

The incapacity of the employee due to illness or injury suspends the implementation of the contract.[128]

§ 1. CONCEPT OF 'INCAPACITY TO WORK'

For there to be a case of incapacity to work it suffices that the employee is incapable of performing the tasks contractually agreed upon. The fact that the employee concerned may be capable to carry out other tasks is of no importance.

In the past there used to be some discussion regarding the requirement of the incapacity for work having to be the result of a 'disease' or 'injury', more specifically with regard to cases of sterilisation or vasectomy. The Court of Cassation ruled that, when an employee chooses to undergo this kind of surgery for a reason other than the preservation or recovery of his/her health, the operation may cause a situation of incapacity to work even though the employee was not ill prior to the treatment.[129] Gross error is the only reason for denying an employee the right to guaranteed wages.

128 Article 31, § 1 Employment Contract Act.

129 Cassation 12 March 1984, *Rechtskundig Weekblad* 1983–84, p. 2539.

§ 2. GUARANTEED WAGES

A. *Blue-collar workers*[130]

1. Condition of seniority

The manual worker must have been employed in the same enterprise for at least one month. The requirement of length of service must be satisfied at the moment the incapacity for work starts.

When the required length of service is reached during the period of guaranteed wages, the worker in question is entitled to the remaining part of the guaranteed wages starting on the day on which the condition of seniority is fulfilled.

2. Extent

On the basis of the Employment Contract Act manual workers can only exert their right to normal wages at the expense of the employer for a period of seven days.[131] Moreover, these wages are only due for the days of normal activity for which the worker could have claimed wages if he/she had not been unable to work.

During the following seven days the employer is obliged to pay the worker a sum of 60% of the wages, insofar as this does not exceed the wage limit taken into account for the calculation of the sickness and invalidity insurance allowances. No social security contributions are due. From the 15th day of the incapacity to work the worker is entitled to an allowance paid out by the sickness and invalidity insurance, corresponding to 60% of his/her lost earnings, also with a maximum limit.

In addition, Collective Agreement No. 12*bis* of 26 February 1979[132] obliges the employer to pay an additional compensation for a period of 23 days following the first seven days of incapacity to work. This extra allowance amounts to 25.88% of the wages insofar as this does not exceed the upper limit in the context of the compulsory sickness and invalidity insurance, and to 85.88% of the wages exceeding said limit.

In summary, this means that manual workers are entitled to 100% of their wages during the first seven days of their incapacity to work, albeit reduced by the regular employer's contributions, and after that, up to the 30th day, to 85.88% of this sum.

---

130 Article 52 Employment Contract Act.

131 The normal wages are calculated on the basis of the Public Holidays Act.

132 This collective agreement is revised by the social partners on a regular basis.

B. *White-collar workers*

Within the group of white-collar workers a distinction must be made between employees on fixed-term employment contracts, contracts for specified tasks of less than three months' duration or during the probationary period on the one hand; and other white-collar workers, on the other.

1. White-collar workers on short-term contracts[133]

To a large extent the arrangement for blue collar-workers also applies to white-collar workers employed for a short term. The guaranteed salary owed to them by virtue of the Employment Contract Act is supplemented on the basis of Collective Agreement No. 13*bis* of 26 February 1979.[134] Only the percentages prescribed by the latter are somewhat divergent, and amount to 26.93% and 86.93% respectively.

The requirements regarding length of service also apply to this group of workers.

2. Other white-collar workers[135]

In the event of incapacity for work due to illness or injury under ordinary law, white-collar workers who have been hired for a long(er) duration receive guaranteed wages equal to – agreed by convention – the salary for the first thirty calendar days of the incapacity to work. In concrete terms this means that during the first thirty days of his/her incapacity to work the employee retains his/her current salary.

C. *Relapsing*[136]

The guaranteed salary is not due again when a new incapacity to work occurs within the first 14 days following the end of the period of incapacity to work which caused the payment of a guaranteed salary.

---

133 Article 71 Employment Contract Act.

134 This collective agreement is revised on a regular basis by the social partners.

135 Article 70 Employment Contract Act.

136 Article 52, § 2 Employment Contract Act and Article 73 Employment Contract Act.

D. *Grounds for exclusion*[137]

Guaranteed wages are not due:

- when the employee has had an accident as a result of a sports competition or sports exhibition for which the organisers charge admission fees and for which the participants receive wages in whatever form;
- when the incapacity to work is the result of a gross error committed by the employee.

E. *Redress*

If the employee is unfit for work as a result of an accident under ordinary law for which a third party is liable, the victim's employer has the right to claim compensation from the liable party for the wages he has had to pay to his employee, as well as for the social contributions that he is obliged to pay under the individual and collective employment agreements.

§ 3. THE EMPLOYEE'S OBLIGATIONS

A. *Informing the employer*[138]

1. Principle

The employee is obliged to notify his/her employer of his/her incapacity to work without delay, i.e. 'as soon as this is possible for the employee'. It goes without saying that in actual practice this is a question of fact which has to be assessed in all reasonableness.

The Employment Contract Act does not mention a specific time limit in this respect, but one may assume that normally notification should take place on the first day of incapacity to work.

2. Manner

The employee is free to choose the manner in which he/she fulfils this notification requirement: by telephone, in writing, by immediately submitting the required medical certificate, by handing in the forms intended for the insurance agency for sickness and invalidity, etc. When the person concerned becomes incapable to

[137] Article 52, §3 Employment Contract Act and Article 73, § 2 Employment Contract Act.
[138] Article 31, § 2 Employment Contract Act.

work while he/she is at work, it may be assumed that the employer is informed of his/her condition right away.

The proof that he/she has acquitted him/herself of this duty rests with the employee.

If so desired, the employee may instruct another person to inform the employer of his/her incapacity to work.

3. Sanctions

The Employment Contract Act does not provide for punitive sanctions if the employee violates this rule. Logically speaking, one could impose a sanction comparable with the sanction for an overdue delivery of the medical certificate, namely withholding the guaranteed wages until the obligation is fulfilled.

B. Proof of illness or injury

1. Principle

As soon as the employee has notified his/her employer of his/her incapacity to work he/she must give evidence of this. This is usually done by means of a medical certificate, but the law does not exclude other means of evidence. Submitting a medical certificate is only necessary insofar as this obligation is included in a collective agreement or in the work rules, or – in the absence of such an explicit provision – if the employer requests this.[139] In the latter case the burden of proof rests with the employer, who has to be able to show that he submitted such a request to the employee.

2. Time limit

Except in the case of *force majeure* the certificate must be sent to or handed in at the enterprise within two working days of the beginning of the incapacity or from the moment of the employer's request, except when collective agreements or the work rules provide for another time limit.[140] This diverging term may both be shorter and longer; if so desired another starting point may be established.

When the certificate is sent by post the legal time limit of two working days refers to the posting date, and not to the date of receipt by the employer.

---

[139] Article 32, § 2, 2 Employment Contract Act.

[140] Article 31, § 2, 3 Employment Contract Act.

3. Manner

The medical certificate must either be sent by the employee or handed in at the enterprise.

The employee is not obliged to send this document by registered post. However, this method is to be recommended in order to prevent disputes regarding overdue submission.

The employee must be able to produce evidence of submitting the required certificate. This proof may be presented by means of all legal remedies.

5. Addressee

The medical certificate must be submitted to the employer, meaning that the employee cannot be obliged, for instance, to send the certificate in question directly to the medical officer.

6. Sanctions

When the medical certificate is handed in too late, the employee may be denied the right to guaranteed wages for the days of incapacity to work prior to the day on which the certificate is handed in or sent.

In principle, non-observance of the time limit for handing in a medical certificate cannot be invoked as a just cause for dismissal. The fact that a short absence because of incapacity to work is not substantiated by the required pieces of evidence and an overdue posting of the medical certificate do not constitute proof of the employee's wish to terminate the employment contract unilaterally.

C. *Extension of the incapacity to work*

The Employment Contract Act does not determine explicitly which formalities have to be fulfilled if the incapacity to work takes longer than foreseen.

§ 4. CONTROL OF INCAPACITY TO WORK[141]

A. *General*

The employer has the right to submit his employees for a medical assessment. He can try to rebut the incapacity to work through all legal means, including witnesses and presumptions. Making use of a medical officer is the most obvious way to do this. When the employee has proven his/her incapacity to work by

[141] Article 31, § 2 Employment Contract Act.

means of a medical certificate, the only way to rebut the existence of incapacity to work is a medical examination.

This kind of examination is possible during the entire period of incapacity to work, so also outside the period in which guaranteed wages are paid.

It does not matter that the employee was not obliged to submit a medical certificate.

For the same period of incapacity to work it is, furthermore, permitted to check on the employee more than once. An employee who refuses to undergo a medical examination – even if it is the fourth – commits an error.

Only when the employment relationship has been terminated does the right to control an employee's incapacity to work expire.

B. Choice of medical officer

The verification of the incapacity to work may only be entrusted to a medical officer,[142] i.e. a person who is qualified to carry out medical assessments[143] by order of the employer with a view to verifying an employee's incapacity to work because of illness or injury.[144]

These medical checks can only be carried out by a doctor who is qualified to practice medicine and who has had five years of experience as a General Practitioner or in a comparable position.[145]

Furthermore, with every assignment the medical officer must sign a statement of independence[146] which serves as a guarantee that the doctor concerned is completely independent both of the employer and the employee in question.[147]

Medical officers acting contrary to these provisions can be prosecuted.[148]

1. Free Choice

The employer may appoint a medical officer associated with the enterprise or rely on several medical officers or ask an occupational health agency to appoint a doctor on his behalf. If so desired, the medical officer may also be appointed by the insurance company insuring the employer against the effects of his legal obligation to pay guaranteed wages.

---

142 Compare Article 31, § 3, 1 and 3 Employment Contract Act.

143 Article 2, 2 Law 13 June 1999 concerning the medical control system. This law applies to the incapacity to work or the extension of the incapacity to work beginning on 1 December 2002 (Royal Decree 20 September 2002, *BS/MB* 3 October 2002).

144 Article 2, § 1 Law 13 June 1999 concerning the medical control system.

145 Article 3, § 1 Law 13 June 1999 concerning the medical control system.

146 Article 2 Royal Decree 18 July 2001 concerning medical officers and medical arbitrators, *BS/MB* 3 August 2001.

147 Article 3, § 2, 1 Law 13 June 1999 concerning the medical control system.

148 Articles 10 through 12 Law 13 June 1999 concerning the medical control system.

Furthermore, the employer is free to change his choice unilaterally at any time, even when a specific medical officer is named in the employment contract or in the work rules.

C. *Costs of control*

The costs related to the medical control of the incapacity to work are entirely for the employer, as are the costs the employee has had to incur to report for the medical assessment, for instance, travel expenses. It is forbidden to include a different provision in the employment contract or in the work rules.

D. *Location*

1. First hypothesis: the employee may not leave the house

If the attending doctor is of the opinion that the employee's state of health does not allow him/her to travel, the medical assessment must take place at the address where the employee resides.

Whether or not the employee's state of health is such that he/she may or may not leave his/her house, is at the discretion of the attending doctor, who will detail this on the medical certificate he issues to substantiate the incapacity to work.

2. Second hypothesis: the employee may leave the house

If the employee's state of health allows him/her to travel, which will be evident from the medical certificate, he/she must report to the medical officer if so requested.[149]

E. *Time of the medical control*

The Employment Contract Act does not offer any instructions with regard to the times at which assessment is possible.

So there is nothing to prevent this from taking place on Saturdays, Sundays, public holidays or other days of inactivity.

Since 1 January 2014 collective agreements or work rules can stipulate that employees have to be available to receive a medical officer at their place of residence or a place of residence known to the employer for a period of four successive hours between 7 a.m. and 8 p.m.

---

[149] Article 31, § 3, 1 Employment Contract Act.

F. Contents

It is the duty of the medical officer to check if the employee concerned is genuinely unfit for work.

To this end the medical officer is required to examine the employee effectively.

The medical check can consist of a physical examination. The medical officer even has the right – which in practice hardly ever occurs – to carry out technical tests. Furthermore, he may ask access to certain documents in the employee's possession, such as x-rays, lab results, etc. It is the employee's duty to permit all of this, but this duty is not absolute. He/she does have the right to refuse certain examinations if they are not necessary, not without risk, or not painless. The actual state of health of the employee must also be taken into account. It goes without saying that the medical officer may not meddle in the therapy or provide any advice with regard to the correctness of the diagnosis.

Furthermore, the medical officer is only allowed to consult the medical file with the agreement of the patient and approval of the attending doctor.

G. Refusal of control by the employee

The employee is obliged to receive the medical officer authorised and paid by the employer, and to allow this doctor to examine him/her.[150]

However, the employee cannot be forced to undergo an examination. In that case he/she will have to accept the sanction attached to such a refusal, more specifically the withholding of guaranteed pay for his/her days of absence because of incapacity to work.

It is generally accepted that unfit employees cannot demand that the examination takes place in the presence of their attending doctor, which does not alter the fact that the medical officer may agree to the presence of the attending doctor.

The employee's duty to receive the medical officer authorised and paid by the employer and to be examined by him also implies that the employee has to allow the control. We already pointed this out with regard to the employee's obligation to make his/her effective place of residence known to the employer.

In the same vein it was decided that an employee's refusal to remove his/her dog, which was necessary to carry out the examination properly, must be put on a par with making it impossible to carry out proper control.

[150] Article 31, § 3, 1 introduction Employment Contract Act.

H. *Effect on the right to guaranteed pay*

A distinction must be made between the situation in which the employee shirks the control or makes this impossible, and the situation in which the medical officer rebuts the incapacity to work as a result of the control.

The Employment Contract Act does not specify which sanction is attached to the refusal or shirking of medical control. As a rule, however, it is assumed that such behaviour by the employee constitutes an error which may be punished with the loss of the right to guaranteed wages. With regard to the question as to from exactly what moment the right to wages is lost, jurisprudence also takes a unanimous point of view: the employee loses his entitlement to guaranteed wages from the first day of his/her incapacity to work.

It needs pointing out that refusing or shirking control in itself is not a just cause for dismissal unless this involves a particular behaviour on the part of the employee. Nor can from such an act by the employee the presumed wish of unilateral termination of the employment contract be deduced.

When on the other hand the incapacity to work is questioned by the medical officer, the right to guaranteed pages can, in our view, only be cancelled from the first day following the examination at the earliest. Indeed, the incapacity to work, as communicated by the employee, must be considered as proven until the moment the employer proceeds to control. This position not only applies when the medical officer judges that the incapacity to work does not exist (any longer) at the time of the examination or will end at a date determined by him, but also if the medical officer were to decide that during the previous days (or weeks) there had not been any incapacity to work either.

§ 5. CONFLICT

A. *Equality of conflicting certificates*

If the consultation between the medical officer and the attending doctor does not lead to a consensus, the value of each of the conflicting medical certificates has to be established. As far as the starting point is concerned, there cannot (can no longer) be any discussion: conflicting certificates from the attending doctor on the one hand, and from the medical officer on the other, relate to equivalent findings and outweigh each other.

B. *Initiative to solve the dispute*

If the parties cannot reach an agreement about the appointment of a medical arbitrator, the initiative to settle the dispute lies with the party that is first to take action, i.e. the party that has the biggest interest in this. Actually, this is an application of the ordinary rules of evidence.

Usually the employee claiming the payment of the guaranteed wages for the days for which his/her incapacity to work is disputed, shall have to present the evidence of incapacity to work for those days. When the medical officer designated by the employer, contrary to the certificate issued by the employee's attending doctor, decides that the employee is fit for work, the necessary evidence of his/her incapacity to work has not been delivered.

C. *Arbitrational procedure*

1. General[151]

The disputes arising between the employee and the medical officer are settled by means of an arbitrational procedure unless the parties choose to turn to the ordinary courts. However, if one chooses to use a medical arbitrator, the latter's decision is definite and binding for all parties.

2. Appointment of a medical arbitrator[152]

In the first place attempts will be made to get the employee and the employer to agree on the choice of a medical arbitrator. If this turns out to be impossible within a period of two working days after delivery of the findings of the medical officer, it is up to the party first to take action to designate a medical arbitrator.

However, delegation is also possible. The employer can explicitly authorise the medical officer to designate the medical arbitrator. Analogously, the employee can authorise the doctor who gave him/her the certificate to designate a medical arbitrator.

This medical arbitrator must comply with the provisions of the Law of 13 June 1999 regarding the medical control system and be registered on a list of medical arbitrators kept at the Federal Public Service for Employment, Labour and Social Dialogue.[153]

3. Special requirements for the medical arbitrator[154]

For medical practitioners to be included in the list of medical arbitrators, the unanimous assent of the Monitoring Committee is necessary. To be eligible, the candidates must comply with the following requirements:

151 Article 31, § 5, 1 Employment Contract Act.
152 Article 31, § 5, 2 Employment Contract Act.
153 Article 6, § 1 Law 13 June 1999 regarding the medical control system.
154 Article 6, § 2 Law 13 June 1999 regarding the medical control system.

- they must be qualified to practice medicine and have five years of experience as General Practitioners or in a similar practice;
- they must undertake to being completely independent *vis-à-vis* the various parties in the conflict, i.e. the employer, the employee, the attending doctor and the medical officer.

It is obvious that an appointment as a medical arbitrator is incompatible with the position of the employee's attending doctor and the position of medical officer or company doctor.

A medical arbitrator who does not fulfil his obligations can – subject to the assent of the Monitoring Committee – be suspended temporarily or removed definitively from the list by the Minister of Employment.[155]

4. Examination and decision by the medical arbitrator

The medical arbitrator shall perform the medical examination and take a decision with regard to the medical dispute within three days of having been designated.[156] He shall inform the person who issued the medical certificate and the medical officer of his decision. The employer and employee will be informed in writing by registered post.[157]

5. Costs

The costs of the arbitrational procedure as well as the travel expenses of the employee will be charged to the losing party.[158]

6. Interaction with guaranteed wages

Guaranteed wages are owed for the period that the employee was acknowledged to be unfit for work as a result of the settlement of the dispute.[159]

7. Divergent arbitrational procedure

By means of a Royal Decree, after approval by the competent joint committee or sub-committee, it is possible to introduce a divergent arbitrational procedure.[160] For employers who do not fall within the scope of the Collective Agreement

---

155 Article 7, § 1 Law 13 June 1999 regarding the medical control system. According to Article 7, § 2 Law 13 June 1999 the way in which that suspension or removal will take place in actual practice will be specified by Royal Decree.

156 Article 31, § 5, 3 Employment Contract Act.

157 Article 31, § 5, 5 Employment Contract Act.

158 Article 31, § 5, 4 Employment Contract Act.

159 Article 31, § 6 Employment Contract Act.

160 Article 31, § 7 Employment Contract Act.

Act there is also the possibility to lay down a divergent arrangement by Royal Decree.[161]

D. *Legal expertise*

The parties have the freedom to turn to the ordinary courts instead of presenting their medical dispute to a medical arbitrator.

SECTION 8. INDUSTRIAL ACCIDENTS AND OCCUPATIONAL DISEASES

§ 1. CONCEPT OF 'INCAPACITY TO WORK'

The rule by virtue of which the employee's incapacity to work due to illness or injury may lead to suspension of the implementation of the employment contract also applies in the event of industrial accidents or occupational diseases, and this because of the fact that no distinction is made with regard to the origin of the incapacity to work.

Indeed, incapacity to work as a result of an industrial accident or an occupational disease amounts to the same thing: a person's incapability of doing his/her regular job.

§ 2. WAGE GUARANTEE

A. *Short-term employment: blue-collar and white-collar workers*

A labourer who has fallen victim to an industrial accident or an occupational disease is entitled to his/her normal wages during the first seven days of his/her incapacity to work. The same applies to white-collar workers hired for a fixed period shorter than three months, or for specified tasks with an expected duration of less than three months.

On the basis of Collective Agreements Nos. 12*bis* and 13*bis* of 26 February 1979 said employees are also granted an extra amount during the 23 following days. This sum is meant as a supplement to the compensations paid by the industrial accident insurer or the Fund for Occupational Diseases so that the employee is guaranteed remuneration equal to the net income he/she would have earned if he/she had continued working.

[161] Article 31, § 8 Employment Contract Act.

B. *Long-term white-collar workers*

In the case of an industrial accident or occupational disease white-collar workers who were hired for an open-ended period or for a fixed period exceeding three months, or for a specified task whose completion normally takes at least three months, are also entitled to a guaranteed monthly salary during the first thirty days of their incapacity to work.

C. *Redress*

The employer has the right to make a legal claim against the third party that caused the industrial accident or occupational disease for compensation of the wages that the employer had to pay due to the incapacity to work, including the social contributions he was obliged to pay.

§ 3. FORMALITIES

In the case of industrial accidents or occupational diseases the employee has the same obligations with regard to informing his/her employer and submitting a medical certificate as in the case of ordinary illness and injury. These obligations are unrelated to the specific terms with regard to the report of an industrial accident or occupational disease.

§ 4. CONTROL

The control of temporary incapacity to work due to industrial accidents or occupational diseases is exactly the same as in the case of incapacity to work due to ordinary illness or injury.

SECTION 9. MATERNITY RIGHTS[162]

The pregnant employee and the employee who has just given birth – married or not – is, as a result of her condition, entitled to specific rights, including during breastfeeding:

- the right to paid absence to undergo pregnancy check-ups;
- leave of absence before and after giving birth;

[162] Jacqmain, J., *Protection de la maternité*, Etudes pratiques de droit social, Brussels, Wolters Kluwer, 2007, 119 pp.

- the prohibition of or exemption from employment in certain circumstances, or a limited right to adapted work;
- maternity allowance;
- restriction of the employer's power of dismissal during the period before and after giving birth;
- right to breastfeeding breaks.

Sometimes the father, too, is protected, more specifically by granting him paternity leave, which under certain circumstances involves the right to a 'paternity allowance'. When this occurs protection against dismissal is included.

§ 1. LEAVE FOR PREGNANCY CHECK-UPS[163]

A pregnant employee has, under certain conditions, the right to be absent from work – without having their wages docked – for the time needed to have pregnancy check-ups. During this absence the implementation of the employment contract is suspended.

A. *Wage guarantee*

During her absence for pregnancy check-ups the employee keeps her regular wages calculated according to the Public Holidays Act. It goes without saying that this only applies when the employee would have been entitled to pay if she had not been incapable of working.

B. *Conditions and formalities*

The leave of absence for pregnancy check-ups has a certain similarity to the rules for the short leave of absence.

The first requirement is that the employee must have informed the employer of her pregnancy.

Moreover, the right of absence for pregnancy check-ups only applies insofar as these check-ups cannot take place outside working hours.

As already pointed out above, their duration is limited to the time required for the said check-ups. In order to be effectively entitled to wages, the employee must notify her employer of her absence beforehand.

As for the possibility of demanding a medical certificate justifying this absence, the rules are identical to those for the incapacity to work. Submitting such a medical certificate can be made obligatory by collective agreement or by

[163] Article 39*bis* Labour Act and Article 28, 2°*bis* Employment Contract Act.

the work rules. In the absence of such an explicit provision it is for the employer to request this.

§ 2. MATERNITY LEAVE[164]

A. *Antenatal rest or pregnancy leave*

If the employee requests it, the employer is obliged to grant her leave starting from the sixth week before the due date of birth. When a multiple birth is expected, the antenatal period may start from the eighth week before the due date.

This period of leave of six or eight weeks is the antenatal rest or pregnancy leave.

At the latest, seven or nine weeks before the due date of birth, the employee must provide her employer with a medical certificate confirming this date. If she gives birth after the date anticipated by the doctor, the leave is extended until the actual date of delivery.

The employee may not work from the seventh day prior to the due date of birth. So, antenatal rest consists of one week of compulsory leave before delivery, and five or seven optional weeks.

B. *Postnatal rest or maternity leave*

For nine weeks after giving birth the employee is not allowed to work. This period is called postnatal leave or maternity leave. The prohibition of employment is absolute. Parties cannot deviate from this. An employer who forces or allows his employee to work can be prosecuted.

At the request of the employee the interruption of employment after the ninth week is extended by a period equal to that during which she has continued to work from the sixth week before the actual date of birth.[165] In the case of a premature birth, this period is cut back by the days during which the employee worked during the period of seven days prior to delivery. So, the part of antenatal leave that has not been used up is transferable, although only up to a maximum of five (or seven) weeks, and without the seven days prior to delivery being transferable.

In the case of extension of the maternity leave, it is assumed that the employee effectively worked during the seven weeks prior to delivery. However, certain periods of suspension of the employment contract are considered equal to periods of work.

At the employee's request the period of interruption of employment after the ninth week can be extended by a maximum of one week (or two weeks in the case

164 Article 39 Labour Act and Article 28, 2° Employment Contract Act.

165 In the case of a multiple birth from the ninth week.

of a multiple birth) when the employee has been unfit for work due to illness or injury during the entire period from the sixth week prior to the actual date of delivery, or the eighth week when a multiple birth is expected.[166]

C. *Extension*

In the case of a multiple birth the postnatal rest may be extended by a maximum of two weeks at the request of the employee, and this independent of the transfer of non-used antenatal leave.

Furthermore, there is a special arrangement if the new-born baby must stay in hospital after the first seven days after his/her birth. In that situation the postnatal rest can be extended by a period equal to the period of the child's hospitalisation exceeding the period of seven days. The duration of this extension may not exceed 24 weeks. For this purpose the employee must:

- provide her employer, at the end of the postnatal rest period, with a certificate supplied by the hospital showing that the infant has been hospitalised after the first seven days since its birth, and stating the duration of the hospitalisation;
- at the end of the previous extension – where appropriate – supply a new certificate from the hospital that shows that the newborn baby has not yet been allowed to leave the hospital, including the duration of hospitalisation.

D. *Staggering of days of leave*[167]

If the employee can extend the interruption of work by at least two weeks after the ninth week, the last two weeks of the postnatal rest can be converted into separate days of postnatal leave. The employee will have to take these days of postnatal leave according to a schedule drawn up by herself within the eight weeks following the end of the uninterrupted period of postnatal rest.

E. *Paternity leave*[168]

If the mother dies or has to stay in hospital after the newborn has left the hospital, the child's father may take up the remainder of the maternity leave in the mother's stead. Paternity leave is optional, but if the father requests this the employer must grant it.

If the mother dies, the duration of the paternity leave is limited to the remainder of the maternity leave which the mother had not yet taken. It goes without saying that it may be requested for a shorter period.

---

166 Article 39 Labour Act.

167 Article 39 Labour Act.

168 Article 39 last paragraph Labour Act and Royal Decree 17 October 1994 (*BS/MB* 9 November 19945; *err. BS/MB* 15 December 1994).

The same principle takes effect when paternity leave is granted because of the mother's hospitalisation. It is also possible for the paternity leave to end sooner, i.e. at the time the mother leaves the hospital. In that case the following additional conditions have to be fulfilled:

- the paternity leave cannot start before the seventh day after birth;
- the newborn baby must have left the hospital;
- hospitalisation must last longer than seven days.

The Law of 13 April 2011[169] has created the possibility to transpose maternity leave into a leave of absence for the (lesbian) co-mother in the case of hospitalisation of the child's birth mother.

§ 3. PROHIBITION OF OR EXEMPTION FROM EMPLOYMENT IN CERTAIN CIRCUMSTANCES[170]

A. *General*

The protection mechanisms described below come into effect as soon as the employee has informed her employer of her condition, namely pregnancy, or the fact that she has chosen to breastfeed.

As a rule, pregnant employees, employees who have given birth, or breastfeed, must be notified of the result of the risk assessment and the general measures to be taken.

B. *Risk assessment*

For all potentially dangerous work during which a specific risk of exposure to agents, processes or work conditions may occur, a risk assessment has to be carried out. The nature, extent and duration of the exposure must be assessed in order to evaluate any risks for health or safety, and their effects on the pregnancy or breastfeeding, as well as on the child's health, and in order to establish what general measures will have to be taken.

The risk assessment shall be carried out by the employer in collaboration with the company doctor and the department for health and safety in the workplace.

The results of the risk assessment have to be recorded in a document and submitted for advice to the Committee for Prevention and Protection at Work, or failing the latter, to the union delegation.

---

169 *BS/MB* 10 May 2011.

170 Article 41 Labour Act.

C. *Prohibition of exposure to certain risks*

A list has been made of physical, biological and chemical agents and certain work conditions which are obviously hazardous for pregnant and breastfeeding employees. Exposure to these is forbidden.[171]

In addition to this absolute prohibition of exposure, appropriate measures have to be taken when the employee reports a danger or ailment which is related to her condition and could have been caused by her work, provided that the risk is confirmed by the company doctor. In this context one could refer to a relative prohibition of exposure.

D. *Night work*

Employees cannot be forced to do night work during a period of eight weeks prior to the due date of delivery. Night work is understood to mean work that is mainly carried out between 8 p.m. and 6 a.m.

During other periods of the pregnancy the employee in question can also be exempted from the obligation to do night work provided that she submits a medical certificate confirming the necessity of this measure for her own, or her child's, health and safety. The same applies for a period of maximum four weeks immediately following the end of the postnatal rest.

In this context we must point out that the generally binding Collective Agreement No. 46 of 23 March 1990[172] had already introduced a comparable protection. However, the content of this Collective Agreement does not fully correspond to the provisions of the Labour Act. On a number of points the abovementioned Collective Agreement goes further, as a result of which this Collective Agreement is preferential for private sector employees. Collective Agreement No. 46 of 23 March 1990 stipulates that employees who submit a written request cannot be obliged to do night work from at least three months before the due date of birth until at least three months after giving birth. Furthermore, if a medical certificate shows that termination of night work is necessary, there is also the possibility of being exempted from night work – as pursuant to the Labour Act – for other periods during the pregnancy, as well as during a period of time to be determined at the doctor's discretion, from three months after having given birth.

E. *Overtime*

The pregnant employee is not allowed to do overtime. However, this rule does not take effect in the public sector, since most of the government administrations and

---

171 Royal Decree of 2 May 1995 concerning the protection of motherhood, *BS/MB* 18 May 1995.

172 See Royal Decree 10 May 1990, *BS/MB* 13 June 1990.

institutions are not bound by the Labour Act rules concerning working hours. For the public employers there is a specific regulation as established in the Law of 14 December 2000 regarding some aspects of the organisation of the working time in the public sector.[173]

F. *Adaptation of work*

1. In the event of prohibition of exposure to certain risks

Taking into account the results of the risk assessment the employer – with a view to avoiding the employee's exposure to the risk – shall take one of the following measures adapted to the situation of the employee concerned:

- a temporary adaptation of the working conditions of the risk-linked working hours of the employee concerned;
- if such an adaptation of the working conditions or of the working hours turns out to be technically or objectively impossible, or for valid reasons cannot in all fairness be demanded, the employer shall see to it that the employee can carry out different tasks that are compatible with her condition;
- if such a transfer is technically or objectively impossible, or for valid reasons cannot in all fairness be demanded, the implementation of the employee's employment contract is suspended.[174]

2. Lifting the obligation of night work

In those cases where the employee cannot be obliged to do night work the employer shall see to it that she gets transferred to a day job. If this measure is technically or objectively not possible, or for valid reasons cannot in all fairness be expected, the implementation of the employment contract of the employee concerned is suspended.[175]

Insofar as employment during the daytime is not possible, the employee concerned will be granted pregnancy leave from the seventh week before the due date of birth.

3. Obligation of means

As the law now stands it is not correct to say that there is a right to adapted work on the part of the employee. Indeed, as far as the employer is concerned, we are

[173] *BS/MB* 5 January 2001; err., *BS/MB* 31 January 2001, first edition.
[174] Article 28, 2° Employment Contract Act.
[175] Article 28, 2° Employment Contract Act.

dealing with an obligation of means, not an obligation of result. Moreover, there is no sanction attached to non-observance of this provision.

This does not alter the fact that compared to the previous arrangement, it is now necessary to prove technical or objective non-feasibility or to produce valid reasons to 'refuse' adapted work. Furthermore, it is not entirely clear what the impact of the judgment of the company doctor is in this respect.

4. Replacement income

Sometimes a pregnant woman is not allowed to work because of the danger to the unborn child. During this period she receives a compensation of 78.23% of her wages (up to a certain maximum) from the Insurance Agency for Sickness and Invalidity Fund (RIZIV/INAMI). After delivery this is reduced to 60%.

5. Suspension

If the employee is offered adapted work, the original employment contract is suspended. This contract will only come into effect again when the employee is once again capable of resuming her initial tasks. There is also suspension of the implementation of the employment contract when the employer proves that he is not capable of providing adapted work. This suspension is justified on the basis of the medical check form which has to be filled in by the company doctor.

6. Reinstatement

As soon as the period concerning the above described measures has expired, the employee must be re-employed under the same conditions as before.

G. *Information to the company doctor*

After the employer has been informed of the pregnancy or breastfeeding, he/she him/herself immediately informs the company doctor of the employee's condition. Generally the latter is the one to propose the measures necessary to avoid exposure to risks.

§ 4. MATERNITY ALLOWANCE

A. *Formalities*

The employee who wants to enjoy her right to antenatal rest shall provide her employer with a medical certificate demonstrating that the due date of delivery lies within the maximum allowed period of six (or eight) weeks. This certificate must be handed in seven (or nine) weeks at the latest prior to the due date of birth.

The Insurance Agency for Sickness and Invalidity – the health insurance fund or the Auxiliary Fund for Sickness and Invalidity Insurance – also has to be informed by means of a certificate. This institution will provide the employee with an 'allowance form'. This form must be handed in as soon as possible after it has been completed and signed by the employer.

After the baby's birth the employee shall send the insurance agency, without delay, a birth certificate issued by the registrar, or a medical declaration confirming the birth.

B. *Amount*

For every working day or equivalent day in the period of the maternity leave the employee entitled receives a so-called maternity allowance from the sickness and invalidity insurance fund.

1. Pregnancy and maternity leave

During the pregnancy and maternity leave the allowance amounts to:

- 82% of the lost wages, unlimited, for the first thirty days;
- from the 31st day of this leave, 75% of the lost wages, but limited to the maximum of the normal allowances for sickness and invalidity.

The maternity allowance may never be lower than the amount of the invalidity allowance to which the employee could have been entitled if she had not been on maternity leave.

C. *Allowances during paternity leave*

In order to obtain paternity leave a number of specific formal requirements have to be complied with, both towards the employer and towards the Insurance Agency for Sickness and Invalidity.

If a part of the post-birth maternity leave is converted into paternity leave, the father may claim 'paternity allowance'. A requirement is that the father himself is entitled to sickness and invalidity allowances as an employee. Two possibilities must be distinguished.

If paternity leave is granted because of the mother's death the father is entitled to the maternity allowances described above.

If the mother is hospitalised she continues to receive the regular maternity allowance. During his paternity leave the father is entitled to an allowance of 60%

of his lost wages with an upper limit – in other words, the regular sickness and invalidity benefits.

§ 5. PROTECTION AGAINST DISMISSAL[176]

A. *Principle*

An employer may not take any action to terminate the employment of a pregnant employee or employee who has given birth, except for reasons which are unrelated to her physical condition as a result of the pregnancy or delivery.

By analogy, an employee on paternity leave cannot be dismissed by his employer unless it is for reasons unrelated to the paternity leave.

As a rule it is assumed that the dismissal of a pregnant employee or new mother is only justified when a just cause has been established, or for reasons of a technical or economic nature. However, in our view it is sufficient that the reason is objective in nature.

In the case of a disputed dismissal, the burden of proof lies with the employer. If the employee requests so the employer must inform her in writing of the reasons for her dismissal.

B. *Period*

The prohibition of dismissal starts at the moment the employer has been notified of the pregnancy. The employer need not be informed by the employee herself; notification by a third party is also possible.

The protection against dismissal ends one month after the pregnancy and maternity leave has expired.

If the employee obtains postponement of the transferable part of her antenatal leave, we hold the view that the protection against dismissal ends after only one month has passed, starting from the last day of this postponed leave.

The employee on paternity leave in turn is protected against dismissal from the day of notification of the conversion from maternity leave to paternity leave, and this ends as soon as the intended leave expires. When paternity leave is granted because of the mother's hospitalisation, the latter, too, continues to enjoy the above described protection against dismissal.

C. *Sanctions*

If the reason invoked to justify the dismissal is not extraneous to the physical condition of the employee or in the absence of a reason, the employer will have

[176] Article 40 Labour Act.

to pay the employee a lump sum amounting to the gross earnings for six months, without prejudice to the compensations due to the employee as a result of the unilateral termination of the employment contract – in other words the regular compensation in lieu of notice.

In that case the compensation in lieu of notice will have to cover the duration of the period of notice due. The part of that term already expired may not be deducted.

The same principles apply to the employee on paternity leave.

§ 6. RIGHT TO BREASTFEEDING BREAKS[177]

A. *A 'right' to paid breastfeeding breaks*

Each employee working in the private sector has the right to interrupt her work to breastfeed her child and/or to express milk.

During these activities the employment contract is suspended. The employee obtains an allowance from the sickness and invalidity insurance. This – by analogue with the first thirty days of the maternity insurance – amounts to 82% of the wages with no upper limit.

B. *Length of the breaks*

A breastfeeding break takes half an hour. An employee is entitled to a maximum of two half hours. There are three possibilities.

The employee works:

- less than four hours a day: she is not entitled to a break;
- at least four hours and maximum of 7 hours and 29 minutes: she is entitled to half an hour;
- more than seven and a half hours: she is entitled to two breaks of half an hour each. She can take this break in one turn or in two turns.

The situation must be looked at from day to day.

C. *When?*

The employee shall agree with her employer at what time the breastfeeding breaks are to be taken. If no agreement is made, the breaks take place before or after the regular breaks laid down in the work rules.

---

[177] Royal Decree No. 80 of 27 November 2001 establishing the right to breastfeeding breaks, declared generally binding by Royal Decree 21 January 2002, *BS/MB* 12 February 2002.

D. Where?

The employer shall ensure there is a discreet, well-aired, clean and properly heated room at the employee's disposal. Under certain circumstances the employer's house may be used as the place where the employee breastfeeds and/or expresses milk.

In shopping malls, the provision of common breastfeeding rooms for the staff of different employers is permitted.

E. Formalities

1. Duty to report

The employee who wishes to make use of this right, shall inform her employer two months beforehand. The period can be shortened by mutual agreement.

The notification must be made by a registered letter or by handing in a document of which the duplicate shall be signed by the employer.

2. Proof

The right is only granted on the condition that the evidence of breastfeeding is confirmed by a certificate issued by a recognised infant health centre or by a medical certificate.

After that, the employee must supply the employer with a monthly certificate, always on the same date in the month as the right to breastfeeding breaks was first exercised.

F. Duration

The right to breastfeeding breaks applies for 7 months after birth. So, the duration of this right is rather relative given that after the nine weeks of compulsory postnatal leave a lot of women also take up the remaining six weeks of the antenatal leave, followed by their annual holidays. As a result, in quite a number of cases the employer shall only have to grant this right for a short period.

In exceptional circumstances related to the child's state of health (e.g. a premature birth), and insofar as this is confirmed by a medical certificate, the total duration of the period in which the employee is entitled to breastfeed can be extended by two months.

G. Protection against dismissal

An employee invoking this right is protected against dismissal. The terms of this protection are similar to those applied to pregnant women.

The employer may not take any action to terminate the employment contract unilaterally starting from the moment that he was informed of the assertion of the right. The protection period runs until the expiry of the month beginning on the day following the expiry of the validity of the last medical certificate.

The protection is not absolute. The only requirement is that the dismissal does not relate to the physical condition resulting from breastfeeding and/or expressing of milk.

When a woman making use of breastfeeding breaks is dismissed, the employer must prove that the dismissal has nothing to do with the fact of her exercising this right. If the employee requests this, the employer will have to inform her of the reasons for dismissal in writing.

If the employer dismisses such an employee without any reason or because of the fact that she exercises her right, he shall have to pay a lump-sum compensation that is equal to the gross earnings for six months, without prejudice to the compensation in lieu of notice.

In the period of one month after the end of the postnatal leave the woman enjoys double protection, more specifically by virtue of the Labour Act as well as by virtue of Collective Agreement No. 80. However, in the event of unfair dismissal, she is only entitled to one lump-sum compensation.

SECTION 10. ADOPTION LEAVE[178]

In the event of the adoption of a child an employee is entitled to adoption leave during a consecutive period of maximum six weeks if the child is younger than three years of age, and a maximum of four weeks for children from three to eight years of age. That maximum period is doubled when the employee adopts a disabled child – in other words a child with an incapacity of at least 66%, or suffering from an ailment which entitles him/her to additional child benefit for disabled children. Anyhow, the right to adoption leave ends as soon as the child has reached the age of eight.

This leave must commence within the two months of the date the adopted child was actually taken in by the employee's family.

When several children are adopted simultaneously the employee is only entitled to adoption leave once.

During the adoption leave the employee obtains an allowance from the health insurance agencies. However, during the first three days of that leave the employee retains his/her right to pay from the employer.[179]

The employee who wishes to use his/her right to adoption leave must inform his/her employer of his/her intention in writing at least one month before taking

178 Article 30*ter* Employment Contract Act.

179 Royal Decree of 21 September 2004, *BS/MB* 18 October 2004.

his/her leave. Furthermore, he/she must observe the requirements with regard to the health insurance.

The employee also enjoys a special protection against dismissal during a certain period, i.e. from two months prior to the adoption leave until one month after its termination. During this time the employer is not allowed to terminate the employment contract unilaterally unless this involves reasons unrelated to the adoption leave. The burden of proof in this respect lies with the employer. In the event of infringement the employee is entitled to a lump-sum compensation amounting to three months' pay, not taking into account the compensation in lieu of notice due. However, accumulation with other special dismissal compensations is not possible.

SECTION 11. LEAVE FOR FOSTER PARENTS[180]

An employee who has been appointed as a foster parent by the court, by foster agencies recognised by the regional governments, by the services of the youth assistance committees (*Comité Bijzondere Jeugdbijstand/Aide à la Jeunesse*) has the right to be absent from work to fulfil obligations and perform tasks, or to cope with situations resulting from the fact that he/she has taken in one or more foster children. The absence may not exceed six days a year. If the foster family consists of two employees appointed to act as foster parents, these days of absence must be divided among them.

The Royal Decree of 27 October 2008[181] determines who is to be considered a foster parent and for what purposes the leave can be used.

The employee taking leave is entitled to compensation from the National Employment Office (RVA/ONEM).

SECTION 12. PREVENTIVE CUSTODY OF THE EMPLOYEE[182, 183]

The employment contract is suspended during the time that the employee is absent because of measures of preventive detention.

Preventive detention cannot be put on a par with a unilateral termination of the employment contract, nor with a case of force majeure or just cause.

(Obviously) there is no guarantee of wages during this suspension.

180 Article 30*quater* Employment Contract Act.

181 *BS/MB* 13 November 2008.

182 Article 28, 5° Employment Contract Act.

183 Vannes, V., 'La détention préventive et le contrat de travail: la loi du 29 novembre 1983', *JTT* 1985, pp. 417–422.

SECTION 13. SERVING AS LAY JUDGE[184]

The contract is suspended during the time the employee acts as a lay judge in the labour courts and labour tribunals.

It is assumed that the employment contract is suspended during the time necessary to travel to and from the court building, as well as the time necessary to serve. Serving not only involves the attendance of the session, but also all acts performed by the judge, for instance, participating in deliberations.

During his/her absence the judge has no right to wages. Nor is he/she entitled to protection against dismissal.

SECTION 14. EDUCATIONAL LEAVE[185]

The employment contract is suspended during the time the employee is absent because of 'educational leave'. Under certain conditions employees can be absent to complete a self-chosen course or to take exams. The competence with regard to this matter was transferred to the communities and regions by the sixth reform of the State. When this book was written it was not yet clear what this new legislation would amount to. Therefore, it is not possible to comment on this.

SECTION 15. CAREER BREAK

The principles governing career breaks are not included in the Employment Contract Act. They are the subject of Articles 99 through 107*bis* of the Recovery of the Economy Act of 22 January 1985 concerning social provisions.[186] The Royal Decree of 2 January 1991 with regard to career break allowances[187] implemented these general provisions further.

On 14 February 2001, in implementation of the multi-industry agreement, the social partners in the National Labour Council concluded Collective Agreement No. 77 with a view to the establishment of a system of time credit, career reduction and a reduction of the labour output to half-time employment.[188] This was adapted several times.

By the Royal Decree of 28 December 2011[189] a new regulation was formulated. This was established in the context of part of the programme of the Di Rupo

184 Article 28, 3° Employment Contract Act.

185 Section 6 of Chapter III of the Economic Recovery Act of 22 January 1985 concerning social provisions, *BS/MB* 24 January 1985. The details are regulated by the Royal Decree of 23 July 1985, *BS/MB* 10 August 1985.

186 *BS/MB* 24 January 1985.

187 *BS/MB* 12 January 1991.

188 Declared generally binding by Royal Decree 13 March 2001 (*BS/MB* 28 March 2001).

189 *BS/MB* 30 December 2011.

Government aimed at stricter conditions for time credit and career reduction. Collective Agreement No. 103, concluded on 27 June 2012, completed this for the private sector. Depending on the reasons, employees are entitled to time credit and a number of variations: full-time time credit, half-time time credit, 1/5 career reduction with and without reasons, as well as older employees' right to an end-of-career job, i.e. the possibility to work in a 4/5 system or half-time regime from a certain age.

It is not within the scope of this article to discuss all the procedures, conditions and the like. Moreover, there is a real chance of all this being changed in the near future. During the time credit period the employee can claim a fixed monthly allowance from the National Employment Office to compensate his/her wage loss or reduced income.

§ 1. COMPASSIONATE LEAVE

A. *Palliative care*

1. Legal framework

The right to a complete career interruption and to a reduction in working hours for palliative care is included in Article 100*bis* and Article 102*bis* of the Recovery of the Economy Act of 22 January 1985 respectively. Further implementation is the subject of the Royal Decree of 22 March 1995.[190]

2. Contents

Palliative care is understood to mean any form of assistance and, in particular, medical, social, administrative and psychological assistance to, and care of, persons who suffer from an incurable illness and find themselves at the terminal stage.

The employee must present evidence of this by means of a certificate issued by the attending doctor of the person who is in need of palliative care. This certificate must demonstrate that the employee is prepared to give palliative care without, however, revealing the patient's identity.

There need not be any family tie or kinship between the employee and the person getting assistance towards the end of his/her life, nor is there any obligation of living under the same roof.

Moreover, an employee may assist more than one person in the final stages of life throughout his/her career.

---

[190] *BS/MB* 5 May 1995.

3. Duration

To provide palliative care employees can assert their right to a complete career break or to a reduction in working hours of half the time or one fifth during one month. This period can be extended by one month.

4. Procedure

It suffices that the employee submits the abovementioned certificate to his/her employer. Subsequently, the right commences on the first day of the week following the week in which the employee provided his/her employer with the certificate. If the employer agrees, that right may even commence earlier.

If the employee wishes to use the one month extension he/she must submit a new certificate. Given the maximum duration it is logical that an employee can only submit two certificates regarding the palliative care of the same person.

5. Protection against dismissal

Employees taking palliative leave can only be dismissed with just cause or for justified reasons. The protection starts on the day of application and lasts until three months after the (partial) suspension of the contract. If this rule is breached the employer has to pay compensation equal to six months' salary. If there was a reduction in working hours, the period of notice will be calculated as if the employee had not worked fewer hours. The severance pay will be calculated on the wages due before the reduction.

B. Assisting or caring for a seriously ill family member or relative

1. Legal framework

The Royal Decree of 6 February 1997 establishing a right to career interruption in implementation of Article 7 § 2, 1° of the Law of 26 July 1996 promoting employment and preventive protection of competitiveness already introduced, more specifically for the period from 1 January 1997 to 31 December 1998, a short-term right to career break for taking care of or giving assistance to a seriously ill family member or relative.[191] A Royal Decree dated 2 December 1997 completed the implementation thereof.[192]

Since 1 January 1999 the right to a career break for assisting or caring for a seriously ill family member or relative is regulated in a separate Royal Decree, i.e.

[191] Article 5 Royal Decree 6 February 1997.

[192] *BS/MB* 12 December 1997.

the Royal Decree of 10 August 1998.[193] This decree, which appears to be operative for an undetermined term, does not – contrary to the Royal Decree of 6 February 1997 – offer the possibility of using a collective agreement to establish a divergent sectoral arrangement regarding the right to career break for assisting or caring for a seriously ill family member or relative.

2. Contents

Employees have the right to suspend their employment contract completely or to reduce their working hours to take care of a seriously ill family member or relative.

This right is restricted to the care of, or assistance to, a seriously ill family member, i.e. any person living with the employee, or a non-live-in relative, both blood relations and in-laws, up to the second removed.

A serious illness is understood to mean any illness or surgery classified as such by the medical attendant, and which according to the doctor requires social assistance, home nursing or emotional assistance or care with a view to recovery of the patient.

The employee must submit evidence of the existence of such an illness by means of a certificate issued by the medical attendant of the seriously ill family member or relative. This must show that the employee is prepared to give assistance to, or take care of, the seriously ill person.

3. Duration

For giving assistance to, or taking care of, a seriously ill family member or relative, the employee is entitled to suspension of the employment contract for a maximum of 12 months per patient. In the case of a reduction in working hours, the limit is 24 months for the same family member or relative.

Such periods of interruption or reduction of working hours can only be taken in periods of minimum one month, and maximum three months, consecutive or not, until the maximum term of 12 or 24 months has been reached. This principle is subject to a whole series of exceptions, which we will not go into here.

4. Protection against dismissal

The protection against dismissal is identical to that for palliative leave. The only difference is that the compensation in lieu of notice is calculated on the basis of the wages paid for the reduced working hours.

---

193 *BS/MB* 8 September 1998, pp. 28.855–28.857.

C. *Parental leave*

1. Legal framework

On 24 July 1996 the Minister of Employment asked the National Labour Council for advice regarding a Royal Decree bill with a view to establishing a right to parental leave. Herewith, the Minister wanted to implement Directive 96/34/EC of 3 June 1996 inspired by European employer and employee organisations.

However, the social partners took over the initiative and concluded a collective agreement, more specifically, Collective Agreement No. 64 of 29 April 1997, which was declared generally binding by the Royal Decree of 29 October 1997.[194] Another Royal Decree, the Decree of 29 October 1997 establishing a right to parental leave in the context of career interruption,[195] clarified the financial consequences. Collective Agreement No. 64 of 29 April 1997 only guarantees the right of suspension of the implementation of the employment contract. People who want to receive compensation during their parental leave must also comply with the provisions of the Royal Decree of 29 October 1997.

On 8 March 2010 the Council of the EU changed the provisions regarding parental leave on the initiative of the European social partners (BUSINESSEUROPE, UEAPME, CEEP and EVV). Directive 96/34/EC was replaced by Directive 2010/18/EC. Its provisions were transposed in to Belgian law by the Royal Decree of 31 May 2012.[196] As a result the duration of parental leave has been increased from three to four months.

2. Contents

Only those employees who in the course of the 15 months prior to the written application for leave were employed by the employer in question for at least 12 months under an employment contract, may assert a right to parental leave.

All employees, men as well as women, are entitled to parental leave. So the fact that the (foster) mother applies for parental leave does not exclude the (foster) father from doing this too.

The right to parental leave is an individual, non-transferable right for parents and foster parents. In other words, if the (foster) father renounces this right the (foster) mother cannot assert this right twice.

The employee is entitled to parental leave:

- from the child's birth until he/she turns 12 years of age;

194 *BS/MB* 7 November 1997.
195 *BS/MB* 7 November 1997.
196 *BS/MB* 1 June 2012.

- in the context of an adoption, during a period starting from the child's registration as a family member at the registrar's or aliens' office of the city or town where the employee resides until the child turns 12 years of age.

For disabled children who meet certain conditions the age is increased to 21 years.

3. Duration

The principle is that all employees have the right to suspend the implementation of their employment contract to look after their children.

The employee can choose between three options:

- suspension of the implementation of the employment contract for a four month period; the employee can choose to subdivide this period into separate months; or
- halving his/her working hours – if he/she is a full-time employee – over a period of eight months; he/she can choose to subdivide this period into periods of two months or a multiple thereof; or
- reducing his/her working hours by one fifth – if he/she is a full-time employee – for a period of 20 months; the employee can choose to subdivide this period into periods of five months or a multiple thereof.

The employee also has the right to combine the various formulas with regard to parental leave.

4. Guarantees

Finally, Collective Agreement No. 64 of 29 April 1997 offers a number of guarantees for the exercise of the right to parental leave.

After the end of the parental leave the employee has the right to return to his/her old job or at least to an equivalent or comparable position pursuant to his/her contract of employment.

In addition, the abovementioned collective agreement includes a protection against dismissal, meaning that the employer is only allowed to terminate the employment contract unilaterally if there is an overriding or sufficient reason.

§ 2. INTERRUPTION ALLOWANCE

Just like in the scheme for career breaks, employees using their right to time credit, career reduction or a reduction in working hours to the level of a part-time job, receive financial compensation from the National Employment Office.

§ 3. RIGHT TO PART-TIME WORK AFTER REDUCTION IN WORKING HOURS

A. *Principle*

By the Law of 22 December 1995 concerning social provisions[197] a provision was inserted into Chapter IV of the Social Recovery Act of 22 January 1985, which acknowledges the right to part-time work after a partial career break. The rule is that the employee who has exhausted the possibilities of reducing his/her working hours within the framework of the legislation regarding career breaks has the right to switch to a part-time employment contract. This transition must link up directly to the period of partial career break.

The right to a part-time job implies that the part-time employment contract concluded with the employee is of the same nature as that which applied to him/her during the periods of reduction in working hours in accordance with the legislation concerning career breaks. The further rules and conditions regarding the exercise of this right are the subject of the Royal Decree of 25 November 1998.[198]

B. *Protection against dismissal*

If the employee uses his/her right to part-time work after a period of reduction in working hours within the framework of the legislation regarding career breaks, he/she enjoys special protection against dismissal. From the beginning of a period of three months before the transition to a part-time employment contract until three months after, the employer can only terminate the employment of his employee unilaterally for just causes. If the employer ignores this he owes the employee a lump-sum compensation of six months' salary in addition to the usual compensation in lieu of notice.

SECTION 16. POLITICAL LEAVE[199]

The arrangement regarding political leave is to be found in the Law of 19 July 1976 establishing a leave to exercise a political mandate,[200] as well as in the Royal Decree of 28 December 1976.[201]

---

197 See Article 17 Law 22 December 1995 concerning social provisions (*BS/MB* 30 December 1995).

198 See Royal Decree 25 November 1998 concerning the right to part-time work after the reduction in working hours within the framework of the legislation on career break has ended (*BS/MB* 23 December 1998).

199 Article 28, 4°, c) Employment Contract Act.

200 *BS/MB* 24 August 1976.

201 *BS/MB* 31 December 1976.

§ 1. SCOPE

Employees who are members of a provincial council, agglomeration council, federation council, local council, district council, the Joint Community Council, the Flemish Community Council, the French Community Council, social welfare committees, the Council of the German Speaking Community, or who hold the chair of one of these institutions or are members of the governing bodies thereof, are entitled to political leave.

Certain employees fall outside the scope of the law:

- public sector employees;
- employees of the subsidised free schools;
- the mayors, aldermen and the chair persons of the Public Social Welfare Centres in cities/towns with over fifty thousand inhabitants;
- the executives of the provincial council.

§ 2. DURATION

The employees exercising one of the above mandates or official duties are entitled to be absent from work during a previously established maximum monthly number of working days or parts of working days.

The employees who exercise the duty or mandate of mayor, alderman, chairperson or member of the bureau of a district council or chairperson of the council for social welfare are entitled to be absent from work for a maximum of two days a week.

However, there is an alternative for these employees. They may suspend the implementation of their employment contract completely during the period of their mandate or official function. This possibility only applies for the exercise of a single mandate or function. The duration of the suspension is fixed at a minimum of 12 months. If necessary, the suspension can be applied several times, with or without interruption between periods, each time for a minimum of 12 months.

§ 3. GUARANTEED PAY

During his/her political leave the abovementioned (para 313) employee retains his/her normal wages. Every three months the employers can get a refund of the wages and employer contributions from the institution where the employee exercises his/her mandate or office.

§ 4. PROTECTION AGAINST DISMISSAL

A. *Principle*

Certain measures have been taken to protect persons standing for political elections against dismissal, whether or not they are elected.

The rule is that for a certain period the employer may not commit any act aimed at the unilateral termination of the employment contract of the abovementioned employee, except for reasons extraneous to the fact that the employee is a candidate or has been elected.

B. *Period*

The employee-candidate must inform his/her employer by registered letter within six months prior to the election. From the date of receipt until the day of the election, he/she is protected against dismissal.

A distinction must be made depending on whether or not the person concerned has been elected:

- insofar as the employee is effectively present on the list of candidates but has not been elected, the protection against dismissal remains in force until three months after the election;
- for the effectively elected employees this protection is effective during the entire period of the mandate and during the six months immediately following it.

C. *Sanctions*

If the employer does dismiss the employee in question without a valid reason he will have to pay the employee a lump-sum compensation equal to the gross earnings for six months in addition to the compensation owed in case of termination of the employment contract.

SECTION 17. LEAVE FOR COMPELLING REASONS

Since 1 January 1990 all employees are entitled to ten days of unpaid leave per calendar year for compelling reasons.

The employees' fundamental right to be absent from work for compelling reasons is provided for in Article 30*bis* Employment Contract Act. The further implementation for the employees of the private sector was completed by Collective Agreement No. 45 of 19 December 1989.[202]

§ 1. CONCEPT

'Compelling reason' is understood to mean every unforeseen incident not related to the job that requires the employee's compelling and necessary intervention and provided his/her job makes this intervention impossible.

Examples of this are:

- illness, injury or hospitalisation of a person living under the same roof or of non-live-in next of kin or relatives in the first degree;
- serious damage to material possessions of the employee;
- appearing in court as a party.

§ 2. PART-TIME WORK

In the case of part-time employment the employee is entitled to leave for compelling reasons in proportion to the duration of his/her working hours.

§ 3. TERMS

The employee is only allowed to be absent during the time necessary to cope with the problems caused by the abovementioned incidents, obviously within the limits of the established maximum length of ten working days per calendar year. This absence is not paid.

The employee is obliged to either inform his/her employer beforehand, or as soon as possible if notification in advance is not possible.

The employee must use the leave of absence for the purpose for which it is granted. At the request of the employer the employee must be able to deliver evidence of the compelling reason.

[202] Declared generally binding by Royal Decree 6 March 1990, *BS/MB* 21 March 1990.

SECTION 18. BAD WEATHER CONDITIONS[203]

If weather conditions make it impossible to work the employment contract of manual labourers may be suspended. For instance, a chocolate factory will probably have to stop production in the event of extremely high temperatures.

§ 1. CONDITIONS

The employer can suspend the implementation of the employment contract because of bad weather conditions if all three of the following conditions are met:

- the bad weather must make it impossible to work;
- the employer must inform the employee;
- the employee must have exhausted all the days in lieu to which he/she is entitled under the Labour Act and Public Holidays Act.

The suspension does not end until the employee has been informed that the work can be resumed. The employee himself/herself is not obliged to judge whether the bad weather conditions have ended.

§ 2. WAGE GUARANTEE

The employer is not compelled to pay wages during the suspension. He must hand the employee a C 3.2 form so that the latter may claim unemployment benefits.

As regards the National Employment Office the employee is considered as 'temporarily unemployed', i.e. as an employee who remains tied to an employer by means of an employment contract, but whose work has been temporarily suspended.

§ 3. NOTIFICATION

In order to prevent abuse the employer is obliged to inform the unemployment section of the National Employment Office, at the municipality where the enterprise has its seat by registered mail or by fax, of a number of details, such as the nature of the bad weather conditions.[204]

---

203 Article 50 Employment Contract Act.

204 Royal Decree 3 May 1999 implementing Article 50, 3 of the Law of 3 July 1978 concerning the employment contracts, *BS/MB* 23 June 1999.

§ 4. NOTICE

The employment contract can be terminated by the worker without notice if the suspension exceeds one month.

SECTION 19. TECHNICAL MALFUNCTION[205]

In the event of a technical malfunction in the enterprise the implementation of the employment contract is suspended. This kind of suspension can only involve manual workers.

§ 1. CONDITIONS

The Employment Contract Act does not give a definition of a technical malfunction. It is usually considered to:

- be a malfunction of a technical nature;
- take place within the enterprise;
- interrupt the activities only temporarily.

In addition to these conditions the employee also has to have exhausted all his/her days off in lieu.

The director of the regional unemployment bureau can object to the reason submitted by the employer for the technical malfunction. In that case, as well as when the employer has not complied with the prescribed formalities, the wage for the entire duration of the technical malfunction is paid entirely at the expense of the employer.

§ 2. WAGE GUARANTEE

During a period of seven days starting on the day of the technical unemployment the labourer is entitled to his/her normal wages. The working day which was interrupted because of the technical malfunction and which is paid on the basis of the arrangement concerning the guaranteed daily wage must be considered as the first day of the seven-day period.

The employee loses the right to his/her normal wages when he/she refuses to accept substitute work suitable to his/her physical and intellectual skills and

[205] Article 49 Employment Contract Act.

compatible with his/her professional qualifications. Nonetheless, this refusal as such is not a just cause justifying termination of the contract.

During the suspension the employer is entitled to unemployment benefits. To this end the employer provides him/her with a C 3.2 form.

The suspension ends from the moment the technical malfunction ceases to exist.

§ 3. NOTIFICATION

In principle the employer is not obliged to inform the employee of the suspension. However, if the latter has not been informed and presents himself/herself for work, the employer is obliged to pay the guaranteed daily wage.

At the latest on the first working day after the day of the technical malfunction the employer must send the regional bureau of the National Employment Office of the municipality where the enterprise is located a registered letter with the following details:

- the date and nature of the technical malfunction;
- the starting date of the suspension of the implementation of the employment contract.

Within six days of the day of the technical malfunction the employer shall provide the regional bureau with a list with the names, first names and addresses of the employees whose employment contracts have been suspended.

The director of the regional bureau of the National Employment Office may refuse to recognise the technical malfunction (e.g. if it could have been foreseen). In that case the employer will have to pay the employees' wages for the entire duration of the suspension.

When the notification takes place outside the term laid down by the law the employer can also be obliged to pay the employees' wages during a period of six days starting on the first day of unemployment.

The employer also has a duty to inform the works council (or in the absence thereof, the trade union delegation) of the nature of the technical malfunction. This report must have taken place at the latest the fourth day following the date of the malfunction.

SECTION 20. ECONOMIC REASONS[206]

The Employment Contract Act provides for the possibility to suspend the employment contract in its entirety or to introduce an arrangement of partial work in the absence of work because of economic reasons. However, this can only be done with regard to the suspension of the employment contracts for blue-collar workers.

§ 1. PROCEDURE

A. *Conventional arrangement*

At the proposal of the joint committee or of the National Labour Council the Crown can lay down the conditions under which the implementation of the contract is suspended in its entirety or an arrangement of part-time work is introduced through lack of work because of economic reasons.

This decree must state:

- the manner in which, and the period within which, the new working arrangement must be communicated;
- the duration of the new arrangement;
- the maximum number of days of unemployment;
- the manner in which, and the period within which, the unemployment bureau of the National Employment Office of the municipality where the enterprise is located is to be informed.

The notification and the report to the National Employment Office must contain certain legally established statements, such as the dates on which the workers will be unemployed.

B. *Supplementary arrangement*

Failing a conventional arrangement the minimum arrangement included in the Employment Contract Act applies.

The implementation of the employment contract can only be suspended for a period of four weeks at the most. When the maximum duration has been reached, the employer must reintroduce the arrangement of full employment before a new full suspension or an arrangement of partial work can start.

206 Article 51 Employment Contract Act.

The notification must contain certain particulars, such as the surname, first names and place of residence of the unemployed workers, and, if this is relevant, the sections of the enterprise where the work has been suspended.

This must be done either by putting up bill posters in a visible spot on the premises of the enterprise, at least seven days in advance, the day of posting not included, or within the same period by means of a written notification addressed to each unemployed employee separately.

On the same day a notification must be sent by registered mail to the unemployment bureau of the National Employment Office of the place where the enterprise is located.

Furthermore, the employer must state the economic reasons justifying the full suspension of the implementation of the contract or the introduction of an arrangement of partial work.

C. *Joint provisions*

On the day of the bill-posting or notification, the employer must inform the works council or – failing the latter – the union delegation of the economic reasons that justify the suspension or the introduction of a system of partial employment.

The arrangement of partial work can be introduced for a maximum period of three months if it consists of less than three working days per week, or less than one working week per two weeks. Moreover, if the employment system of one week out of two amounts to less than two working days, the rules are the same as in the complete suspension of the employment contract.

When the arrangement of partial employment has reached the maximum duration of three months, the employer must introduce, once again, the arrangement of complete employment before a full suspension or a new arrangement of partial employment can commence. On the advice of the competent joint committee or the National Labour Council the Crown may deviate from this period.

If the partial employment consists of at least three working days per week, or one working week per two weeks, it can be introduced for a period exceeding three months.

To calculate the duration of a complete suspension of the implementation of the contract or of the arrangement of partial employment, the duration which the employer mentioned in his notification is taken into account.

Whenever the employer changes the arrangement he must inform both the employees and the National Employment Office in the manner described above.

§ 2. WAGE GUARANTEE

During the suspension the employee is temporarily unemployed. The unemployment arrangement is similar to that of the suspension because of bad weather conditions.

If the employer ignores the formalities he will be compelled to pay wages for seven days starting from the first day of the effective suspension of the implementation of the contract.

If he were to suspend the contract for a longer period than legally permitted, he will have to pay wages during the period that exceeds the legally established limits.

§ 3. RESIGNATION

In the periods of complete suspension of the implementation of the contract or of partial employment the worker has the right to terminate the contract without giving notice.

§ 4. PROHIBITION OF EMPLOYMENT

The employer is not allowed to contract out to third parties the work which is normally done by employees who are temporarily unemployed during the period of temporary unemployment.[207]

SECTION 21. EXCEPTION TO THE RULE

In the past, suspension of the employment contract for economic reasons was only possible for blue-collar workers. In 2009, because of the crisis, the government felt it necessary to introduce an analogous suspension for white-collar workers. In 2011 this arrangement became permanent, and with a view to this Articles 77 (1) through 77(8) were added to the Employment Contract Act. This arrangement does not apply to all employers, but only to undertakings meeting certain conditions, e.g. having suffered a decrease in turnover of more than 10% in the four previous quarters, bound by a collective agreement or business plan. This possibility is subject to very strict restrictions.

[207] Article 2 Collective Agreement of 23 February 1993, declared generally binding by the Royal Decree of 2 April 1993, *BS/MB* 29 April 1993.

IV

TERMINATION OF EMPLOYMENT[208]

The most important forms of lawful dismissal are notice (with a period of notice) and dismissal for just cause. Categorised as unlawful dismissal are dismissal with payment of compensation in lieu of notice (because of non-observance of the rules of dismissal) and the unilateral change of an essential element of the contract of employment.

CHAPTER 1

TERMINATION OF THE EMPLOYMENT CONTRACT

SECTION 1. MANNERS OF TERMINATION IN ACCORDANCE WITH CIVIL LAW

Sometimes the term 'dismissal' is used in the sense of 'termination' and therefore also includes the methods of termination according to civil law.

The most common civil law techniques are:

- the dissolution of the employment contract;
- mutual consent;
- termination as a result of *force majeure*;
- nullity.

208 Westrade, M. en Gilson, S. (ed.), *Quelques propos sur la rupture du contrat de travail. Hommage à Pierre Blondiau*, Louvain-la-Neuve, Anthemis, 2008, 529 pp.

§ 1. DISSOLUTION OF THE EMPLOYMENT CONTRACT[209]

A. *Forms*

The term 'dissolution' refers to a complex of techniques, approached in different ways that lead to the termination of the contract, whether or not this is after judicial intervention.

Legal doctrine usually distinguishes between the resolutory term, the judicial dissolution because of inadequacy, the express avoidance clause and the resolutive condition.

B. *Resolutory term*

A resolutory term is understood to mean the future and certain event on which the claimability and liquidation of the debt depend. The occurrence and completion of the event may not emanate from one of the contracting parties.

In accordance with Article 32 Employment Contract Act it is permitted to include a resolutory term in an employment contract. Usually employment contracts with a resolutory term are fixed-term employment contracts. However, the legislator has seen to it that the use of such a provision is prohibited in certain situations.

For instance, the parties are not allowed to include a clause in the employment contract introducing a resolutory effect when an employee reaches the retirement age.[210] In addition, both the Civil Code[211] and the Employment Contract Act[212] forbid the conclusion of an employment contract for life.

---

209 Davagle, M., 'La résolution judiciaire du contrat de travail', *Ors.* 2008/9, pp. 1–13; Funck, J., 'Résolution judiciaire du contrat de travail: nouvelles perspectives', *Chron. D.S.* 2005, pp. 185–189; Wantiez, C., 'La résolution judiciaire du contrat de travail: quelques précisions', *JTT* 1989, pp. 137–139; De Theux, A., 'Résolution judiciaire: principes et applications en droit du travail' in E. Vogel-Polsky (ed.), *Permanence du droit civil en droit du travail*, Brussels, Ed. de l'Université de Bruxelles, 1983, pp. 94–175; Gadot, F., 'Résolution judiciaire et rupture pour motif grave' in E. Vogel-Polsky (ed.), *Permanence du droit civil en droit du travail*, Brussels, Ed. de l'Université de Bruxelles, 1983, pp. 176–187; Huisman, F., 'La condition résolutoire expresse' in E. Vogel-Polsky (ed.), *Permanence du droit civil en droit du travail*, Brussels, Ed. de l'Université de Bruxelles, 1983, pp. 208–242; Paternostre, B., 'Résolution judiciaire et acte équivalent à rupture' in E. Vogel-Polsky (ed.), *Permanence du droit civil en droit du travail*, Brussels, Ed. de l'Université de Bruxelles, 1983, pp. 188–207; Plas, D., 'Les protections spéciales contre le licenciement et la résolution judiciaire' in E. Vogel-Polsy (ed.), *Permanence du droit civil en droit du travail*, Brussels, Ed. de l'Université de Bruxelles, 1983, pp. 243–269.

210 Article 36 Employment Contract Act.

211 Article 1780 Civil Code.

212 Article 7 Employment Contract Act.

C. *Judicial dissolution because of inadequate performance*

Article 1184 Civil Code stipulates that in all reciprocal agreements the 'resolutive condition' is always present. However, the judicial dissolution of the contract is only possible if there is a sufficiently serious inadequate performance on the side of the defaulting party.

A procedure for judicial dissolution of the employment contract has advantages as well as disadvantages.

An advantage compared to the other methods of termination, such as, for instance, dismissal for just cause, is that the employment contract continues to exist until the possible pronouncement of dissolution. If the judge does not consider the contractual inadequacy as sufficiently serious he may impose a different sanction on the defaulting party. Naturally, this will not entitle the party because of whom the dissolution was requested, to claim compensation from the party asking for the dissolution. In the event of dismissal for just cause of which the legitimacy was not accepted by the court the party wrongfully invoking just cause will have to pay a severance allowance.

The judicial dissolution because of inadequate performance is a method of termination that is not applied very often in actual practice, not least because it is difficult to give it a place in labour law as a whole. Indeed, the suspension of the employment contract during the procedure with a view to dissolution on the basis of the non-implementation clause does raise problems with regard to the continuing existence of other rights stemming from the employment relationship. Furthermore, during the period of suspension the employee will not receive wages. By virtue of an explicit legal provision the judicial dissolution of an employment contract of a workers' representative in the works council is not possible.[213]

Sometimes, i.e. if the employer or the employee in the event of a fault on the part of the other party does not want to run the risk of an irrevocable unlawful dismissal for just cause, Article 1184 Civil Code is applied. In a number of cases employees demand judicial dissolution if they are the victim of a unilateral change of the employment contract.

D. *Express avoidance clause*

As a rule, two types of avoidance clauses are distinguished: the ordinary express avoidance clause and the express avoidance clause *ipso jure*.

[213] Article 2, § 6 Law on Special Dismissal Arrangement Staff Representatives of 19 March 1991.

1. Ordinary express avoidance clause

The ordinary express avoidance clause amounts to explicating the possibility of judicial dissolution because of inadequate performance regarding the reciprocal agreement as described in Article 1184 Civil Code.

The basis of the application of the express avoidance clause is a contractual non-implementation whose gravity must be assessed by the courts.

2. Express avoidance clause *ipso jure*

Conversely, under civil law, intervention and assessment by the court are said to be impossible when the parties included an express avoidance clause *ipso jure* in the agreement. The dissolution takes place automatically and the judge does not need to give a verdict to this effect.

In principle legal doctrine accepts the possibility of the express avoidance clause *ipso jure* in employment contracts, but is opposed to the exclusion of judicial assessment. The doctrine wants the express avoidance clause *ipso jure* to be treated in the same way as the conventionally stipulated just cause. In both cases it is for the court to assess the seriousness of the facts invoked.

E. The resolutory condition

The resolutory condition is a future and uncertain event whose realisation leads to the dissolution of the agreement.

In principle the use of the resolutory condition in the context of individual employment contracts is not prohibited.

However, the legislator has excluded some of its applications. The clauses – regardless of whether these involve a resolutory condition or an express avoidance clause because of non-implementation – in which it is stated that marriage or motherhood end the agreement, are null and void.[214]

The law also forbids any clause ending the agreement in the event of wage garnishment as a result of consumer credit.[215]

Outside the resolutory conditions explicitly forbidden by the law the parties of the employment contract can agree on a resolutory condition as a term for termination. In the past, legal doctrine and jurisprudence always stated that to be valid the effect of the condition should result in an undermining of the legal arrangements with regard to probation clauses, suspension and termination.

Thus considered as invalid is the purely potestative resolutory clause, i.e. the termination solely depending on the will of one of the parties without observance

---

[214] Article 36 Employment Contract Act.

[215] Article 36*bis* Employment Contract Act.

of the mandatory rules with regard to dismissal/resignation.[216] Furthermore, the validity of an avoidance clause consisting of a legal ground for suspension, e.g. incapacity to work, is usually rejected.

§ 2. TERMINATION OF THE EMPLOYMENT CONTRACT BY MUTUAL CONSENT[217]

Just like any agreement, an employment contract can also end by mutual consent of the parties. That which has been established by mutual agreement can also be ended by mutual agreement.

Parties may agree that the employment contract will end either immediately or after a certain period has passed.

The termination by mutual agreement can be invoked for any type of employment contract, in other words, not only in the context of an open-ended employment contract, but also for a fixed-term employment contract, an employment contract for a specified task, for replacement, etc.

A document as such is not necessary but it is advisable (in duplicate).

Termination by mutual agreement in itself does not lead to indebtedness of any compensation. If it is agreed that a party – usually the employer – does have to pay compensation, this is neither a severance allowance nor compensation in lieu of notice.

Just as for the conclusion of the employment contract, the normal validity requirements imposed by general contract law must be implemented for the termination of the contract by mutual consent.

The greatest difficulties are to be found at the level of the consent. Error, deceit and violence can affect its validity.

Violence will chiefly occur in the form of moral coercion. Usually it will be the employee who is morally forced by the employer to agree with termination by mutual consent.

§ 3. *FORCE MAJEURE*[218]

A. *Principle*

Depending on its duration *force majeure* can have a suspending or terminating effect on the employment contract. A situation of *force majeure* which is limited in time only entails the suspension of the implementation of the employment

216 Cassation 18 January 1993, *JTT* 1993, p. 141.

217 Paternostre, B. en De Muynck, S., 'La rupture de commun accord au contrat de travail', *Ors.* 2004/12, pp. 1–10.

218 Paternostre, B., 'La rupture du contrat de travail pour force majeure', *Ors.* 2013, pp. 2–17.

contract. Conversely, when the situation has a definite character it has a terminating effect.

Bankruptcy, apparent insolvency of the employer, and closure of the firm ensuing from measures taken in application of ecological legislation, are in themselves not cases of *force majeure* leading to the termination of an employment contract.

B. *Incapacity to work*

In the Employment Contract Act a new article, Article 34, has been inserted with regard to permanent incapacity to work.

Incapacity to work as a result of illness or injury as a result of which the employee is permanently unable to carry out the agreed work no longer in itself ends the contract for reasons of *force majeure*. The permanent incapacity to work must be established either by the employee's attending doctor or by the company doctor. If the diagnosis is made by the employee's doctor this still needs to be confirmed by the company doctor. Failing this, the permanent incapacity to work confirmed by the attending doctor cannot be used to establish the termination of the employment contract as a result of *force majeure*.

The Crown is qualified, by virtue of a decision made in the Council of Ministers, to lay down further procedural rules regarding the employee's permanent incapacity to carry out the agreed work referred to in the previous paragraph.

If an employee is declared permanently unfit for the agreed work, the employer is obliged to keep the employee working in accordance with the recommendations of the company doctor by adapting his/her work, or, if this is impossible, by giving him/her a different job, unless this is technically or objectively impossible, or when this, in all fairness, cannot reasonably be demanded.

If it is technically or objectively impossible to adapt the working conditions, or if this cannot be demanded for valid reasons, or if the employer cannot offer another job corresponding to the employee's capacity, or if the employee refuses the offer of a different job in accordance with his/her capacities, the termination of the contract because of *force majeure* can only be established after attestation of the permanent incapacity to work by the competent doctor of the General Directorate Supervision of Well-Being in the Workplace of the Federal Public Service for Employment, Labour and Social Dialogue.

This does not detract from the employer's right to terminate the employment contract provided he observes a period of notice or pays compensation in accordance with the provisions of this law.

However, Article 34 Employment Contract Act is not yet effective, so civil law continues to be applicable. This implies that the employer can terminate the employment contract because of *force majeure* insofar as he can produce proof that the incapacity to work has a permanent character. In that case the contract is terminated immediately without notice or compensation.

§ 4. NULLITY OF THE EMPLOYMENT CONTRACT

An employment contract can end as a result of nullity. This can stem from:

- failure to respect the validity requirements of the employment contract;
- non-observance of the legislation with regard to the use of languages in social relations;
- contravention of a law of public policy (*ordre public*).

Annulment of an implemented employment contract only has effect for the future *(ex nunc)*.

Nullity stemming from non-observance of the validity requirements of the employment contract usually concerns a relative nullity. This means that it can only be invoked by the interested party. Moreover, it is also possible to renege this or to confirm the situation, for instance, by effectively implementing the employment contract.

Nullity as a result of a breach of the language legislation or another law of public policy usually is an absolute nullity. This must be raised by the judge by virtue of his office. One cannot renounce it, nor is it possible to confirm it.

Nullity is a manner of termination pertaining to civil law that affects the parties of an employment contract in an unequal way and that may have serious consequences for the economically weaker party. Because of this the legislator took some tempering measures by limiting the consequences and the applicability of the nullity.

SECTION 2. END OF THE CONTRACT BY EXPIRY OF THE TERM OR COMPLETION OF THE AGREED WORK[219]

If the employment contract is concluded for a fixed term or specified task, the party terminating the contract before expiry of the term without just cause owes the other party compensation equal to the amount of the wages due until the end of that term, however, without exceeding twice the amount of the wages corresponding to the period of notice which should have been observed if the contract had been an open-ended contract.

However, a new deviation of this rule is that all parties can terminate an employment concluded for a fixed term or specified task before the expiry date, provided they respect the periods of notice. Still this is only possible during the first half of the agreed term, and the period in which notice can be given may not exceed six months.

219 Article 40 Employment Contract Act.

The party terminating the contract before expiry of the term, during the first half of the agreed term of the contract and without exceeding the period of six months, has to pay the other party compensation corresponding either to the duration of the period of notice or to the remaining part of that term.

If the parties have concluded several consecutive employment contracts for a fixed term or a specified task of which the consecutiveness is justified pursuant to Article 10 or Article 10*bis*, the possibility of notice can only be applied to the first of these contracts.

SECTION 3. DEATH OF ONE OF THE PARTIES[220]

In principle, only the death of the employee ends the employment contract. Theoretically, the death of an employer does not result in the end of the employment except:

- when the contract has been concluded *intuitu personae*, i.e. because of the person of the employer;
- or when the employer's death also immediately amounts to the end of the activity.

In those cases Article 33 Employment Contract Act permits the possibility to pay the employee compensation through judicial intervention. The judge assesses *ex aequo et bono* if there is a ground for compensation and is also free to determine the amount.

SECTION 4. TERMINATION BY NOTICE[221]

§ 1. CONCEPTS

Notice means that one of the parties of the employment contract notifies the other party of the unilateral termination of the contract after a certain time has passed and with due regard for a certain period. In other words, notice is dismissal or resignation with observance of a valid term. Within the context of Belgian employment contract law termination by giving notice is only possible in the case of open-ended employment contracts, and under certain conditions during the probationary period.

---

220 Wantiez, C. en Neven, J., 'La mort de l'employeur: art. 33 de la Loi du 3 juillet 1978', *JTT* 1990, pp. 209–212.

221 Capart, R., Massart, G. en Strongylos, M., *Le statut unique ouvriers-employés: commentaire pratique de la loi du 26 décembre 2013*, Limal, Anthemis, 2014, 298 pp.; Verwilghen, M. en Van Kerrebroeck, N., *Harmonisation des statuts ouvriers-employés*, Brussels, Larcier, 2014, 349 pp.

The period of notice is the period after which the employment contract ends.

The compensation in lieu of notice is the compensation owed by the party unilaterally ending the contract without observing a period of notice or observing too short a period of notice.

§ 2. NOTICE OF TERMINATION

A. *Formal requirements*[222]

Notice of termination is a unilateral formal legal act. The fact that there are some obligatory formal requirements is not only the result of the wish to facilitate the furnishing of proof, but also of the intention to provide the employee with more adequate protection.

1. Documents

Notice of termination has to be given in writing. Oral notice is null and void. The letter of notice must be signed by the person who gives notice – either the employee or the employer or his representative. The signature, too, is a matter of mandatory law, meaning that without this the notice is invalid. It is also assumed that the letter should be dated.

Notice of termination is an individual act on the basis of an individual document.

Giving notice of termination to a group of employees by means of a collective document is not possible.

2. Terms[223]

There are three different ways in which notice of termination can be served. A distinction must be made between notice given by the employee and notice given by the employer.

The employee can use either a registered letter, a writ or a normal letter, which is handed over to the other party and of which a copy is signed for receipt.

Since 1 January 1988 the employer can only terminate the employment contract by means of a registered letter or a writ. The legal prohibition for the employer to hand over a letter of notice was prompted by the aim to prevent antedating of the notice to the prejudice of the National Employment Office. The legislator wants to prevent the employee from claiming employment benefits prematurely.

[222] Article 37 Employment Contract Act.

[223] Article 37 Employment Contract Act.

3. Manual delivery

Manual delivery is only possible for the employee. It means that the employee hands the employer a letter in which he/she expresses his/her decision to end the contract unilaterally.

A copy of this letter must be signed by the employer. The mere fact of signing without adding any other statement only proves that he has received the letter. So this does not mean that the employer agrees with the content of the letter. Only insofar as the other party adds the handwritten declaration 'agreed' or 'seen and approved' is the acceptance of the period of notice a fact.

If the employer refuses to sign the letter of resignation, the letter of resignation has not been served. In that case the employee will have to rely on one of the other means of notification.

4. Registered letter

When using a registered letter the receipt of the post office suffices to prove the existence of the notification.

It is possible that a registered letter is not accepted, either because it was refused or was not collected, or because it was addressed wrongly.

Refusal or not collecting has no impact whatsoever on the effect of the notice of termination.

If the address is wrong, there are two possibilities. Either the letter of notice was sent to the employee's old address and the latter failed to inform the employer of his/her change of address. In that case the letter of notice which was served at the old address is valid, or it was just a matter of a wrong address, and in that case the notice must be sent again to the correct address.

5. Writ

It is also possible to use a bailiff to serve a notice of termination.

6. Language

The letter of notice must be written in the appropriate language. When this rule is violated, the notice is absolutely null and void.

7. Contents

a. Obligatory statements[224]

Under penalty of nullity the beginning of the period of notice and its duration must be mentioned in the document.

So far the courts have applied this legal rule with due flexibility and accepted letters of notice from which the details required by law could be derived. For instance, the indication of the beginning of the period of notice can be implicitly apparent from the statement regarding the duration of the period of notice and of the date of its expiry. The legally required details can also become apparent from the precise mentioning of the date of commencement and termination of the period of notice.

If there are inaccuracies in the obligatory statements this does not detract from the validity of the notice. If a wrong, i.e. premature date of commencement has been given, the commencement of the period of notice will only be adjourned to the correct legally provided date of commencement. If, on the other hand, an error has crept into the duration of the notice, and too short a term of notice has been laid down, this will result in compensation in lieu of notice for the part of the term of notice that has been disregarded unless both parties can reach an agreement.

It is not necessary – and even inadvisable – to mention the end date. Because of the suspending effect of certain absences in the course of the term of notice, at least when notice is given by the employer, it is not possible to determine the end date with certainty at the time the notice is served.

b. Reason for the dismissal/resignation

In the context of the so-called Unified Status, the social partners in the National Labour Council were asked to reach a consensus on the reason for dismissal. This led to Collective Agreement No. 109 of 12 February 2014. Whereas in the past dismissal did not have to have a reason behind it, this is now obligatory. An employee who is dismissed has the right to be informed by his/her employer of the concrete reasons leading to his/her dismissal. To this end he/she must send a registered letter to his/her employer within two months of the termination of the employment contract.

If the employment contract is terminated by the employer with observance of a period of notice, the employee has to send his/her request to the employer within six months of the notification by the employer, without, however, being allowed to exceed a term of two months after the termination of the employment contract.

---

[224] Article 37 Employment Contract Act.

The employer receiving such a request informs the employee by registered letter of the concrete reasons that led to the dismissal within two months of receipt of the employee's registered letter.

The letter must contain the necessary elements to enable the employee to know the exact reasons for his/her dismissal. If the employer had already informed the employee in writing of the reasons for dismissal, he is not obliged to respond to the employee's request, provided that this letter contained the necessary elements to inform the employee of the reasons for his/her dismissal.

If the employer does not inform the employee requesting concrete reasons of the reasons for his/her dismissal a fine corresponding to two weeks' wages is due. It goes without saying that this fine is not owed if the employer has communicated the reasons of his own free will.

Collective Agreement No. 109 contains a number of exceptions to the obligation to provide reasons. The employer does not have to justify the dismissal in the following cases:

- dismissal during the first six months of employment;
- if the employee is employed with a temporary agency contract or a student's contract;
- if the employee is dismissed in the context of unemployment with company allowances (early retirement);
- if the employee is dismissed to terminate the open-ended employment contract from the first day of the month following the month in which he/she reaches the legal retirement age;
- if the employee is dismissed because of the permanent termination of the activity, closure of the enterprise, collective dismissal or multiple dismissal in the event of restructuring as defined at the sectoral level;
- if the employer has to comply with a special dismissal procedure laid down by law or a collective agreement, more specifically the special dismissal arrangement in favour of personnel representatives in the works council and the prevention committee, or for the dismissal of prevention advisers;
- in case of dismissal for just cause;
- if the employee is a blue-collar worker of a joint committee where it is possible to apply a shortened term in the context of the new arrangement regarding the Unified Status.

B. *Nature and consequences of the notice of termination*

The notice of termination has a definitive and irrevocable character. Of course there is nothing to stop both parties from cancelling the notice by mutual agreement. This can take place explicitly but also tacitly, for instance, by continuing to implement the employment contract after notice has been given.

The notice of termination does not change the character of the employment contract. The rights of the parties remain unimpaired, nor are there any changes regarding the mutual obligations.

C. *Moment*

The manner in which notice is given determines the moment at which the notice is considered to be given.

In the case of a registered letter the moment of notice occurs three days after the date of posting, regardless of the moment at which the actual notification takes place.[225]

This principle remains unimpaired when the addressee refuses to accept the registered letter or fails to collect it, or in case of wrong addressing, for which the addressee is to blame.

As soon as the letter of notice is handed over, notice is considered to be given. This also applies when a writ is issued. Even if in the absence of the person concerned, the bailiff puts a copy of the writ in this person's letterbox, the day on which the writ was filed remains the day of notification.

D. *Nullity of notice of termination*

If the notice of termination does not meet one of the above described formal validity requirements this may result in nullity of the act.

There is much diversity of opinion about the consequences of the nullity of the notice of termination for the validity of the dismissal itself.

§3. TERM OF NOTICE

Before 1 January 2014 dismissal/resignation law was different for blue-collar workers and white-collar workers. We will restrict ourselves to the current rules and regulations.

A. *Start of the Period of Notice*

The period of notice starts on the Monday following the week in which notice was given.[226]

225 Article 37 Employment Contract Act.
226 Article 37(1) Employment Contract Act.

B. Employment Contracts Concluded After 1 January 2014

1. Periods

For those having concluded an employment contract after 1 January 2014, the following periods of notice apply.[227]

Seniority	Notice by the employer (in weeks)	Notice by the employee (in weeks)
From 0 to less than 3 months	2	1
From 3 months to less than 6 months	4	2
From 6 months to less than 9 months	6	3
From 9 months to less than 12 months	7	3
From 12 months to less than 15 months	8	4
From 15 months to less than 18 months	9	4
From 18 months to less than 21 months	10	5
From 21 months to less than 24 months	11	5
From 2 years to less than 3 years	12	6
From 3 years to less than 4 years	13	6
From 4 years to less than 5 years	15	7
From 5 years to less than 6 years	18	9
From 6 years to less than 7 years	21	10
From 7 years to less than 8 years	24	12
From 8 years to less than 9 years	27	13
From 9 years to less than 10 years	30	13
From 10 years to less than 11 years	33	13
From 11 years to less than 12 years	36	13
From 12 years to less than 13 years	39	13
From 13 years to less than 14 years	42	13
From 14 years to less than 15 years	45	13
From 15 years to less than 16 years	48	13
From 16 years to less than 17 years	51	13
From 17 years to less than 18 years	54	13
From 18 years to less than 19 years	57	13
From 19 years to less than 20 years	60	13
From 20 years to less than 21 years	62	13
From 21 years to less than 22 years	63	13
From 22 years to less than 23 years	64	13
From a seniority of 21 years the term of notice is increased by one week per year.		

These terms cannot be changed by means of a sectoral agreement.[228] However, collective agreements at company level and individual agreements with regard to the term of notice are allowed.

227 Article 37(2) Employment Contract Act.
228 Article 37(2) Employment Contract Act.

2. Counter notice[229]

An employee who has been given notice by his/her employer can terminate the employment contract with a shorter term of notice when he/she has found another job.

This term of counter notice has been established as follows:

- one week for employees with less than three months seniority;
- two weeks for employees with a seniority of between three months and six months;
- three weeks for employees with a seniority of between six months and one year;
- four weeks for employees with a seniority of one year or more.

3. Shortened terms of notice

- The term of notice to be observed by employees can be reduced to seven days in the context of re-employment programmes;[230]
- if notice is given to terminate an open-ended employment contract from the first day of the month following the month in which the employee reaches the legal retirement age, the term of notice amounts to a maximum of 26 weeks when it is the employer who gives notice;[231]
- employees whose employment contract has been suspended for economic reasons have the right to terminate the contract immediately. The same goes for employees whose employment contract has been suspended for longer than one month because of bad weather. If the employee in the above cases resigns or has resigned (in the normal way), the term of notice takes effect during the suspension. This is not the case when the employer has given notice;[232]
- in the case of dismissal with a view to the system of unemployment with extra company benefits, the terms of notice can be reduced to a minimum of 26 weeks, provided the company has been recognised as a company in difficulties or engaged in restructuring operations.

4. Concurrence with sickness/injury[233]

In the case of incapacity to work as a result of sickness or injury occurring after the employer's notification of dismissal by means of a term of notice, the

229 Article 37(2)(3) Employment Contract Act.
230 Article 37(5) Employment Contract Act.
231 Article 37(6) Employment Contract Act.
232 Article 37(7) Employment Contract Act.
233 Article 37(8) Employment Contract Act.

cancellation of the employment contract by the employer entitles the employee to compensation corresponding to the term of notice still to be observed.

If the contract has been concluded for a fixed term of less than three months, or for a specified task whose completion normally takes less than three months, the employer is allowed, in case of incapacity to work because of illness or injury lasting more than seven days, to terminate the contract without compensation. This arrangement can only be applied if there is no longer the possibility of giving notice as provided for in Article, § 2 Employment Contract Act.[234] This means that the first half of the agreed duration of the contract must have been exceeded.

If the incapacity to work as a result of illness or injury of an employee hired for a fixed term of at least three months, or for a specified task whose completion normally takes at least three months exceeds six months, and if the duration laid down in the contract has not been exceeded, or if the task specified in the contract has not been completed, the employer can terminate the contract at any time, provided he pays compensation. This equals the wage that should have been paid during the agreed time or during the term still necessary to complete the task for which the employee was hired, with a maximum of three months' pay and after deduction of the amount paid since the beginning of the incapacity to work.

5. Seniority[235]

The terms of notice are calculated with due regard for the acquired seniority at the moment the term of notice starts.

Seniority is understood to mean the period during which the employee has been employed without interruption by the same employer.

If notice is given by the employer, the employee's previous period of employment as a temporary agency worker for the same employer also qualifies for the calculation of his/her seniority to a maximum of one year, provided that his/her actual recruitment followed the period of temping, and his/her function is the same. All periods of inactivity of seven days or less are counted as a period of employment as a temporary agency worker.

6. Application leave[236]

During the term of notice the employee is allowed to take a leave of absence whilst retaining wages to find a new job.

During the last 26 weeks of the term of notice the employee can use this right to be absent from work once or twice a week, provided that the duration of this

234 Article 37/9 Employment Contract Act.
235 Article 37/4 Employment Contract Act.
236 Article 41 Employment Contract Act.

absence does not exceed one working day. During the period prior to this he/she may only be absent for half a day per week.

Employees entitled to an outplacement arrangement (see *infra*) can be absent from work once or twice a week during the full term of notice, provided that the absence does not exceed one working day per week.

C. *Transitional Provisions*[237]

For employees employed before 1 January 2014 but dismissed after this date, the terms of notice before and after are added.

1. White-collar workers

However, for 'more senior' white-collar workers the method of calculation before 1 January 2014 is no longer in use and has been replaced by the following arrangement.

For white-collar workers whose annual income exceeded € 32,254 on 31 December 2013, this term is laid down at one month per started year of seniority in the case of notice by the employer, with a minimum of three months.

For white-collar workers whose annual income exceeded € 32,254 on 31 December 2013, this term is laid down at one and a half months per started period of five years of seniority in the case of notice by the employee, with a maximum of four and a half months if his/her annual income did not exceed € 64,508 on 31 December 2013, or six months if his/her annual income exceeded € 64,508 on 31 December 2013.

For the rule that for employees employed before 1 January 2014 but dismissed after that date the terms of notice from before and after have to be added, there is also an exception in the case of resignation.[238] The result of the second part of the calculation (term of notice from 1 January 2014) may not be added to the result of the first part of the calculation when at 31 December 2013 the following maximum levels were reached:

- 3 months if the annual income on 31 December 2013 was less than € 32,254;
- 4.5 months if the annual income on 31 December 2013 was higher than € 32,254 but did not exceed € 64,508;
- 6 months if the annual income on 31 December 2013 was higher € 64,508.

If on 31 December 2013 (i.e. the first part of the calculation) these maximum levels were not reached, the sum of the two parts may not exceed 13 weeks.

237 Article 67 Employment Contract Act.
238 Article 69 Employment Contract Act.

2. Blue-collar workers

a. *Gleichschaltung*

For blue-collar workers a gradual introduction into the new system has been provided:

1 January 2014: 20 years of seniority;
1 January 2015: 15 years of seniority;
1 January 2016: 10 years of seniority;
1 January 2017: others

b. Exceptions to the rule[239]

It was the intention that in some sectors this regulation would be deviated from and that the old regulation would continue to apply after 2017. This was, *inter alia*, the case for the building industry. However, this regulation did not stand the Constitutional Court's test.

D. Rights and duties during the period of notice

During the period of notice the employment contract continues to exist. So both parties must continue to comply with their normal obligations.

This has as a result that, for instance, the employer cannot change the employee's job specification unilaterally. Conversely, certain gross errors on the part of the employee can constitute a just cause which – provided the applicable procedure is observed – can result in the immediate termination of the employment contract without compensation.

§ 4. COMPENSATION IN LIEU OF NOTICE[240]

Compensation in lieu of notice is the compensation that has to be paid if no period of notice or too short a period of notice is observed. The law considers the compensation in lieu of notice as a sanction for not observing a period of notice, although in practice notice is often accompanied by compensation in lieu as an alternative for notice with a period of notice.

Compensation in lieu of notice is a lump-sum compensation determined on the basis of the non-observed periods of notice. That way the right to compensation in lieu of notice is not influenced by the scope of the damage caused by the

[239] Article 70 Employment Contract Act.
[240] Article 39 Employment Contract Act.

dismissal, nor by the possible absence of damage. In principle, the mistakes of the dismissed party are also irrelevant to determining the compensation in lieu of notice.

A. *Calculation*

Compensation in lieu of notice is proportionate to the duration of the period of notice, or if this method of termination is chosen after the employment contract has been terminated in accordance with the usual conditions, proportionate to the part of the period still to be covered.

Article 39, § 1 Employment Contract Act states that the 'current wages' must be taken as a basis for the calculation of the compensation in lieu of notice; in other words, the income the employee has already earned. Wage and index increases are not considered. This means that for an employee who has been dismissed without a period of notice, the compensation in lieu of notice will be calculated without taking into account the possible pay and index increases he/she might have enjoyed if he/she had continued to work during the period of notice.

The current wages also include the end-of-year bonus, even if this is only granted at the end of the year under certain conditions.

If the remuneration is entirely or partially variable, the basis is the average of the variable wages earned during the 12 months prior to the date of termination.

Among other things, this refers to the so-called double holiday allowance, shift and production bonuses, overtime insofar as this is worked regularly, benefits in kind, the employer's contributions to the group insurance, etc.

Article 39, § 1 Employment Contract Act further stipulates that the compensation in lieu of notice not only comprises the current pay, but also the benefits acquired by virtue of the employment contract, e.g. the value of a studio provided by the employer. As a result of the change in dismissal/resignation law the terms of notice are now expressed in weeks. For the employees receiving fixed wages, the weekly pay necessary to calculate the severance pay is determined by first multiplying the monthly pay by three and then dividing this by thirteen.

B. *Payment*

The compensation in lieu of notice must be paid at the moment the employee leaves the company or at the latest on the first regular pay day following this.

As a rule the compensation in lieu of notice must be paid in full. There is an exception to this rule:[241] for a company in difficulties or in extremely unfavourable circumstances the employer may obtain permission to pay the compensation in lieu of notice in monthly instalments.

---

[241] Article 39*bis* Royal Decree 29 August 1985.

Interlude: golden parachutes

As a result of the financial crisis there has been a lot of discussion about the golden handshakes for top managers. By the Law of 6 April 2010,[242] the so-called Corporate Governance Law, 'golden parachutes' were created. For some firms these departure bonuses were limited. They can only amount to a maximum of 12 months' wage (and very exceptionally 18 months). However, if the manager is bound by an employment contract the Employment Contract Act prevails (meaning that the compensation can be higher). In practice the interaction between labour law and corporate law raises a lot of questions.

SECTION 5. DISMISSAL FOR JUST CAUSE[243]

§ 1. CONCEPT

Just cause is understood to mean a serious shortcoming that makes any professional cooperation between employer and employee impossible immediately and permanently.[244]

Usually this will involve a mistake made during the implementation of the employment contract. Just cause requires a mistake. Yet Article 35 Employment Contract Act does not require the serious shortcoming to be of a contractual nature, nor for this to have been committed *vis-à-vis* the employer, or harming the latter. Therefore, in principle, serious shortcomings that occurred in the private sphere can also result in just cause for dismissal. In other words, it is not an absolute requirement for the shortcoming to be of a contractual nature.

The error must have been committed effectively. The mere intention, even if this was expressed, does not suffice. On the other hand, to be able to refer to a just cause, actual damage is not necessary either.

A just cause, which requires immediate dismissal, is incompatible with further activities by the employee in question, at least if the work is carried out under the authority of the employer. If the employer allows the employee to carry out further tasks it is obvious that the collaboration is not impossible right away.

---

242 *BS/MB* 23 April 2010; Niesten, N. en Coulon, D., 'L'encadrement juridique des politiques de rémunération dans les institutions financières et dans les sociétés cotées', *Ors.* 2011/2, pp. 19–30.

243 Wantiez, C. and Votquenne, D., *Le licenciement pour motif grave*, Brussels, Larcier, 2012,151 pp.; Gilson, S., *Le congé pour motif grave: notion, évolutions, questions spéciales*, Louvain-la-Neuve, Anthemis, 2011, 549 pp.; Westrade, M. en Gilson, S. (red.), *Le congé pour motif grave*, Limal, Anthemis, 2011, 549 pp.; Wantiez, C., *Le congé pour motif grave*, Brussels, Larcier, 1998, 126 pp.; Wantiez, C., *Le congé pour motif grave*, Brussels, Larcier, 1998, 126 pp.; Jamoulle, M. en Jadot, F., *Licenciement et démission pour motif grave*, Liège, Law Faculty, 1977, 248 pp.

244 Article 35 Employment Contract Act.

§ 2. EVIDENCE

The person invoking just cause must produce evidence of the facts he/she puts forward. This evidence may be produced with all remedies at law, including witnesses.

Moreover, the party who dismisses someone or resigns for just cause must prove that they observed the terms for dismissal/resignation as well as the notification of the grounds.

§ 3. ASSESSMENT

When the other party challenges the gravity of the motives invoked for the dismissal/resignation for just cause, that party can appeal to the labour tribunal. The judge will then assess if there is a just cause.

Even when individual employment contracts or the work rules list acts or facts that can be invoked as just cause, the judge retains his full power of judgment. However, he can include this in his assessment of the importance parties attach to certain shortcomings.

If the judge decides that the facts invoked do not constitute just cause, the party ruled against will have to pay compensation corresponding to the period of notice that would have had to be complied with in the normal course of events.

Although, in principle, the labour tribunals in their capacity as trial courts decide irreversibly whether or not certain facts constitute just cause, just cause remains a legal concept. This means that the Court of Cassation is competent to examine whether or not the trial court was able to deduce from the established facts that the just cause in question is a just cause within the meaning of Article 35 Employment Contract Act.

It is not easy to give a clear-cut definition of just cause. A given case will always have to be assessed with regard to the actual and specific circumstances. Some aspects will be considered as mitigating circumstances on one occasion, and as aggravating circumstances on another occasion.

Mitigating circumstances could be the absence of the intention to cause damage, the young age of the employee, his/her high seniority, the lax or provocative attitude of the employer or his delegate, the once-only occurrence, etc.

Aggravating circumstances could be previous warnings, the intention to cause damage, the qualification as a blue-collar worker or white-collar worker, the recurring nature of the error, etc.

§ 4. PROCEDURE

In the case of termination of the employment contract for just cause strict requirements as to form and periods must be observed. Basically, dismissal for just cause takes place in two stages, in each of which a term of three working days is to be strictly complied with.

The first stage is the actual termination of the employment contract. This is followed by the confirmation with a specification of the reasons for the termination.

A. *Term*

The person wishing to terminate the employment contract for just cause must give notice within a term of three working days, following the day on which sufficient certainty has been obtained regarding the facts involved.

The term commences at the moment when the party taking the initiative has sufficient certainty regarding the fact constituting a dismissal/resignation for just cause. So this term does not necessarily start at the moment the serious shortcoming occurs. Nor does it begin at the moment when the other party is first notified of the facts, and only has presumptions to go on.

So, waiting until enough evidence has been collected is permitted, unless the certainty regarding the facts and their gravity was already present before all the evidence has been gathered by the party invoking just cause. This means, *inter alia*, that the party concerned is allowed to begin an investigation into the accuracy of the fact or to postpone the termination until he/she has had the opportunity to hear the other party with regard to the fact with which he/she has been charged. Yet one must be careful not to wait too long, for instance, for elements of proof that do not add anything to the knowledge one already has.

In the case of recurring shortcomings the term of three working days commences, at the latest, after the shortcoming invoked has ended.

The period of three working days for dismissal only starts when the mistake constituting the just cause has been communicated to the person authorised to give notice. The period is counted in days. It involves an absolute term, meaning that the party must act within three working days, regardless of the circumstances. For instance, the term will not be suspended in the event of absence of the employee for whatever reason, such as illness, annual holidays, etc.

Except for Sundays and public holidays, all days are working days.

B. *Authorised person*

Dismissal must be carried out by the person authorised to do this. However, sometimes this is done by an unauthorised person. Case law usually only considers this kind of dismissal to be valid when it is confirmed in time – i.e. within three working days following the dismissal carried out by the unauthorised person – by the authorised person.

C. *Formal requirements*

Dismissal for just cause is not subject to any specific custom. It suffices that the party clearly informs the other party of their wish to terminate the contract without notice. This means, for instance, that the employer can inform the employee orally of the fact that he/she has to leave the workplace immediately and is not permitted to return.

Dismissal for just cause terminates the employment contract at the moment the party giving it notifies the other party of their wish to terminate the contract. Nonetheless, the dismissal can only be presented to the other party at the moment that the latter has been given the opportunity to take cognizance of this dismissal. Among other things, this is important with regard to the right to wages and possibly the right to industrial accident compensation in the period of the notification of dismissal for just cause, but in which the other party has not yet had the possibility to take note thereof.

§ 5. NOTIFICATION OF THE 'JUST CAUSE'

Within three working days following the day on which notice was given, the party by whom the dismissal/resignation for just cause was communicated must notify the other party of the gross shortcomings that they are charged with.

The Employment Contract Act clearly distinguishes between the dismissal/resignation and the notification of the reasons behind it. Naturally, there is nothing against informing the person concerned of the dismissal and the just cause at the same time, which in any case has to take place within three working days after the facts have been clarified with certainty.

A. *Formal requirements*

Whereas the dismissal itself is not subject to any formalities the notification of the reasons for the dismissal must be made in writing.

On pain of nullity, the relevant documents must be served in one of the following three ways:

- by means of a registered letter of which the posting date is the qualifying factor to establish whether or not the notification took place within the prescribed time;
- by means of a writ;

– by handing over the document and the other party signing a copy for receipt. If the other party refuses to sign this document, it will be necessary to resort to one of the two abovementioned means without this refusal being able to be invoked to extend the term of three working days.

B. Contents

The notice of dismissal must describe the facts that constitute the just cause. It is of critical importance that these be worded clearly. Often a dismissal for just cause is considered unlawful, merely because the notification was insufficiently clear.

The content of a letter of notice must enable the other party to know the facts they are charged with and allow the judge to assess its gravity and to examine whether the facts invoked are the same as those mentioned in the notice.

The judge may only take cognizance of the facts specified in the document. Elements not mentioned in the notice cannot be retained as just cause. However, these may be involved in the assessment of the just cause by the judge if they clarify the just cause invoked, even if the unmentioned elements are of a different nature than the just cause invoked.

C. Language

For dismissal for just cause the language provisions have to be complied with as well.

§ 6. SANCTIONS

The person invoking just cause not only has to produce the evidence of the existence of the gross shortcoming constituting the just cause, but he/she also has to prove that the prescribed periods and formalities have been observed.

If a procedural mistake is made, the employment contract has been terminated unlawfully, meaning that payment of compensation in lieu of notice is due.

SECTION 6. UNILATERAL AND SUBSTANTIAL MODIFICATION OF AN ESSENTIAL WORKING CONDITION[245]

The concept of the unilateral and substantial modification of (an) essential working condition(s) fits in with a theory developed by case law and doctrine which says

[245] Gilson, S. (ed.), *La modification unilatérale du contrat de travail*, Louvain-la-Neuve, Anthemis, 2010, 187 pp.

that certain acts and certain behaviour of the parties of an employment contract show that it is likely that there is a wish to terminate the contract.

Given the binding force of the employment contract as laid down in Article 1134 Civil Code, neither the employer nor the employee has the right to change the agreement unilaterally.

It is significant that the conditions regarding the essence of the employment contract can only be changed by mutual consent. Nevertheless, if the employer does proceed to make a major unilateral modification, case law assumes that this is the expression of the wish to change the employment contract unilaterally – in other words, an implicit immediate unlawful dismissal.

Inadequate performance on the other hand, even involving essential obligations according to the employment contract, in itself does not terminate the employment contract. Nonetheless, this kind of inadequate performance can be an indication, or evidence, of the wish to terminate the contract unilaterally and therefore unlawfully.

The two main problems in this regard are the notion of 'essential working condition(s)' and the manner in which an employee whose employment contract undergoes such a modification, can react to this.

§ 1. ESSENTIAL WORKING CONDITION

To distinguish essential from non-essential working conditions, case law and doctrine developed three criteria.

According to the first criterion a working condition must be considered to be essential when in its modified form it would have prevented the employee from concluding the contract.

The second criterion refers to the damage factor, stating that a working condition is essential if its modification harms the employee, either materially or morally.

The third and last criterion indicates that the judge must weigh two elements against one another: on the one hand the company's interest, which sometimes may require an adaptation of the manner in which the work is organised and therefore the working conditions; and on the other hand, the employee's expectations.

Furthermore, case law requires that the essential working conditions are changed substantially. Usually the following terms are considered to be essential: the working hours, the place of employment, wages, etc. To a certain extent parties are allowed to determine whether or not an element of the employment contract is essential. For instance, the working hours, which directly determine the work agreed upon, constitute an absolutely essential element. The location, on the other hand, is not necessarily an essential element.

§ 2. POSSIBILITIES FOR THE EMPLOYEE

An employee holding the view that a working condition essential to him/her has been altered substantially and unilaterally by the employer has three ways in which to react.

First of all he/she can resign with just cause. However, doing so has a disadvantage. The employee not only loses his/her job, but in no way will he/she be able to obtain compensation.

A second possibility open to him/her is to ask the court for a legal annulment of the contract. This solution has the advantage that the employment contract continues to exist as long as the procedure is pending and no annulment has been pronounced. Moreover, if the shortcoming on the part of the employer is not serious enough for an annulment, it is possible that damages will be awarded. The disadvantage is that it is not easy to apply this solution within the context of an employment contract.

The third and most commonly chosen method is that of a unilateral termination by the employer. The employee regards the unilateral and substantial alteration of an essential working condition by the employer as an expression of the wish to terminate the agreement. Consequently, the employee will claim the normal compensation in lieu of notice from the employer. To this end, the employee must invoke the unilateral modification of an essential element as unlawful dismissal within a reasonable time for reflection after the alteration has been made. If the employee exceeds this time for reflection and continues to work, he/she renounces his/her right to invoke breach of contract, even if the further implementation of the employment contract takes place under continued protest.

SECTION 7. APPARENT UNREASONABLE DISMISSAL AND IMPROPER USE OF DISMISSAL LAW

§ 1. APPARENT UNREASONABLE DISMISSAL

Above, we already referred to the obligation to state the grounds for dismissal and the sanctions in the event of non-compliance. In addition, Collective Agreement No. 109[246] provides for a verification of the reason given. In this context the concept of 'apparent unreasonable dismissal' is the key element. This kind of dismissal is the dismissal of an employee with an open-ended employment contract based on reasons that are not related to his/her suitability or behaviour, or have nothing to do with requirements with regard to the operations of the enterprise, institute

[246] Wantiez, M. and Lemaire, G., 'Quelques questions relatives à la convention collective n° 109 concernant la motivation du licenciement', *JTT* 2014, pp. 261–269.

or service, and which would never have been given by a normal and reasonable employer.

In the case of an apparent unreasonable dismissal the employer owes the employee damages amounting to a minimum of 3 weeks' wages and a maximum of 17 weeks' wages.

A provision with regard to the burden of proof was included:

- if the employer has communicated the reasons for the dismissal, the burden of proof lies with the party contesting this;
- the employer must deliver proof of the reasons he cited for the dismissal but did not communicate to the employee and which demonstrate that the dismissal is not unreasonable;
- the employee must deliver proof of elements that seem to indicate the apparent unreasonableness of the dismissal if he/she has not submitted a request to be informed of the reasons for his/her dismissal.

The compensation cannot be combined with any other compensation owed by the employer because of the termination of the employment contract, with the exception of compensation in lieu of notice, a non-competition compensation, goodwill indemnity or a supplementary compensation paid in addition to the social benefits.

§ 2. MISUSE OF THE RIGHT OF DISMISSAL

The above described rules only refer to the dismissal of a worker hired for an open-ended period. In other situations of dismissal or resignation ordinary law theory on the prohibition of abuse of rights applies. In contractual relations this is based on good faith, as laid down in Article 1134, 3 Civil Code.

Given the fact that in the general arrangement regarding the misuse of the right of dismissal there is no reversal of the burden of proof, the party invoking misuse of the right of dismissal (usually the employee) must prove this misuse.

Entitlement to compensation for misuse of the right to dismissal requires the existence of damage that is not compensated by the lump-sum compensation in lieu of notice.[247] This must concern damage that does not result from the dismissal itself, but instead, from the circumstances accompanying the dismissal.[248]

247 Cassation 19 February 1975, *Bull.* 1975, p. 685.

248 Cassation 26 September 2005, AR S.04.0176N, *Bull.* 2005, p. 1742.

SECTION 8. SPECIAL DISMISSAL PROCEDURES

For certain categories of employees there are special dismissal procedures. However, we will not discuss these in detail. The special procedures apply to:

- the personnel representatives and candidate-personnel representatives in the works councils and workplace health and safety committees;
- trade union representatives;
- health and safety advisers;
- the environment coordinator;
- the medical insurance advisers;[249]
- the employees working for an employer who does not comply with the consultation rules in the event of the introduction of new technologies;[250]
- etc.

SECTION 9. DOCUMENTS

When the employee leaves the company – regardless of the way in which the employment contract was terminated – the employer must issue the following so-called social documents:

- the financial statement for the last work done;
- the individual account for the current year;
- the holiday certificate for white-collar workers, which must allow them to claim their right to annual holidays from their new employer;
- taxation card 281.10 for the declaration of income tax;
- unemployment statement form C4;
- employment statement which only mentions the beginning and the end of the employment contract as well as the nature of the work done. This document may not include any other statement unless the employee expressly requests so.

SECTION 10. OUTPLACEMENT

Dismissal often involves outplacement. This is a complex of coaching services for employees who have been made redundant or run the risk of being made redundant. Outplacement helps them to find a new job or to start a business

[249] Article 154 Sickness and Invalidity Insurance Act 14 July 1994 and Royal Decree No. 35 of 20 July 1967, *BS/MB* 29 July 1967.

[250] National Labour Council Collective Agreement No. 39 of 13 December 1983, declared generally binding by Royal Decree 25 January 1984, *BS/MB* 8 February 1984.

of their own. A distinction must be made between voluntary and compulsory outplacement.

An employer who wants to offer his employees outplacement assistance must comply with the provisions of Collective Agreement No. 51.[251] This implies, among other things, that he has to consult with the works council or union delegation.

Employees who have reached the age of 45 when they are dismissed are entitled to outplacement assistance.[252] This scheme was laid down in Collective Agreement No. 82 of 10 July 2002.[253] However, this right is rather limited. The assistance may not exceed three times 20 hours during a period of 12 months.

Employers who do not observe these obligations have to make a contribution to the National Employment Office.

Through Article 76 Unified Status Act 'a general outplacement arrangement' has been included in the Law. By and large, this means that an employee whose employment contract is terminated by the employer by means of a term of notice of at least 30 weeks, or by means of a compensation equalling the current wage corresponding to the duration of a term of notice of at least 30 weeks, or the remaining part of that term, is entitled to outplacement except when she/he has been dismissed with just cause.

SECTION 11. THE COMPETITION CLAUSE[254]

The competition clause is the clause according to which an employee (blue-collar worker, white-collar worker or sales representative), upon his departure from the company, undertakes not to engage in similar activities, either by running a company of his/her own, or by entering the service of a rival company, as a result of which he/she would have the possibility of damaging the firm he/she has left, by using the industrial or trading knowledge of the company and which he/she acquired, for himself/herself, or for the benefit of the rival company.

---

251 Collective Agreement No. 51 of 10 February 1992, declared generally binding by the Royal Decree of 10 April 1992, *BS/MB* 1 May 1992.

252 Articles 12 *et seq.* Law 5 September 2001 with a view to improving the level of employment, *BS/MB* 15 September 2001.

253 Declared generally binding by the Royal Decree of 20 September 2002, *BS/MB* 5 October 2002; the Collective Agreement was amended by Collective Agreement 82*bis* of 17 July 2007, declared generally binding by the Royal Decree of 3 October 2007, *BS/MB* 21 November 2007.

254 Wantiez, C., *Les clauses de non-concurrence et le contrat de travail*, Brussels, Larcier, 2001, 110 p.

§ 1. THE COMPETITION CLAUSE FOR BLUE-COLLAR WORKERS

A. *Formal requirements*

Under penalty of nullity the competition clause must be put down in writing. The document must include the application terms. The legal application terms can be developed further by means of a collective agreement concluded in the competent joint (sub-)committee.[255]

B. *The possibility of including a competition clause in an employment contract depends on the employee's annual income*

1. Gross earnings under €33,221

When the gross earnings do not exceed €33,221 the competition clause is considered to be non-existent.

2. Gross earnings over €33,221 and under €66,441

In this case the competition clause may only be applied to positions or categories of positions determined by collective agreement concluded in a joint (sub-) committee. Lacking such an agreement, either because the aforementioned bodies are not active or because they were unable to reach an agreement and conciliation procedures failed, the (categories of) positions may be designated at the request of the first party to decide at enterprise level, provided there is an agreement between the employer and the representative employee organisations. If the difference of opinion between the employer and the employee organisations continues to exist, either party can seek the advice of the Committee of Good Services.

3. Gross earnings over €66,441

If the gross annual income exceeds €66,441 the competition clause may be included in the employment contract in a legally valid way, except for the (categories of) positions excluded by a collective agreement concluded in a joint (sub-)committee.

---

255 Article 65, § 2 Employment Contract Act.

C. *Validity requirements regarding the clause*

1. Effectiveness limited in time and space

The effectiveness of the clause is geographically restricted to the locations where the worker can effectively compete with his/her former employer because of the nature of the enterprise and its sphere of influence. The clause can never apply outside the national borders.

Its range is also limited in time, more specifically to a maximum of 12 months from the day the employment ended.

2. The competition clause must relate to similar activities

In order to be able to invoke the competition clause against the employee it is not enough that the latter enters into service with a rival firm. He/she must carry out similar work.

The employer has to prove that the activities of his/her former employee cause him/her harm and that this harm is the result of the employee's use of industrial or technical knowledge acquired within the enterprise of his/her former employer. A final requirement is that the employee used this knowledge to his/her own advantage or to the advantage of the competing employer.

If he/she uses his knowledge to the benefit of a third person who is not the competing employer, the clause does not apply. However this does not preclude the employer from claiming damages on the basis of Article 1382 Civil Code.

3. The clause must provide for a one-off lump-sum compensation

The clause must provide for the payment of a one-off lump-sum compensation by the employer. The minimum amount of the compensation is equal to half of the gross wage due for the period during which the clause applies. The basis of this amount is the gross income the worker received during the month prior to the day on which the employment ended.

For workers with completely or partially variable wages, the amount for the variable part is calculated on the basis of the average gross income of the 12 months prior to the termination of the contract.

D. *The effectiveness of the competition clause*

1. Cases in which the competition clause does not take effect

The clause does not take effect when the employment contract was terminated within the probationary period or was terminated by the employer outside the probationary period without just cause, or for just cause by the employee.

2. The employee is subjected to the competition clause

If the employee is subjected to the competition clause, i.e. when as a result of the competition clause he/she must remain inactive during a period of 12 months, he/she may claim the abovementioned lump-sum compensation. The employer is not obliged to pay the compensation if he/she goes back on the application of the clause within 15 days of the termination of the contract.

3. Violation of the competition clause

If this is the case, the employee owes his/her former employer the abovementioned amount as compensation. If he/she already received a lump-sum compensation as a result of being subjected to the clause he/she has to pay back this amount as well. However, this will only occur for that part of the amount that corresponds to the period that he/she did not observe the clause.

The employer is entitled to a higher compensation than the lump sum if he proves the existence and the extent of the harm done.

E. Sanction when one of the validity requirements is not observed

If the clause does not meet one of the validity requirements it is completely null and void, and not just the part that relates to the non-observed requirement. This means that the court is not allowed to reduce the clause to the legal limits when it transgresses these.

§ 2. THE COMPETITION CLAUSE FOR WHITE-COLLAR WORKERS

In the case of white-collar workers a distinction must be made between the legal clause and the derogation clause.

A. The legal clause

The arrangement regarding the legal competition clause is identical to that for blue-collar workers.[256]

[256] Article 86, § 1 Employment Contract Act.

B. *The derogation clause*

1. Enterprises for which a derogation is possible

A derogation clause can be applied to enterprises that meet one or both of the following conditions:

- an international sphere of influence or important economic, technical or financial interests on the international markets;
- an internal service for research.

In those enterprises the derogation clause can be applied to white-collar workers employed in positions enabling them, directly or indirectly, to obtain knowledge of practices typical of the enterprise and whose use, outside the enterprise, can be harmful to the latter.[257]

2. Elements of the legal system that may be deviated from

The following elements of the legal arrangement may be deviated from:

- the validity and application in space: the effectiveness of the clause can go beyond the national borders;
- time: the clause can be effective for more than 12 months;
- the application terms: one is allowed to deviate from the principle according to which the clause does not apply in the event of dismissal during the probationary period, dismissal by the employer without just cause after the probationary period, or resignation by the employee for just cause.

3. The structures and conditions of the derogation clause

The structures and conditions of the derogation clause are formulated in Collective Agreement No. 1*ter*. This Collective Agreement determines that, just like for the legal clause, the deviation clause must be put down in writing. The terms for establishing a derogation clause must be present:

- in a collective agreement concluded at the level of the branch of industry;
- in the absence of a collective agreement at branch level, in an agreement concluded at enterprise level;
- in the absence of a collective agreement at enterprise level, in an individual employment contract.

[257] Article 86, § 2 Employment Contract Act.

Within the framework of Collective Agreement No. 1 a Committee for Good Services was established. This Committee consists of experts (partially designated by employees' and employers' organisations within the National Labour Council, partially co-opted). It gives advice with regard to the validity and application of derogation clauses because of individual conflicts. The Committee's competence does not exclude the competence of labour tribunals.

§ 3. THE COMPETITION CLAUSE IN THE EMPLOYMENT CONTRACT FOR SALES REPRESENTATIVES

See *infra*.

§ 4. CONCLUSION

The usefulness of a competition clause is marginal except with regard to sales representatives. The objective of the legislator, i.e. preventing an employee from competing with his/her employer by means of knowledge acquired from the latter, is only rarely achieved. The financial benefits resulting from immediate employment with a competing employer are usually bigger than the lump sum so that a lot of employers are prepared to pay this amount instead of paying the employee.

SECTION 12. THE ARBITRATION CLAUSE

Employees and employers are not allowed to agree in advance that they intend to submit the disputes resulting from the employment contract to an arbitrator.[258] A prohibition on relying on an arbitrator for settling individual disputes is also mentioned in Article 9 Collective Agreement Act, Article 10 Work Rules Act, and Article 1678 Judicial Code.

Article 69 Employment Contract Act accepts two exceptions to this prohibition. The arbitration clause can be used for a white-collar worker who:

- has a gross income of over € 66,441;
- is in charge of the executive management of the company, or who has managerial responsibility in a department or unit comparable to that for the entire company.

258 Article 13 Employment Contract Act.

Case law and legal doctrine accept the possibility of relying on arbitrators once the dispute resulting from the employment contract occurs. At that moment the employee is no longer in a subordinate position.

SECTION 13. THE TRAINING CLAUSE[259]

An employer often invests in an employee. The latter could be inclined to resign soon after he/she has completed expensive training and start working somewhere else (for better pay). To avoid this, parties may conclude an agreement under which part of the costs is recovered: the training clause.

According to Article 22*bis* Employment Contract Act the training clause is understood to mean that the employee who completes a course during the implementation of his/her employment contract at the expense of the employer undertakes to reimburse part of the training costs to the latter if he/she leaves the company before the end of the agreed period. Certain categories of employees and/or courses may be excluded from the application of the training clause by virtue of a collective agreement concluded in the responsible joint committee and declared generally binding by the Crown.

Under penalty of nullity the clause must be laid down in writing for each employee separately, at the latest, at the moment that the course in question starts. It can only be established in the context of an open-ended employment contract.

The document must include the following details:

1. a description of the agreed training, its duration and the location where it will take place;
2. the costs of the course or, if it is not possible to determine the full amount, the elements permitting an estimate to be made. Neither the compensation due to the employee in the context of the implementation of the employment contract nor travel expenses or accommodation can be considered as part of the training costs;
3. the starting date and the period of validity of the training clause. If the training results in a certificate being awarded, the starting date of the validity of the training clause coincides with the date the certificate is presented;
4. the amount to be refunded, i.e. the part of the training costs paid for by the employer which the employee undertakes to pay after completion of the course. This amount must be expressed degressively in terms of the validity of the training clause. The amount is limited.

---

259 De Ridder, S., 'La clause d'écolage une formation bien méritée !' in Claeys & Engels, *Arbeidsovereenkomstenwet na 30 jaar... anders bekeken*, Brussels, Larcier, 2008, pp. 99–111; Mairy, C., 'La clause d'écolage', *Ors.* 2007/8, pp. 20–27.

The training clause is considered to be non-existent:

- when the indexed annual pay does not exceed € 33,221;[260]
- when this does not involve a specific course allowing a person to acquire new professional skills that may also be used outside the company;
- when the training given to the employee follows from a legal or regulatory provision with a view to the position for which the worker was recruited, when the course does not take 80 hours, or has a monetary value equal to double the average minimum monthly pay as established for employees of 21 years or older by virtue of a collective agreement concluded by the National Labour Council.

The validity of the training clause may not exceed a period of three years and must be determined taking account of the costs and the duration of the training.

The amount to be paid back by the employee when the duration agreed in the training clause is not complied with may not exceed:

- 80% of the costs of the course if the employee leaves before 1/3 of the agreed period has passed;
- 50% of the costs of the course if the employee leaves between 1/3 and at the latest 2/3 of the agreed period;
- 20% of the costs of the course if the employee leaves after 2/3 of the agreed period have passed. In this case the amount may never exceed 30% of the employee's annual pay.

The training clause does not take effect when the agreement is terminated, either during the probationary period or after this period by the employer without just cause, or by the employee for just cause.

It does not take effect either when the employment contract is terminated in the context of a restructuring operation as referred to in the Generation Pact.

The employee continues to be the owner of his/her diplomas or certificates and must be in the possession of the original or a copy certified by the training centre, regardless of whether or not the training clause takes effect.

[260] Amount for 2016. This is indexed annually.

SECTION 14. LIMITATION OF THE EMPLOYMENT CONTRACT ACTIONS

§ 1. LEGAL ACTIONS *EX CONTRACTU*

The legal actions resulting from the employment contract are limited to one year after the termination of this contract or 5 years after the fact that led to this action, provided that this term does not exceed a period of one year after the termination of the contract.[261]

The limitation does not fall under public policy (*ordre public*). It can be invoked both by the employee and the employer but not by the court of its own volition.

§ 2. LEGAL ACTIONS *EX DELICTO*

In labour law many provisions are subject to punitive sanctions. Examples of offences pertaining to labour law are non-payment of holiday allowances, public holiday allowances and the minimum wage established in a generally binding collective agreement.

If the offence causes damage, the aggrieved employee is entitled to damages/compensation. The limitation of this civil legal action is not regulated by the Employment Contract Act. After all, this does not involve a contractual claim, but rather an extra-contractual claim whose limitation is governed by Article 26 Introductory Title Code of Criminal Procedure and Article 2262*bis* Civil Code; this means five years from the day following the day on which the injured party became aware of the damage. However, some authors hold the view that Article 15 Employment Contract Act also applies.

Quite often the concept of the continued or collective offence is invoked, i.e. the totality of offences that in themselves are expiring but which, because of the unity of criminal perception, are considered to be one offence. By connecting the civil claim to damages/compensation to the continued offence a category of almost imprescriptible actions is created *de facto*.

[261] Article 15 Employment Contract Act.

CHAPTER 2
RESTRUCTURING OF ENTERPRISES

In case of the restructuring of an enterprise there are provisions that deviate from 'ordinary' dismissal law.

Employers who proceed to collective dismissal, closure of the enterprise or who transfer their enterprise, either completely or partially, must – depending on the case – inform the public authorities and employees' organisations beforehand. Apart from this, in certain cases employees receive specific compensation. In the case of bankruptcy, too, there is a special arrangement for regulating employees' rights after the take-over of the healthy parts of the bankrupt company. This arrangement was inspired by Chapter 11 of the US Bankruptcy Code. Because of the specificity this matter will not be discussed further. Those interested can find more information on the following governmental website: www.herstructureringen.be/restructuration/fr/homepage/index.html.

V

SPECIAL AND DEVIATING TYPES OF EMPLOYMENT CONTRACTS

CHAPTER 1

EMPLOYMENT CONTRACTS WITHIN THE SCOPE OF THE LAW OF 3 JULY 1978

SECTION 1. THE EMPLOYMENT CONTRACT FOR SALES REPRESENTATIVES

The provisions of the Employment Contract Act regarding white-collar workers also apply to sales representatives, except for the rules on the competition clause. However, since this group of employees deliver very specific services, the Employment Contract Act devotes a separate title (Title IV) to them.

§ 1. WHAT IS A SALES REPRESENTATIVE?

The employment contract for sales representatives is the agreement under which an employee, i.e. the sales representative, undertakes, in return for wages, to find and visit customers with a view to negotiating and completing transactions, with the exception of insurance policies, under the authority of, chargeable to, and on behalf of, one or more principals.[262]

A number of persons working for principals and performing activities bearing resemblance to those of sales representatives are nonetheless not considered to be sales representatives. The legislator specifically stipulated this for: persons working in the insurance business, agents, brokers, concessionaires, middlemen allowed to pass on their orders to whomever they like, and the commercial agents bound to their employer by a contracting agreement within the meaning of the law regarding an agency agreement, a mandate for wages or any other agreement

262 Article 4 Employment Contract Act.

pursuant to which a commercial agent does not act under the authority of his/her principal.

Despite any explicit or implicit provision of the agreement, a contract concluded between a principal and a middleman, whatever his description, is considered to be an employment contract for sales representatives unless proof to the contrary is given. Thus, the judge is not bound by the qualification the parties themselves allocated to the contract.

§ 2. THE SALES REPRESENTATIVE'S WAGES

The wages of a sales representative consist of a fixed salary, a commission, or partly a fixed salary and partly commission.[263]

A. *Commission: concept and basis for calculations*

A commission is a variable wage calculated on the basis of the turnover made by the sales representative, the work done, etc.

A distinction is made between *direct* and *indirect* commissions.

Direct commissions are due for orders completed by the sales representative himself/herself. Indirect commissions are due for orders completed without his/her intervention but for which remuneration is due because an exclusivity clause was included in the agreement.

In principle, the agreement determines how the commission is calculated. Failing contractual provisions the calculation is made according to the rules formulated in Article 96 Employment Contract Act, i.e.:

- on the basis of the price mentioned on the order form or in the order accepted by the employer;
- failing the former, on the basis of the price lists, price rates or scales;
- failing the former, on the basis of the prices obtained.

Evidence can be produced by means of the statements and documents the employer monthly issues to the sales representative and which contain the details regarding the commission due for the previous month.[264]

263 Article 89 Employment Contract Act.

264 Article 97 Employment Contract Act.

B. *The right to commission*

1. During the implementation of the contract

Direct commissions:[265] the commission is due for each order accepted by the employer, even if this is not followed by execution, except in the case of non-execution through fault of the sales representative.

Each order is assumed to be accepted except for refusal or reservations of which the employer shall notify his sales representative in writing within a period established in the employment contract. If no such period has been laid down, then it amounts to one month starting on the day the order is passed on.

Indirect commissions:[266] during the implementation of his/her contract the sales representative who has to visit certain customers or branches on his/her own, is entitled to commission for deals which the employer completes without the representative's intervention in the sector for which exclusivity was granted.

2. During the suspension or after the termination of the contract

Direct commissions: the sales representative is entitled to commission for the orders he/she brought in even if they are accepted during the suspension or after the termination of the contract.[267] Furthermore, he/she is entitled to commission for the orders made by the customers during the entire duration of the suspension, or during a period of three months following the termination of the contract, if he/she can prove that during the implementation of the contract he/she has established contact with the customer that was followed by facts leading to the acceptance of the said orders.[268]

Indirect commissions: the sales representative is also entitled to commission for deals made during the suspension or after termination of the contract insofar as the order was passed on during the implementation of the contract.[269]

Staggered deliveries: if the accepted orders refer to staggered deliveries the sales representative is entitled to commission for the deliveries that were made during a period of six months after the termination of the contract.[270]

---

[265] Article 90 Employment Contract Act.
[266] Article 93 Employment Contract Act.
[267] Article 91 Employment Contract Act.
[268] Article 92 Employment Contract Act.
[269] Article 93 Employment Contract Act.
[270] Article 94 Employment Contract Act.

C. *Payment of the commission*

1. During the implementation and suspension of the contract

In the absence of contractual provisions the commission is collectable 15 days after the statement and, possibly, the documents included in Article 97 Employment Contract have been submitted.[271]

The direct and indirect commissions for which there is a right despite the suspension, must be paid within thirty days of acceptance of the order.[272]

2. After the termination of the contract

Orders accepted before the termination of the contract: the commission on all accepted orders must be paid within a term of thirty days following the termination of the contract.[273]

Orders made before the termination of the contract, but accepted afterwards: payment within thirty days following the acceptance of the order.[274]

Commissions for orders made by the customer during a period of three months after the termination of the contract, of which it can be proven that the sales representative made the necessary contacts during the implementation of the contract: payment, at the latest, the fourth month after the termination of the contract.[275]

Commissions owed for staggered deliveries: payment, at the latest, the seventh month after termination of the contract.[276]

§ 3. GOODWILL INDEMNITY

When an employment contract is terminated by the employer without just cause or by the sales representative for just cause, the sales representative is owed goodwill compensation unless the employer proves that the termination of the contract does not in any way damage the sales representative.[277] This indemnity is a compensation for the loss of customers. It is only due:

- when the employee has been employed as a sales representative for at least one year;

---

271 Article 98 Employment Contract Act.
272 Article 99, 2 Employment Contract Act.
273 Article 99, 2 Employment Contract Act.
274 Article 99, 2 Employment Contract Act.
275 Article 99, 3 Employment Contract Act.
276 Article 99, 3 Employment Contract Act.
277 Article 101 Employment Contract Act.

- when customers have been brought in;
- when the employer cannot prove that the sales representative does not suffer any harm from the termination of the contract.

The goodwill indemnity equals three months' wages for the sales representative who was employed by the same employer during a period of one to five years.

It is increased by one month's wages for every extra five-year period of employment for the same employer.

If the sales representative's income consists entirely or partly of commission, the goodwill indemnity is calculated entirely or partly on the basis of the monthly average of the commission earned during the 12 months prior to the termination of the contract. The goodwill indemnity does not only take into account the current wage but also the benefits acquired by virtue of the contract.

If the contract is terminated because of a just cause for which the employer is to be blamed, and the amount of the lump-sum goodwill indemnity does not fully compensate the actual damage suffered, the sales representative, provided that he/she proves the extent of the alleged damage, can obtain damages on top of the lump-sum compensation to the amount of the difference between the sum of the actual damage and the sum of the compensation.[278]

§ 4. THE COMPETITION CLAUSE

A competition clause can only be agreed upon if the annual wages exceed € 33,221. If this threshold is not reached the clause is considered to be non-existent.

In contracts providing for an annual wage exceeding € 33,221 the validity of the competition clause depends on three conditions: it must relate to similar activities, it cannot cover more than 12 months and is restricted to the area within which the sales representative carries out his/her activities.

Under penalty of nullity the clause must be put down in writing.

It does not have effect if either during the probationary period or after the probationary period the contract is terminated by the employer without just cause, or by the sales representative for just cause.

The lump-sum compensation provided for in the contract in case of a breach of the competition clause may not exceed the amount of three months' wages. However, the employer can demand a higher compensation if he can prove the existence and extent of the harm done.

If the employee violates the clause he/she is obliged to pay the employer the lump-sum compensation, unless the latter can prove that the real harm done is much more significant. Contrary to the scheme applying to white-collar and blue-collar workers, the sales representative is not entitled to compensation if he/

278 Article 103 Employment Contract Act.

she does not violate the clause. To compensate, the law includes the presumption that the sales representative has brought in customers. The employer can produce proof to the contrary.[279]

§ 5. THE *DELCREDERE* CLAUSE

The sales representative is liable for the customer's creditworthiness. This so-called *Delcredere* clause must always be included in writing.

However, liability is limited. The clause can – except in the event of gross error or deceit – only have effect to the amount of a sum equal to the commission relating to irrecoverable claims at the expense of the customer.[280] Moreover, it can only relate to non-payment, and never to the annulment of an order.

SECTION 2. THE EMPLOYMENT CONTRACT FOR DOMESTIC SERVANTS[281]

The employment contract for domestic servants is the contract pursuant to which an employee, a servant, undertakes to perform, in return for wages and under the authority of an employer, predominantly housekeeping work at the home of the employer or his family.[282] However, not all domestic personnel can be considered as domestic servants. Employees mainly performing intellectual work – e.g. home tutors – are regarded as white-collar workers, and employees performing non-domestic labour, e.g. the driver and gardener, can be qualified as blue-collar workers.

Since domestic servants are just a small group of employees we will not discuss this further.

SECTION 3. THE EMPLOYMENT CONTRACT FOR STUDENTS

Although this subject is regulated in a separate title of the Employment Contract Act, there is no 'employment contract for students' *stricto sensu*. Depending on the nature of the work the student will be considered as a blue-collar worker, a white-collar worker, a sales representative or a domestic servant.

---

279 Article 105 Employment Contract Act.

280 Article 107 Employment Contract Act.

281 Jacqmain, J., 'Réflexions sur le travail domestique', *Chron. D.S.* 1983, pp. 337–367; Germain-Poclet, M. and Servais, J., 'La loi sur le contrat de travail domestique', *JTT* 1971, pp. 37–40; Danse, A., 'Le contrat de louage de services domestiques', *JT* 1963, pp. 221–223.

282 Article 5 Employment Contract Act.

Therefore he/she is subject to all legal rules applicable to the category to which he/she belongs provided this is not contrary to the specific provisions of Articles 120 *et seq*. Employment Contract Act.

§ 1. WHAT IS A STUDENT?

A definition of 'student' has not been included in the law. In practice this concept is interpreted quite broadly.

Certain categories of students are excluded from the scope by the Crown:

- students who have been working for the same employer for a period of six months and therefore have become regular employees;
- students who are enrolled in evening classes or receive a training with a limited curriculum;
- students doing a teaching placement as part of their course.

Students who are still minors can only conclude a contract if they:

- are at least 15 years old and are in full-time secondary education;
- are minors but no longer subject to compulsory education and still go to school;
- minors of 15 years and older in part-time education or training, do not receive a tideover allowance and carry out the work during the school holidays.

Notwithstanding all express provisions the contract concluded between an employer and a student is presumed to be an employment contract, whatever name it is given. Proof to the contrary is permitted.

§ 2. FORMAL REQUIREMENTS AND COMPULSORY STATEMENTS

The contract must be put down in writing for each student separately, at the latest, on the date he/she starts[283] working. Apart from this it must include a number of statements.[284] The document is not a validity requirement. So, even if none is made, an employment contract may be established. In that case the employer will be sanctioned.

---

[283] Article 123 Employment Contract Act.

[284] Article 124 Employment Contract Act.

The student must be provided with a copy of the rules of work.

A copy of the contract and a copy of the receipt of the rules of work must be presented to a civil servant designated by the Crown within seven days of the beginning of the implementation of the contract.[285] This obligation on the part of the employer is cancelled when the employer registers the employment immediately – possibly electronically – with the Crossroad Bank for Social Security.

If the document does not include the compulsory statements or if the administration does not receive copies of the contract and the receipt, the employment contract can be terminated by the student at any time without observance of a period of notice or compensation.[286]

If there is no document, or the document does not contain the statements with regard to the date of the beginning and end of the contract, the work roster or reference to the work roster in the rules of work, then the same conditions apply as for an open-ended employment contract. However, this sanction does not take effect if the employer can prove that the absence of the statements regarding the work roster has not harmed the student.[287]

Taking into account that the student contract is a so-called social document, the employer can also be prosecuted.

§ 3. THE PROBATION CLAUSE[288]

The employment contract may include a probation clause.[289] The first three working days are considered to be a probationary period. Until that period has expired either party may terminate the agreement without notice or compensation.

§ 4. SUSPENSION OF THE EMPLOYMENT CONTRACT BECAUSE OF INCAPACITY

The employer shall provide the living-in student who is unfit for work with proper accommodation and appropriate care as long as this is needed.

The medical costs, however, are not payable by the employer.

At the student's behest the employer shall inform the person designated by the student of the latter's state.

---

285 Article 125 Employment Contract Act.
286 Article 126 Employment Contract Act.
287 *Ibid.*
288 Article 127 Employment Contract Act.
289 Article 127 Employment Contract Act.

If the student is a minor under guardianship the employer must notify the person in whose care the student usually remains.[290]

If he/she is not living in, the student must notify the employer and possibly submit a medical certificate to him. As regards the payment of the guaranteed minimum wage, the rules of the category the student belongs to apply.

If the incapacity to work lasts longer than seven days the employer can terminate the employment contract, provided he pays compensation equal to the wages corresponding either to the duration of the period of notice or the part of that period still to be covered.[291]

§ 5. TERMINATION BY GIVING NOTICE

In principle, the employment contract ends on the expiry date. However, each of the parties has the right to terminate the contract sooner by giving notice.

When the duration of the agreement does not exceed one month the period of notice to be observed by the employer is three days, and the period to be observed by the student is one day. These periods are seven days and three days respectively when the agreement exceeds one month.

Notice must be given, under penalty of nullity, by means of a registered letter, a writ or manual delivery of a letter. The period commences on the Monday following the week in which the notice of termination is served.

SECTION 4. THE EMPLOYMENT CONTRACT FOR HOME WORKERS

Home work, i.e. work one performs at home without the supervision of an employer, is considered by many as a relic from days long gone. Yet this phenomenon has been gaining renewed interest in recent years. Indeed, new technologies make it possible to organise work in such a way that it is no longer necessary to leave one's home.

For a long time it was not very clear which legislation was applicable to home workers. The legislator ended this uncertainty by including Article 119 concerning this category of employees in the Employment Contract Act.

290 Article 118 Employment Contract Act.

291 Article 129 Employment Contract Act.

§ 1. WHAT IS HOME WORK?

Article 119/1 Employment Contract Act defines home work as work done by employees 'who for wages perform work under the authority of an employer in their home or any other place chosen by them without them being under the supervision or direct control of this employer'.

Home work can be carried out as blue-collar worker or as white-collar worker. For teleworkers there is a separate scheme.

§ 2. THE EMPLOYMENT CONTRACT ACT AS RESIDUARY LEGISLATION

For matters not explicitly regulated, the provisions of the Employment Contract Act apply (depending on the case, the provisions for blue-collar workers or white-collar workers).

If so desired, employees can work at home for a couple of days a week only. In that case they are subject to the new Article 119 for their work at home while for their other work they are subject to the other provisions of, *inter alia*, the Employment Contract Act.

§ 3. FORMAL REQUIREMENTS AND COMPULSORY STATEMENTS

The contract for the employment of home workers must be laid down in writing for each worker separately, at the latest, at the time the employee commences employment.

The document must include a number of obligatory statements which, if necessary, can be changed or completed by the competent joint committee:

1. the employer's surname, first names and main place of residence (if this concerns a natural person), or the name of the company and the registered office; and if applicable, the name by which the employer addresses the public;
2. the employee's surname, first names and main place of residence;
3. the wages agreed upon or (e.g. in the case of piece-wages) the manner and the basis for the calculation of the wages;
4. reimbursement of expenses connected to the home work. In the absence of individual or collective agreements a fixed amount of 10% of the wages are due unless the employee can prove with documents that his/her real expenses are higher;
5. the place or places chosen by the home worker to do his/her job;
6. a brief description of the work agreed upon;

7. the agreed work arrangement and/or roster and/or the agreed minimum amount of work to be done;
8. the competent joint committee.

If no document is made or if the document does not include the abovementioned statements (except for the reimbursement of the expenses connected to the home work), the home worker can terminate the contract of employment at any time without observing the period of notice or payment of compensation in lieu of notice.

The employment contract can be concluded for a fixed period or an open-ended period, either part time or full time. In the case of a part-time fixed term agreement, this means that the provisions of Articles 10 and 11*bis* have to be complied with as well.

§ 4. THE EMPLOYERS' OBLIGATIONS

The employer's obligations *vis-à-vis* the home worker are limited. The provisions of Article 20 Employment Contract Act do not apply, except for two obvious exceptions: making appliances and material available, as well as payment of wages.

§ 5. SUSPENSION OF THE CONTRACT

For home workers the suspension of the contract because of technical malfunction and bad weather conditions cannot be invoked. The arrangement with regard to *force majeure* by virtue of which the National Employment Office can decide to grant employment benefits, on the other hand, does apply.

An employee who receives fixed wages and cannot start or continue his/her job for a reason independent of his/her will is entitled to a guaranteed daily wage.

When a home worker produces evidence that, for instance, the equipment he/she works with is broken, he/she is entitled to guaranteed wages. This applies for each day of malfunction.

In the event of illness the employee must notify his/her employer without delay and – except when provided for differently in the collective agreement or work rules – provide him with a medical certificate within two days.

For blue-collar workers the Crown can change or adapt the arrangement with regard to unpaid sick days at the proposal of the competent joint committee.

The guaranteed wages of employees who do not receive fixed wages amount to 1/7 of a regular weekly wage, except if the implementation of the agreement had already been suspended or if the employee is entitled to other wages.

Home workers who receive fixed wages have – in the event of notice – the right to be absent from work according to the terms of Article 41 Employment Contract Act.

§ 6. HOME WORKERS' RIGHT OF PRECEDENCE

Employees who are employed as home workers are to be given preferential treatment with regard to jobs within the company. To this end they must submit a written application comparable to the arrangement for part-time employees.

Obviously, employers have the freedom to refuse to employ the home workers on the premises provided they can justify the refusal, e.g. if an employee who is a home worker does not perform adequately.

CHAPTER 2
SPECIAL EMPLOYMENT CONTRACTS

SECTION 1. TEMPORARY WORK, TEMPORARY AGENCY WORK AND HIRING OUT[292]

Article 11*ter* Employment Contract Act offers the opportunity to replace an employee whose employment contract has been suspended for another reason than lack of work for economic reasons, bad weather conditions, strike or lockout. Apart from that there are a number of employment schemes which can also offer a solution to a temporary lack of personnel, more specifically the employment contract for the performance of temporary work, temporary agency work and the hiring-out of employees.

This matter is regulated by the Law of 24 July 1987 regarding temporary work, temporary agency work and the hiring-out of employees on behalf of the user,[293] and Collective Agreement No. 108 of 16 July 2013 concluded in the National Labour Council regarding temporary work and temporary agency work.

§ 1. TEMPORARY WORK

Temporary work is the activity that is carried out on the basis of an employment contract and whose aim it is to see to the replacement of a permanent employee or to meet with a temporary increase in the work load or to carry out an exceptional task.

An employer cannot use the system of temporary work if the suspension is the result of a lack of work for economic reasons or bad weather conditions.

The employment contract for the performance of temporary work is concluded for a fixed term, for a specified task, or to replace a permanent employee.

The contract must be laid down in writing, at the latest, at the time the employee commences work. The reason for the replacement and, if applicable, the duration of the agreement, must be included in the contract. In the absence of a document the rules of open-ended employment contracts apply.

---

292 Moreno, O., *Travail temporaire, travail intérimaire et mise à disposition de travailleurs*, Brussels, Kluwer, 2005, 234 pp.

293 *BS/MB* 20 August 1987.

However, in such a case the employee can terminate the contract within seven days of the commencement of employment without giving notice or paying compensation.

Barring a conflicting contract, the first three days are considered to be a probationary period. Until the expiry of that period each of the parties may terminate the contract without notice or compensation.

The procedure to be followed and the duration of temporary jobs are established by Collective Agreement No. 108.

§ 2. TEMPORARY AGENCY WORK

An employment contract for temporary agency work is a contract by which a temporary agency worker undertakes, *vis-à-vis* an employment agency, to carry out temporary work for wages for an agency client. A temporary agency worker can only be employed if certain conditions are met. An employment agency may not employ agency workers at a client's or keep them working there when there is a strike or lockout.[294] Temporary agency work is only allowed for permitted temporary work. It is allowed for replacing a permanent employee, for responding to a temporary increase in the work load, or for carrying out extraordinary work.

The Law of 26 June 2013[295] added a fourth possibility: the so-called intake, i.e. employment agency work aimed at making a temporary agency worker available to a client to fill a vacancy with the intention of hiring this worker for the same job after this temporary period has ended.

The intention of concluding an employment contract for temporary agency work must be put in writing by both parties for each employee separately, at the latest, at the moment at which the employee starts working for the temporary employment agency.

Consecutive day contracts for temporary agency work at the same client's are only allowed if the necessity of this kind of flexibility can be demonstrated by the client. If he/she fails to do so, the temporary employment agency owes the temporary worker employed on consecutive day contracts, not only wages, but also compensation corresponding to the wages that should have been paid if an employment contract for two weeks had been concluded.

Consecutive day contracts for employment agency work are understood to mean employment contracts for temporary employment agency work for the same client which do not exceed 24 hours and succeed each other, or, at the most, are separated by a public holiday or the normal days of inactivity in the client's company applicable to the category of workers to which the temporary agency worker belongs. If consecutive day contracts are used, an information

294 Article 19 Collective Agreement No 108.

295 *BS/MB* 16 July 2013.

and consultation procedure is required that will differ depending on whether or not a works council or trade union representation is active within the company. If it is found that improper use has been made of day contracts for temporary employment agency work, the dispute will be submitted to the joint committee. The courts can only be addressed if this procedure has been followed.

The actual contract must be put in writing, at the latest, within two working days from the moment at which the employee starts working. In the absence of these two documents the rules regarding open-ended employment contracts apply. However, in such a case the employee can terminate the contract within seven days following the expiry of the term of two days without notice or compensation.

The contract for temporary employment agency work contains a number of compulsory statements, such as the name of the client, the reason, etc.

The temporary agency worker's wages may not be lower than the wages he/she would have be entitled to if he/she had been hired by the employer as a permanent employee under the same conditions.

During the period in which the temporary employment agency worker works for the client, he/she is, under the same conditions as the permanent employees, entitled to access to the facilities or services available in the client's company, such as canteens, child care and transport facilities, unless the difference in treatment is justified for objective reasons.

If the contract is concluded for a certain period or a specific task, the party unilaterally terminating the contract before the expiry of the term, and without just cause, will have to pay the other party compensation equal to the amount of wages owed until the end of the term, however, without exceeding double the wages corresponding to the duration of the term of notice that should have been considered if an open-ended employment contract had been concluded.

Compensation is not due if the temporary employment agency provides the temporary agency worker with a replacement job for the period he/she was hired for the same wages and under the same working conditions.

If the contract was concluded to replace a permanent employee for an indefinite period, the temporary employment agency unilaterally terminating the contract before the end of the replacement, and without just cause, must pay the temporary agency worker compensation corresponding to the gross wage of three months.

Subject to a term of notice of seven days the employment agency work can end the contract if he/she has found a permanent job.

If the client employs a temporary agency worker because of other circumstances than those laid down in the law, the employment contract is considered to be an open-ended employment contract. The same applies when the employment continues after the temporary employment agency has decided to withdraw the worker.

The organisation of temporary employment agency work is a matter belonging to the competence of the regions. So in Flanders, trading as a temporary employment agency is subject to the approval of the Flemish Government.

§ 3. HIRING OUT EMPLOYEES

In principle it is forbidden for an employer to hire out employees employed by him/her to users who have partial authority over these employees.[296, 297] The main objective of this prohibition is to fight labour traffickers who have no other activity than hiring-out workers. Usually this involves persons who do not observe the social security obligations and fail to transfer the advance tax payment to the Treasury.

In addition to his/her normal activities, a *bona fide* employer can hire out employees for a limited period, and on the condition of prior permission being granted by a civil servant designated by the Crown and with the consent of the union delegation.[298]

In a number of cases specifically listed in the law the employer may hire out employees without permission, e.g. in the context of collaboration between companies of the same economic and financial unit. In such cases the civil servant must be notified at least 24 hours prior to this.[299]

Principals often rely on (sub-)contractors. Given the fact that sometimes there is a dispute regarding the question as to whether one is dealing with (sub-)contracting or with hiring-out, an article was added to the Temporary Agency Work Act, which stipulates that compliance by the principal of the obligations regarding well-being in the workplace, both with regard to working hours and rest periods and the performance of the agreed work, should not be considered as the exercise of authority.

SECTION 2. THE CONTRACT FOR TELEWORKERS

In 2001 the European social partners started negotiating on the subject of telework. On 16 July 2002 the talks led to the 'Framework Agreement on Telework'. Collective Agreement No. 85 of 9 November 2005 converted the Agreement to national law.

---

296 Article 31, § 1 Employment Agency Work Act.

297 This fundamental prohibition was tempered in 2000 by the erosion of the notion of 'exercise of authority' (Article 181 Programme Act 12 August 2000, *BS/MB* 31 August 2000).

298 Article 32, § 1, 1 Employment Agency Work Act j° Article 32, § 3 Employment Agency Work Act.

299 Article 32, § 1, 2 Employment Agency Work Act.

§ 1. DEFINITION AND SCOPE

Telework is a form of organisation and/or performance of work within the context of an employment contract in which, using information technology, activities that could be carried out on the company premises, are carried outside the company premises on a regular basis instead of incidentally.

Telework can take place in the home of the teleworker or at any other place chosen by him/her.

Falling outside the scope of the Collective Agreement are:

- the mobile teleworker, i.e. an employee whose mobility is part of the method of implementation of the contract (e.g. a community nurse); and
- telework performed in a satellite office of the employer, i.e. a (decentralised) room provided for by the employer.

§ 2. THE CONTRACT

Telework is based on voluntariness. It can be agreed upon at the moment the contract is concluded (and therefore included in the original job description) or it can be agreed upon during the implementation of the contract.

A written contract must be concluded for each teleworker separately, at the latest, at the moment the implementation of the contract commences. For running employment contracts a written addendum is required.

The document must contain a number of obligatory statements, such as the frequency of the telework and the times when the teleworker must be reachable.

In the absence of a written agreement the teleworker has the right to carry out his/her work at the company premises or to return there.

Collective Agreement No. 85*bis* added a significant change. The document must mention the location(s) where the teleworker will/can perform his/her work. Apart from that it is also possible to mention within which time span the work will be done. That way it becomes possible to determine whether or not a teleworker has had an industrial accident.

§ 3. WORKING CONDITIONS

Teleworkers have the same working conditions as other employees. However, if additional contracts are concluded with regard to the telework, the employee must be notified of this. For instance, agreements can be made with regard to reporting.

§ 4. ORGANISATION OF THE TELEWORK

Within the framework of the working hours applied in the enterprise the teleworker organises his/her own working schedule.

He/she is subject to the same workload and standards of performance as the employees who perform their activities within the company.

The employer must see to it that the teleworker is not isolated within the enterprise. With a view to this he/she may recall the teleworker to the company at specific times.

§ 5. EQUIPMENT AND DEFECTS

In the Collective Agreement a number of provisions are included with regard to the hardware and software used.

The employer bears the costs of the equipment. If the employee uses his/her own equipment, the costs attached to the use thereof (e.g. depreciation) are also for the employer.

As regards the costs, an agreement shall be made before the telework commences.

The employer provides technical support and pays the costs stemming from loss of or damage to the equipment.

If the teleworker is unable to work because of *force majeure* the employer must pay the wages. However, agreements can be made regarding substitute work (in the case of *force majeure*) and a (temporary) return to the company premises.

§ 6. DATA PROTECTION

The teleworker is only allowed to use the equipment for professional purposes. He/she cannot spread material via the Internet that falls outside the description of the activities to be performed by him/her. As for control, the provisions of Collective Agreement No. 81 also apply to the teleworker.

§ 7. HEALTH AND SAFETY

The teleworker works with display screen equipment and thus falls within the scope of the relevant legislation. Therefore the health and safety advisers of the internal service have access to the teleworker's workplace. If the visit takes place in an occupied room, the employee must consent to the visit and the visit must be announced beforehand.

§ 8. TRAINING

Teleworkers must receive adequate training with a view to using the equipment.

As far as training is concerned, but also as far as the assessment policy is concerned, teleworkers must be subjected to the same rules as persons working at the company premises.

SECTION 3. MISCELLANEOUS

In addition to the above discussed deviations to the Employment Contract Act there are also employment contracts for sportsmen, trainees, dockworkers, barge skippers, offshore fishermen, mariners on board of sea-faring vessels, etc.

PART II

INDUSTRIAL RELATIONS LAW

I
FREEDOM OF ASSOCIATION

CHAPTER 1
HISTORICAL OVERVIEW

The provisions on the freedom of work and industry set out in the Le Chapelier Law were upheld in Article 6 of the Law of 22 Germinal year XI and subsequently adopted in the Napoleonic Penal Code of 1810.

Article 414 of the Penal Code penalised any employer coalition devised to lower wages, with prison sentences ranging from six days to one month, and a fine of between 200 and 3,000 francs. Work stoppages and preventing persons willing to work from working were prohibited by Article 415. Violations were punished with one to three months' imprisonment, and leaders risked two to five years' imprisonment. Such penalties were also imposed by Article 416 on employees who threatened employers and their representatives with industrial action.

The Governmental Decree of 16 October 1830 lifted all bans on the freedom of association. This was confirmed by Article 27 of the Constitution,[300] which grants the right to enter into an association or partnership, a right that is not subject to any preventative measures. The Penal Code of 1810 nevertheless retained Articles 414, 414 and 416 because politicians in the 1830s were concerned with political freedom rather than with freedom of association.

The Law of 31 May 1866 abolished these Articles and allowed workers to associate and set up unions. However, the newly added Article 310 of the Penal Code forbade any form of physical or moral coercion which might injure the freedom of work and industry; picketing remained unlawful, thus making effective union action impossible.

[300] Initially Article 20 of the Constitution.

On 11 June 1919 the Minister of Justice, Emile Vandervelde, introduced a government bill abolishing Article 310 of the Penal Code, but this expired when Parliament was dissolved on 13 January 1920. It was re-introduced after being amended to cover not only the right to organise and set up a union, but also freedom of association in the broad sense of the word, leading to the Law of 24 May 1921[301] on the protection of freedom of association. A second law passed on the same day abolished Article 310 of the Penal Code.

[301] *BS/MB* 18 May 1921.

CHAPTER 2
THE RIGHT TO ORGANISE

SECTION 1. ARTICLE 27 OF THE CONSTITUTION

Article 27 of the Constitution provides that citizens have the right to enter into an association or partnership; this right cannot be subject to any preventative measures. In principle, it covers all social activities provided they do not breach public order and/or morality, and therefore also covers the right to set up a union or professional association.

SECTION 2. THE FREEDOM OF ASSOCIATION ACT OF 24 MAY 1921

The Freedom of Association Act of 24 May 1921 governs, firstly, the protection of the freedom of association, and secondly, the consequences of joining an association. Although general in scope and not confined to the right to set up a union, it is clear that the legislature of 1921 sought to recognise and regulate this freedom.

The law guarantees both positive and negative freedom of association.

Positive freedom of association grants persons the right to set up and join a professional association (Articles 1, 2 and 3). Negative freedom of association is a person's right not to join a professional association (Articles 1, 3 and 4).

The principle that no one can be forced to join an association is a public order issue. The contracting parties cannot relinquish this right, either by individual or by collective consensus.

Any individual or collective agreement containing a clause breaching this principle is regarded as void.

In addition, the legislature imposed a penalty under criminal law for violating freedom of association, in this case the right to join a union.

Any person found guilty of forcing people to join, or preventing them from joining an association through acts of violence, threats or assault, or by threatening them with dismissal or damage to their family, person or assets (Article 3), is punishable by prison sentences of eight days to one month and a fine of € 50 to

€ 500. The same penalty is imposed on all those who maliciously and purposefully violate the freedom of association by subjecting the conclusion, execution or continued existence of an employment or service contract to affiliation or non-affiliation of a professional association (Article 4).

SECTION 3. INTERNATIONAL SOURCES

Belgium has ratified a number of treaties that guarantee, one way or another, trade union freedom: the ILO Convention Nos. 87 and 98, the ICCPR, the ECOSOC Treaty, the ECHR, the Revised European Social Charter. In addition, we are also bound by the provisions of the Charter of Fundamental Rights of the EU. A number of these provisions have been successfully invoked in national courts.

II

TRADE UNIONS AND EMPLOYERS' ASSOCIATIONS

Employers and unions[302] are organised in professional associations.

Article 10 of ILO Convention No. 87 defines a professional organisation as any organisation of workers or employers aimed at furthering and defending the interests of workers or employers. However, there is no actual definition in Belgian law. This is the result of two facts:

Firstly, workers' organisations have always refused to adopt legal personality. Secondly, the public authorities are committed to the natural balance of power and never intervene directly in industrial relations.

This does not mean that unions operate in a legal void. Some have actually been specifically integrated into the system. Our study will be confined to these 'representative' organisations.

CHAPTER 1

TRADE UNIONS[303]

SECTION 1. THE LEGAL POSITION OF REPRESENTATIVE UNIONS[304]

§ 1. FUNCTIONAL LEGAL PERSONALITY

Unions can acquire legal personality provided their articles of association comply with the Law of 31 March 1889 on professional associations (hereafter referred

302 In Belgium employers and unions are referred to as 'social partners'.

303 Faniel, J., 'Caractéristiques et spécificités des syndicats belges', in Arcq, E., Capron, M., Leonard, E. and Reman P. (eds.), *Dynamiques de la concertation sociale*, Brussels, CRISP, 2010, pp. 93–119.

304 François, L., 'Les syndicats et la personnalité juridique', *RCJB* 1968, pp. 39–65.

to as the Professional Associations Act)[305] or the Law of 27 June 1921 on non-profit organisations (hereafter referred to as the Non-profit Organisations Act). For various reasons they have not used this possibility to date.

After the Second World War, the public authorities realised that unions had to be formally involved in the socio-economic decision-making process and granted them certain powers, i.e. functional legal personality. This covers a wide range of union powers. The most important is undoubtedly the competence to conclude contracts and act as agents.

In the framework of the Law on Collective Labour Agreements of 5 December 1968[306] (hereafter the Collective Labour Agreements Act), representative unions were awarded, *inter alia*, the competence to draw up legally binding collective labour agreements.

§ 2. REPRESENTATIVE WORKERS' ORGANISATIONS

The concept 'most representative workers' organisation' was first used in the framework of the Constitution of the International Labour Organization and adopted in various Western European countries in the period between the two World Wars. It became commonly used in Belgium after 1945, when the legislature proceeded to structure industrial relations in consultation with the social partners.

In order to facilitate social dialogue, the public authorities decided to negotiate only with representative workers' organisations. To qualify as representative, they had to meet a number of conditions. Article 3 of the Collective Labour Agreements Act, for instance, provides that multi-industry organisations set up at national level and represented in the National Economic Council[307] and the National Labour Council[308] are representative. Other laws contain similar provisions.

As a result, only three workers' organisations are involved in social consultations at all levels, i.e. the Federation of Liberal Trade Unions,[309] the Confederation of Christian Trade Unions,[310] the Belgian General Federation of Labour[311] and the occupational associations affiliated to the latter two.

The National Confederation of Managerial Staff[312] only acquired representativeness in the framework of the law on works councils. In contrast

305 *BS/MB* 8 April 1898.

306 Collective Agreements and Joint Committees Act of 5 December 1968, *BS/MB* 15 January 1969.

307 Centrale Raad voor het Bedrijfsleven – Conseil central de l'économie (see *infra*).

308 Nationale Arbeidsraad – Conseil national du travail (see *infra*).

309 ACLVB-CGSLB (300,000 members).

310 ACV-CSC (1.7 million members).

311 ABVV-FGTB (1.2 million members).

312 NCK-CNC.

to the three other organisations, it is not allowed to conclude collective labour agreements or designate union representatives.

SECTION 2. STRUCTURES

The Belgian General Federation of Labour and the Confederation of Christian Trade Unions are union federations or confederations. Workers are organised according to groups of connected branches of industry. These organisations are affiliated to the multi-industry union.

The Federation of Liberal Trade Unions of Belgium does not centralise professional organisations. It is a general organisation grouping workers from different occupations and sectors into one organisation. Public sector workers fall under the Public Sector Workers' Union,[313] which has structural links with the Federation of Liberal Trade Unions.

The National Confederation of Managers has a multi-industry structure.

SECTION 3. LIABILITY OF REPRESENTATIVE WORKERS' ORGANISATIONS

§ 1. PENAL AND CIVIL LIABILITY

As unions do not have legal personality, they cannot be held liable under penal law for criminal acts committed by their members. In the absence of collective responsibility, individual members are personally liable for their acts. *Mutatis mutandis*, this also holds true for civil liability. Not the union as such, but rather individual members will be held liable for third-party damage.

§ 2. CONTRACTUAL LIABILITY OF UNIONS IN THE FRAMEWORK OF THE COLLECTIVE LABOUR AGREEMENTS ACT

According to the Collective Labour Agreements Act, representative workers' organisations are allowed to conclude collective labour agreements.

If one of the contracting parties fails to respect its obligations, in this case the representative unions, it will be held accountable, thus giving the other party various remedies in law, such as action for rescission of a contract pursuant to

313 VSOA-SLFP.

Article 1184 of the Civil Code, the right to claim damages, etc. However, the legislature sought to limit liability by adding statutory restrictions to Article 4, paragraph 2 of the Collective Labour Agreements Act.

Damage claims for failure to comply with obligatory provisions can only be brought against representative unions if this possibility is provided for by collective agreement. Whilst damages cannot be claimed on the grounds of contractual liability without explicit provisions, Article 4(2) of the Collective Agreements Act cannot prevent a party from seeking enforcement and dissolution or from invoking *exceptio non adimpleti contractus*.

SECTION 4. UNION MEMBERSHIP[314]

Organisations may refuse membership if there are serious indications that a candidate member is not willing to pursue the union's social objective. Given that the *affectio societatis* is an essential part of a contract of association, they can also exclude members for the same reason.

SECTION 5. INTERNATIONAL WORKERS' ORGANISATIONS

The ABVV/FGTB used to be a member of the International Confederation of Free Trade Unions. The ACV/CSC joined the Christian inspired World Confederation of Labour, and on 3 November 2006, in Vienna, the two organisations merged to form the ITUC (International Trade Union Confederation).

The European Trade Union Confederation is the most important union at European level; the Belgian General Federation of Labour, the Confederation of Christian Trade Unions and the Federation of Liberal Trade Unions of Belgium are affiliated. NCK/CNC is a member of the *Confédération européenne des cadres* (CEC).

[314] Dorssemont, F., 'Le droit des syndicats d'expulser des membres en raison de leur conviction politique', *Rev. Trim. Dr. H.* 2008, pp. 549–572.

CHAPTER 2
EMPLOYERS' ASSOCIATIONS[315]

SECTION 1. STRUCTURES

Employers' associations also distinguish between industrial and multi-industry organisations.

Employers join the professional association of the branch of industry in which they are active. These associations are geographically organised at local, regional and national levels.

At the national level, industrial federations are centralised by the multi-industry organisation. These federations, rather than individual employers, are members of the multi-industry organisation.

The Belgian Federation of Enterprises[316] groups the different industrial organisations, such as Agoria (metal sector), Fedustria (a.o. textile sector), Essencia (chemical sector) and CEPA (port of Antwerp).

The interests of the self-employed are defended by UNIZO and UCM; the agricultural employers are united in the *Boerenbond* and the *Fédération Wallonne de l'Agriculture.*

Apart from these structures there are some important regional employers' organisations, such as the *Vlaams netwerk van ondernemingen*[317] and the *Union Wallone des Entreprises.*[318] ETION and the *Association chrétienne des dirigeants et cadres*[319] organise employers on the basis of their (Christian) ideology.

Although the Belgian Federation of Enterprises and its main affiliated federations are actually associations just like representative workers' organisations, a certain

315 Arcq, E., 'Les organisations patronales', in Arcq E., Capron, M., Leonard, E. and Reman, P. (eds.), *Dynamiques de la concertation sociale*, Brussels, CRISP, 2010, pp. 121–146.

316 VBO-FEB.

317 VOKA.

318 UWE.

319 ADIC.

number have adopted either the status of professional association or non-profit organisation.

Provided they are representative, employers' organisations can also participate in social consultations. Indeed, the provisions of Article 3 of the Collective Labour Agreements Act apply to both employers' associations and unions. This means that only multi-industry organisations set up at national level with representatives in the National Economic Council and the National Labour Council are representative. Professional organisations can be awarded representative status on the recommendation of the National Labour Council. They do not have to meet the same quantitative criteria as employers' associations.

SECTION 2. INTERNATIONAL EMPLOYERS' ORGANISATIONS

The Belgian Federation of Enterprises is a member of the International Organisation of Employers. At the European level, it is affiliated to Business-europe, which defends employers' interests in the European Union.

UNIZO and UCM are members of the European Association of Craft, Small and Medium-sized Enterprises.[320] The employers of the semi-public sector are united in the European Centre of Employers and Enterprises providing Public Services.[321]

A lot of sectoral employers' organisations also reside under a larger European or international structure.

---

320 UEAPME.

321 CEEP.

III
INSTRUMENTS FOR SOCIAL DIALOGUE

CHAPTER 1
GENERAL OVERVIEW

In the past, during periods of great social conflict, the public authorities summoned employees' and employers' representatives to round table conferences to to jointly seek solutions. Such tripartite concertation was the norm before and immediately after the Second World War. However, its importance gradually decreased as joint consultations gained a more structural basis following the establishment of permanent consultative bodies.

Although some of these bodies are rooted in the 19th century, the foundation for structured collective bargaining was laid primarily during the German occupation. Employees and employers clandestinely concluded the 'Draft Agreement on Social Solidarity'.[322] This document contained a blueprint for industrial relations after the War, one of which was the establishment of joint cooperation at national, sectoral and enterprise levels.

The first step taken in this direction was the Joint Committees Act of 1945, followed in 1946 by the Regent Decrees establishing Health and Safety Committees. In 1947, a national agreement between employees' and employers' organisations laid down the status of trade unions. Subsequently, the Law of 20 September 1948 with regard to the organisation of the economy (hereinafter Organisation of the Economy Act) established the National Economic Council and works councils.

The National Labour Council was set up in 1952.

Parallel to these joint bodies, high level negotiations were also held between the Belgian Federation of Enterprises and the unions, resulting in multi-industry

322 Ontwerp van overeenkomst tot sociale solidariteit – Projet d'accord de la solidarité sociale.

agreements. Between 1960 and 1975 social dialogue was at its zenith. After 1975, state intervention increased as a result of the changing socio-economic climate, so much so that it effectively became a third party. Concertation evolved from bipartite to tripartite.

As a result of the regionalization of state structures from 1980 onwards, the governments and regional ministries can also be parties to social consultations. To this end, Flanders' Social and Economic Council and its Walloon counterpart, the Walloon Economic and Social Council were set up, in addition to the Flemish Economic and Social Consultative Committee and the Brussels Regional and Social Council for the Brussels region.

CHAPTER 2

STRUCTURED BIPARTITE NEGOTIATION

SECTION 1. INTRODUCTION

The public law industrial regulatory body[323] controls the composition, the organisation and powers of official bodies relating to the organisation of the economy. It has jurisdiction at three levels: national, (federal and regional), sectoral and at enterprise levels. Given that industrial relations are still mainly a federal matter, the importance of the regional consultative bodies is limited.

	Economic	**Social**	**Prevention and protection/well-being**
At national level	National Economic Council (CRB/CCE)	National Labour Council (NAR/CNT)	High Council on Prevention and Protection (*Hoge Raad/ Conseil Supérieur*)
Flanders	Flanders Social and Economic Council (SERV)	SERV/VESOC	
Wallonia	Walloon Economic and Social Council (CESRW)	CESRW	
Brussels	Brussels Regional and Social Council	CBRS/BGESR	
Sector	Special Advisory Committees	Joint Committees and Sub-committees	
Enterprise	Works Council/ union delegation (OR/VA – CE/DS)	OR/VA – CE/DS	CPBW/CPPT

323 PBO – Publiekrechtelijke bedrijfsorganisatie / Organisation de l'économie en droit public.

SECTION 2. NATIONAL LEVEL

§ 1. THE NATIONAL ECONOMIC COUNCIL[324, 325]

A. *Definition and position*

The National Economic Council (NEC) is an autonomous and joint public law body. In addition to advising the public authorities on issues relating to the national economy, it is an important intermediary between economic interest groups and policy-makers.

B. *Composition*

The NEC is composed of:

- an equal number of employer and union representatives designated by their interest group;
- six members co-opted by the Council; and
- an independent chairperson.

Its members and chairperson are appointed by Royal Decree.

C. *Competence*

The NEC has the task of submitting to the government and Parliament, at their request and on their own initiative, formal opinions on all national and economic issues. It has also been entrusted with specific tasks. Since 1996, the National Economic Council and the National Labour Council have been required to issue annual reports on employment and the development of earnings in order to set wage margins.

324 CRB (Centrale Raad voor het Bedrijfsleven) – CCE (Conseil central de l'économie).

325 Van Den Broeck, M., 'Le Conseil central de l'économie', in Arcq, E., Capron, M., Leonard, E. and Reman, P. (eds.), *Dynamiques de la concertation sociale*, Brussels, CRISP, 2010, pp. 191–209.

§ 2. THE NATIONAL LABOUR COUNCIL[326, 327]

A. *Definition and position*

The National Labour Council (NLC) is a public law body entrusted with the task of submitting to a Minister or employer, on request or on its own initiative, opinions or proposals relating to issues affecting employers and employees. It also delivers opinions on any problems of jurisdiction arising between joint committees. The Council's opinions and proposals must be submitted in the form of reports showing the various viewpoints expressed during discussions.

The NLC has had three predecessors: the Supreme Labour Council, the Supreme Council for Labour, and the Social Welfare and the National Joint Council.

The Supreme Labour Council was set up in 1892 as a central body for the Councils on Labour and Industry established in 1887. It was created to give recommendations to the government on the employment and living conditions of the working classes. Abolished in 1935, it was replaced by a similar consultative body, the Supreme Council for Labour and Social Well-being, composed of two divisions competent for employment and social security respectively.

The National Joint Council was set up in 1944 by representative employers' associations and unions. Its main task was to implement decisions and resolutions of the National Employment Conferences. Although an informal body without legal status *stricto sensu,* it was highly regarded.

In 1950, the Chamber submitted a law proposal which ultimately led to the National Labour Council Act of 1952. Its signatories sought to set up a body to advise Parliament on social matters. However, after the Collective Labour Agreements Act, which granted the National Labour Council the power to conclude collective labour agreements at national level, the Council has steadily eroded Parliament's competence in this regard.

B. *Composition*

The National Labour Council is composed of a number of active members and deputy members, designated by representative employers' associations and trade unions, and appointed by Royal Decree for four years. It also has a chairperson, four co-chairpersons and a secretary.

---

326 Nationale Arbeidsraad (NAR) – Conseil national du travail (CNT).

327 De Cuyper, G., 'Le Conseil National du Travail', *Rev.Trav.* 1951, pp. 1012–1039 Palsterman, P., 'Le Conseil national du travail', in Arcq, E., Capron, M., Leonard, E. and Reman, P. (eds.), *Dynamiques de la concertation sociale*, Brussels, CRISP, 2010, pp. 211–223.

The chairperson is appointed by Royal Decree from a number of independent individuals specialised in social and economic matters.

The Council chooses four co-chairpersons from its members: two from the representative employers' associations and two from the representative trade unions.

The composition and working of the executive committee are set out in the rules of procedure drafted by the Council and approved by Royal Decree. The executive committee has a number of specific managerial tasks and represents the Council.

The secretary, assisted by staff, deals with the daily management. The secretariat provides services such as registry and collates documentation relating to the Council's activities.

The National Labour Council also has a number of committees composed of several experts from employers' associations and trade unions. These committees play a very important role in terms of drafting advisory opinions.

C. Competence

1. Delivering opinions

The National Labour Council is mainly charged with delivering or drafting opinions on general social issues that affect employers and employees. It does not deal with other issues or matters not affecting all employees or only a group of employers or workers.

Where the law provides that the Crown has to consult the National Labour Council, the latter is obliged to submit an opinion within two months of receiving the request. A decision can be taken without further formalities after expiry of this term. If the opinion is not obligatory, the requesting party is allowed to set the term.

These opinions are very important for the development of social law and are taken into account by the government and parliament to a considerable extent. Since 1952 more than 1900 opinions have been given.

2. The conclusion of collective labour agreements

The National Labour Council is empowered to conclude national and multi-industry collective labour agreements. In some cases, the Council can also conclude collective labour agreements for certain branches of industry that either have no joint committee or in which the existing one does not function properly because its members refuse to meet. However, the Council cannot act when the agreement is not approved in a normally functioning joint committee or when the latter ignores a draft agreement.

Collective labour agreements concluded by the National Labour Council are very important. They are usually declared generally binding,[328] thus giving them legal effect.

Sometimes representative employers' associations and unions conclude agreements at national and multi-industry level outside the public law industrial regulatory bodies. In these cases they are not collective labour agreements, but multi-industry agreements. Where possible the National Labour Council will try to convert the items agreed on in principle by the social partners into collective labour agreements.

Collective agreements can be concluded in the National Labour Council by organisations that are represented by at least 90% of the members representing the employers and at least 90% of the members representing the employees.

3. Conciliation

One of the tasks of the National Labour Council is to prevent or solve industrial conflicts. It also mediates during jurisdiction disputes arising between joint committees.

D. Functioning

When the National Labour Council meets with a view to concluding a collective labour agreement, at least half the members or deputy members representing employers and half the members or deputy members representing employees have to be present for the arbitration or decisions to be valid. After a second convocation, the Council's decision is final, regardless of the number of members present.

Only members representing employers or employees have decisive votes.

Deputy members are invited to attend the meeting, but are only allowed to vote when replacing effective members.

328 See above.

The procedure for delivering opinions and recommendations is as follows:

a. opinions on general social issues are not put to the vote. They are either approved unanimously or by recording the names of the groups, organisations or individual members approving them;
b. opinions concerning jurisdiction disputes arising between national joint committees are voted by roll call (and approved by majority);
c. the procedure listed under b. is also applied to proposals issued by the Council.

The Council can be assisted by representatives from the administration, public institutions or public utility institutions, or by experts.

§ 3. THE HIGH COUNCIL FOR WORKPLACE SAFETY[329]

The High Council is composed of:

- 12 full members and 12 deputy members designated by the most representative employers' associations;
- 12 full members and 12 deputy members designated by the most representative unions; and
- a number of permanent experts: civil servants, independent experts and representatives of professional organisations.

The High Council's authority is confined to submitting opinions on matters relating to employee welfare.

SECTION 3. REGIONAL LEVEL[330]

Regional consultative bodies were established to deal with employment matters for which the regions are competent.

---

[329] Hoge Raad voor Preventie en Bescherming op het Werk – Conseil supérieur pour la prévention et la protection au travail.

[330] Installé, M., Ongen, O. and Verlinden, M., 'La concertation socio-économique au sein des Régions et Communautés', in Arcq, E., Capron, M., Leonard, E. and Reman, P. (eds.), *Dynamiques de la concertation sociale*, Brussels, CRISP, 2010, pp. 291–319.

§ 1. FLANDERS

A. *Flanders' Social and Economic Council (FSEC)*[331]

The FSEC replaces the Regional Economic Council for Flanders, which was founded in 1970.

The body consists of twenty members, ten of whom are nominated by the representative trade unions and ten by employers' organisations, organisations for small and medium-sized businesses, and agricultural organisations. These members are appointed by the Flemish government, which also appoints a deputy for each member.

The FSEC is authorised to advise the Flemish Council and the Flemish government on matters of a socio-economic nature.

Within the FSEC, a number of autonomously working committees and institutions are active, for instance the Innovation and Work Foundation.

B. *Flemish Economic and Social Consultative Committee*[332] *(FESCC)*

The Flemish Economic and Social Consultative Committee is composed of:

- representatives of the Flemish government;
- 16 members, 8 of which are nominated by the representative employees' organisations; the other 8 represent the employers, the self-employed and agriculture.

Within the FESCC all policy issues with a socio-economic dimension and for which the Flemish Community is competent can be conferred on. In a protocol the Flemish Community promised to carry out any consensus achieved within this consultative body.

§ 2. WALLONIA: WALLOON ECONOMIC AND SOCIAL COUNCIL (WESC)

This joint council has a threefold mission:

1. studying and giving advice on all matters belonging to the regional competence and relating to the economic and social life in the Walloon region;

---

331 Sociaal-Economische Raad van Vlaanderen (SERV).

332 Vlaams Economisch Sociaal Overlegcomité (VESOC).

2. consultation between the regional social partners and the government; and
3. acting as secretariat for the *Conseils consultatifs*, i.e. committees with alternate composition advising on specific regional issues (e.g. the environment).

§ 3. BRUSSELS: BRUSSELS REGIONAL AND SOCIAL COUNCIL

This body is composed of representatives of employees, employers and self-employed persons.

Its first competence is advisory. Another of its competences concerns the consultation between the social partners and the government on issues regarding regional development. Furthermore, the Council has a number of specific competences. For instance, it has to be consulted with regard to applications to set up a temporary employment agency.

SECTION 4. THE SECTORAL LEVEL: JOINT (SUB-)COMMITTEES[333]

Collective bargaining at branch level is conducted almost entirely within joint committees that form the backbone of the system of constant social dialogue. Collective bargaining and conflict mediation are by and large incorporated in this public-law regulatory body.

§ 1. CONCEPT AND BACKGROUND

As they are not defined legally, joint committees can be described as sectoral concertation bodies where employer and union representatives meet on equal terms to discuss common problems.

The first joint committees were set up in 1919. Initially, they were fora attended by employers' associations and unions to jointly examine problems at the social level (for example, the national committee for studying the issue of shorter working hours in the mines). These committees evolved, first forming reconciliation committees and finally joint committees. Some were private initiatives; others were set up by Royal Decree.

[333] Verly, J. and Martinez, E., 'La négociation sectorielle', in Arcq, E., Capron, M., Leonard, E. and Reman, P. (eds.), *Dynamiques de la concertation sociale*, Brussels, CRISP, 2010, pp. 257–274.

The status of joint committees was developed in the Decree Law of 9 June 1945 and amended in 1954. An entirely new set of regulations was introduced by the 1968 Collective Agreements and Joint Committees Act (hereafter Collective Agreements Act), which still applies today.

Joint committees are not a strictly federal matter. Some decrees relating to education provide that the regional governments can set up specific joint committees for the private school sector and oversee their composition, mission and decision-making. Under certain conditions, the regional government may declare the decision of such a joint committee generally binding. These special joint committees will not be discussed here.

§ 2. COMPOSITION

The composition of joint (sub-)committees is as follows:

a. a chairperson and deputy chairperson;
b. an equal number of representatives from employers' associations and trade unions respectively; and
c. two or more secretaries.

The number of members (there are no minimum requirements) is established by Royal Decree, in accordance with the relative importance of the activities falling under the scope of the joint committee, the number of organisations and the power relations between the various organisations. Applications to sit on the committee are published in the Official Belgian Journal.

The competent Minister designates the organisations that will be represented as well as the number of mandates awarded to individual organisations. Mandates are determined either by the results of the last social elections or in proportion to the number of union members of the relevant branch of industry, or by way of an agreement between the unions involved.

As regards employers' associations, the number of mandates depends on their representative value and numerical strength. The designated organisations have one month to present two candidates (one full member and one deputy member) for each mandate.

Members are appointed by Royal Decree for a period of four years. The chairperson and vice-chairperson are also appointed by Royal Decree. They must be impartial and experienced in industrial relations.

In the absence of the chairperson, the vice-chairperson will take the chair. The latter in turn is replaced by an official designated by the Minister. Both the chairperson and the vice-chairperson operate under the Minister's authority. He/she also appoints the secretaries and may, on his/her own initiative and at the committee's request, appoint one or more officials to advise him/her.

The members of a joint (sub-)committee may be assisted by technical advisers, the number of which is established by the rules of procedure.

§ 3. ESTABLISHMENT

A. *Joint Committees*

Joint committees are set up by Royal Decree, either on the Crown's initiative or at the request of one or more representative employers' associations or trade unions.

Joint committees can be set up:

- for blue-collar and white-collar workers;
- for employees who are neither blue- nor white-collar workers, for example, domestic staff, home workers, temping staff, etc.;
- for specific occupations, for example, taxi drivers; or
- for the entire country or for particular regions.

Although most joint committees are established in accordance with the Collective Labour Agreements Act, some are set up by specific laws, for example, the National Joint Committee for Sport and the Joint Committee for Temping Staff.

If the Minister of Employment wishes to create a joint committee, the organisations concerned are notified in the Official Belgian Journal.

This consultation is subject to strict formal rules and failure to respect them leads to nullity. Joint committees can be dissolved by Royal Decree. In such cases the Minister also consults the professional organisations. Prior consultation of a national joint committee cannot replace consultation with the professional organisations concerned.

B. *Joint sub-committees*

At the request of a joint committee, the Crown may set up one or more joint sub-committees.

On their establishment and acting on the committee's unanimous recommendation, the Crown decides whether the collective labour agreements concluded in the sub-committee are subject to approval by the joint committee.

If the sub-committee is granted independent status, it does not have to inform the joint committee of the conclusion of any collective labour agreements or their substance. The joint committee has one month to present objections; after this period the collective agreement is regarded as approved.

If the sub-committee neglects to present the collective labour agreement for approval, it cannot be declared generally binding. Although its provisions apply to the contracting parties, they will be regarded as collective agreements concluded outside a joint committee.

§ 4. COMPETENCE

The tasks of a joint committee and joint sub-committee are as follows:

a. overseeing the conclusion of collective labour agreements by the representative organisations;
b. preventing and settling disputes between employers and employees.
   A conciliation bureau can be set up within a joint committee (or sub-committee). Some of its members can also be delegated to sit on a restricted committee. The aim of both the conciliation bureau and the restricted group is to prevent or settle disputes between employers and employees;
c. advising the government, the National Labour Council, the National Economic Council or Works Councils on all matters falling within their sphere of responsibility at their request or on its own initiative; and
d. fulfilling any other function entrusted to it by or in execution of the law.

During the last few years, both the legislature and the social partners have increasingly used joint committees to implement laws and collective labour agreements, thus making this body the cornerstone of Belgian industrial relations.

§ 5. JOINT COMMITTEES – JURISDICTION

A. *General overview*

Given that joint committees play an important role in a lot of different areas (for example in fixing wages), knowing which employers and employees fall under the jurisdiction of a particular joint committee is crucial.

As a general rule, a joint committee has jurisdiction for workers employed by an employer whose enterprise belongs to the branch of industry for which the joint committee has been set up, regardless of the worker's individual occupation. A carpenter may therefore fall under the jurisdiction of a joint committee for the textile sector.

Where a joint committee has been set up for a specific group, jurisdiction is determined by the type of activity actually practised. For example, workers fall under Joint Committee No. 223 as soon as they exercise an activity as professional sportsperson. Then there are the residuary committees, such as the Auxiliary National Committee for White-collar Workers (No. 200).

B. *Establishing the competent joint committee*

Employers have a duty to respect a collective labour agreement declared generally binding.[334] *De facto,* this means that they have to know to which joint committee their enterprise belongs. This is easily ascertained by bodies such as the National Office for Social Security.[335] As the National Office is entrusted with collecting social security contributions, it must know to which joint committee employers belong in order to establish whether or not they are liable for contributions.

In the event of a dispute, the parties involved may:

– request an opinion from the Federal Public Service Employment, Labour and Social Dialogue. The parties submit a request for an opinion to the Service for Industrial Relations of the Ministry of Employment. The Service examines whether an opinion has already been requested, and if so, whether or not it has been amended in any way. If not, it will set up an inquiry, where necessary, accompanied by an inquiry by the Social Laws Inspectorate. Objections can be lodged within two weeks of notification, leading where necessary to review and a new opinion. This procedure is informal and based on administrative

334 *Infra.*

335 RSZ/ONSS.

guidelines and customs rather than on formal rules. The parties involved usually regard such opinions as arbitral decisions and accept them;

- request an opinion from a national joint committee and in the event of disputes between two joint committees, request an opinion from the National Labour Council; or
- refer to a labour tribunal: if the former fail to solve the dispute the parties can go to court and seek an opinion. Its judgments are wholly independent and not bound by the opinion given by the Service for Industrial Relations.

Disputes with regard to jurisdiction have to be based on certain criteria.

Firstly, an enterprise falls under one joint committee. Derogations from this principle are only allowed when different, non-interrelated types of work are performed within the enterprise in separate and distant locations with individually appointed personnel, or if valid arguments can be invoked.

Secondly, secondary activities are in principle subject to the same rules as the main activity as regards the establishment of enterprise activity.

What is important and what is not? There are two possibilities:

- the joint committee is determined either on the basis of the enterprise activity employing the largest number of workers; or
- according to the principal economic activity.

C. *Consequences*

In its judgment of 14 February 1983, the Court of Cassation[336] ruled that the criterion establishing under which joint committee an enterprise falls, is the activity exercised by the enterprise itself. Activities not carried out by its personnel, but on behalf of the enterprise (i.e. sub-contracted), fall outside its scope. In other words, four carpenters engaged in similar work may be paid disparate hourly rates if they are employed by sub-contractors with distinct principal activities. Consequently, it may be interesting for employers to outsource activities to sub-contractors they control themselves.

---

[336] Cass. 14 February 1983, *JTT* 1984, p. 132.

§ 6. PROCEEDINGS

Joint (sub-)committees' consultations and decisions are valid only when at least half of the full or deputy members representing employers and at least half of the full or deputy members representing employees are present.

An equal number of employer and employee representatives is not required. Mandated organisations do not have to be present.

Only members are entitled to vote. Deputy members can only vote in the absence of full members. The issue of valid voting by a deputy member together with a full member is set out in the rules of procedure.

In the absence of specific provisions to the contrary, decisions are taken by a unanimous vote of the members present.

The working of joint (sub-)committees is established by the Royal Decree of 6 November 1969. They may draw up rules of procedure containing secondary rules specific to a certain type of sector.

SECTION 5. AT ENTERPRISE LEVEL

§ 1. THE WORKS COUNCIL

A. *Definition and background*

A works council is a joint committee at enterprise level designed to organise employer and employee concertation and collaboration.

The legal framework for setting up a joint committee within the enterprise, i.e. a works council, was established by the Act of 20 September 1948.[337] This law met the unions' demand for greater employee involvement in the enterprise's decision-making process and the request to be informed of its social and economic situation. Even though designed to create a new relationship between employment, capital and management, the law has not fundamentally changed existing structures or affected employer authority.

337 Organisation of the Economy Act, *BS/MB* 27/28 September 1948.

B. *Composition*

The works council is composed of the CEO, assisted by a number of senior executives, and an (elected) workers' delegation.

The CEO or his/her legally designated representative acts as chairman.

The members of the employer delegation (i.e. the executive staff) are designated by the latter for a period of four years. However, their mandate expires when they cease to hold a managerial position.

Executive staff are persons entrusted with the daily management of the enterprise, authorised to represent the employer, as well as their direct subordinates, when they, too, perform tasks of general management.

The number of employer delegates may not exceed the number of employee delegates. A lower number is allowed.

The workers' delegation consists of a number of full and deputy members, elected by the enterprise's employees for a four-year term.

Blue- and white-collar workers have separate electoral bodies and elect their own representatives. Enterprises employing at least 25 young workers (i.e. under the age of 25 on the day of the election), are also entitled to their own electoral body and representation in the council.

Delegates representing low-ranking managerial personnel (*cadres*) and employee representatives are elected at the same time. The law defines *cadres* as white-collar workers not forming part of the senior management who have an executive position in the undertaking generally reserved to holders of a university degree or persons with equivalent job experience.

The enterprise must employ at least 15 low-ranking managerial personnel to elect their own representatives.

Candidates representing *cadres* are nominated as follows:

a. by the representative employer's association;
b. by the representative organisations representing managerial staff;
c. by at least 10% of the number of the enterprise's low-ranking executive personnel members with the caveat that the number of signatories may not be less than 5 if the enterprise employs less than 50, and not less than 10 if it employs less than 100 *cadres*. The latter can back only one list.

C. *Establishment*

1. Where and when?

Works councils must be set up in the private sector, regardless of whether or not the undertaking has a commercial or industrial objective, i.e. also in non-profit organisations, private universities, private schools or institutions with a social objective (e.g. hospitals).

Article 14 of the Organisation of the Economy Act provides that works councils have to be set up in enterprises habitually employing an average of at least 50 workers. However, this is a 'target number'; each time social elections are held new thresholds for setting up a works council are established by a separate law. During the social elections of 2016, elections had to be held in enterprises habitually employing an average of 100 workers. The same applies to enterprises where a council was or should have been set up during the last elections, provided they employed at least 50 workers. Undertakings employing less than 100 workers do not have to hold works council elections. Their mandate is carried out by the elected members of the Committee for Prevention and Protection at Work.[338]

A number of parameters have to be distinguished in the general rule given above.

Habitually an average: the average number of workers employed in the enterprise is calculated on the basis of the number of calendar days individual workers were registered on the staff register (or another document if no staff register has to be kept) divided by 365.

Workers: all persons employed by virtue of an employment or apprentice contract. Therefore the calculations also have to take low-ranking managerial staff and senior management into account.

Some categories of workers are excluded from the calculation, for example, workers replacing persons who have taken a full-time career break whereas some other persons are considered as workers, such as trainees.

Enterprise or undertaking: is synonymous with *'technical operating unit'* (TOU). Generally, this unit designates the part of the enterprise that has acquired a certain degree of autonomy. It is defined by the courts on the basis of social and economic criteria. If there are any doubts, social elements prevail over economic ones.

---

[338] *Infra.*

Until proof of the contrary is provided, various legal bodies are presumed to form a technical operating unit when:[339]

(1) either the legal units form part of the same economic group or are controlled by the same person or persons with common economic ties; these legal units perform the same activity or interrelated activities; and
(2) there are elements establishing social cohesion between these legal units, such as:
    - a community of people working in the same or nearby buildings;
    - common personnel management;
    - common personnel policy; or
    - common work rules or similar collective agreements.

If proof is provided that one of the conditions referred to in point (1) and certain elements considered in point (2) have not been met, the legal entities will not be regarded as a technical operating unit if the employer submits proof that their personnel management and personnel policy do not constitute social criteria characteristic of a technical operating unit. This presumption may not prejudice the continuity, operation or scope of the existing bodies.

2. Organisation of elections

So-called 'social' elections are held every four years by the employer (head of the enterprise) who is statutorily obliged to do so. Electoral guidelines are regulated by law or by Royal Decree, largely along established lines.

Elections are held over a 60-day period before notification of the election date until 13 days after notification of the composition of the works council. During this strictly regulated period disputes can be submitted to a labour tribunal.

- Shortlist
  Only representative unions pursuant to the conditions set out in the Collective Labour Agreements Act can shortlist candidates. Organisations representing managerial personnel can only nominate candidates when they are national, multi-industry organisations and have more than 10,000 members. Managers organised within the enterprise can also submit a shortlist.

339 Article 14 paragraph 2 b) of the Organisation of the Economy Act and Article 50 paragraph 3 of the Workers' Health and Safety Act.

- Elections
  All workers of an enterprise engaged by an employment or apprenticeship contract – except managerial staff – have to satisfy the following conditions on the election date:
  - they must hold Belgian nationality or be a national of an EU State. Non-EU subjects have to be employed in accordance with the laws governing the employment of foreigners;
  - they must have worked for at least three months in the corporate body or the technical unit formed by various legal entities. In the case of a transfer of enterprise, account is taken of seniority acquired before the transfer.
    The reasons for suspending the employment contract do not affect seniority.
- Electoral eligibility
  To be elected, persons:
  - must be at least 18 years old. Delegates representing young workers must be at least 16 years old and under 25 years of age;
  - may not belong to the management;[340]
  - must have been employed for at least six months in the legal entity of the enterprise or the legal unit formed by various legal entities;
  - must be employed either in the legal entity to which the enterprise belongs or in the technical work unit in the year preceding the elections, for a total period of at least nine months. This enables candidates with atypical employment contracts who would not normally be eligible because their employment was interrupted to stand for elections;
  - must be under 65.

  Non-EU nationals may sit on the works council if they are employed in accordance with the laws governing the employment of foreigners.
- Incompatibilities
  In view of their position, prevention advisers are not allowed to sit on the works council.
- Number of mandates
  The number of members in the works council is subject to the number of workers employed when social elections are held. This varies between six (enterprises employing 101–500 workers) and 22 (enterprises employing 8,000 workers).
  The number of full members is established by adding managerial staff to the number of workers.

[340] Here, management means all persons entitled to participate in, and sit on, the employer delegation.

D. *Competence of the works council*[341]

The works council has competence at four levels:

- the right to information;
- advisory competence;
- decisive competence; and
- managerial competence.

In terms of content, they are competent at the technical, economic and social levels.

1. The right to information

a. Economic and financial information

The provisions of Collective Labour Agreement No. 9 of 9 March 1972[342] and the Royal Decree of 27 November 1973[343] state that employers are obliged to provide four different types of information.

- General information

General information has to be communicated at the works council's establishment or at the renewal of the mandates. The relevant documents have to provide workers with general information about the enterprise.

- Annual information

Annual information is required to give the works council an insight into the enterprise's financial situation and future outlook. Comparing general information and previous results with annual information allows the works council to assess managerial policies and their impact on the enterprise's performance.

- Periodical information

Periodical information enables the works council to monitor the enterprise's business performance. This is essential to ascertain whether its business targets and objectives have been achieved. Periodical information has to be provided at least every three months.

---

341 Blanpain, R. and Eyskens, M., 'La compétence des conseils d'entreprise en Belgique d'après la loi et les négociations collectives', *Rev.Trav.* 1972, pp. 1–59 and pp. 203–248.

342 Declared generally binding by the Royal Decree of 12 September 1972, *BS/MB* 25 November 1972.

343 *BS/MB* 28 November 1973.

– Occasional information

Occasional information is needed to permit members of the works council to keep abreast of new developments affecting the continuity of the enterprise. These events may be the result of circumstances beyond the enterprise's control, such as a fire in one of its units, or a managerial decision, such as a merger.

Occasional information should be communicated as quickly as possible. When this is the result of a decision of the central management, the works council has to be informed before the decision is taken.

The Royal Decree of 27 November 1973 sets out the minimum information to be communicated. Derogations from this obligation are sometimes allowed, albeit subject to a special procedure and the authorisation of the competent official.

b. SOCIAL INFORMATION

Collective Labour Agreement No. 9 has a chapter on information at the social level. This is broadly similar to the regulation on economic and financial information. Annual and quarterly social information is given to the works council at the same time as financial and economic information.

– Annual information

Every year central management has to provide data to enable the members of the works council to form a clear picture of employment in the enterprise, likely developments and future outlook.

– Quarterly information

Every three months, a progress report is submitted on projected economic targets, the reasons why they may not have been achieved, and any changes in outlook compared to the last quarter.

– Occasional information

Should central management derogate from the employment targets projected in its annual or quarterly information and be obliged to collectively dismiss or recruit workers on economic or technical grounds, the works council has to be informed as soon as possible, and at least before the final decision is taken.

– Social balance sheet

A social balance sheet was rendered obligatory by the Law of 22 December 1995.[344] Its implementation is set out in the Royal Decree of 4 August 1996.[345] The social

344 *BS/MB* 30 December 1995.

345 *BS/MB* 30 August 1996.

plan is annexed to the annual financial statement and contains information about employment issues.

Enterprises have to submit a balance sheet with their annual financial statements to the Belgian National Bank. Such information also has to be communicated to the works council and, failing this, to the union delegation. In the absence of such bodies, the social report can be consulted by the workers at the place where the rules of work are kept. The data is controlled by the enterprise's auditor.

The public authorities may access these figures for statistical processing, studies on employment, etc.

c. The auditor

As the employees' representatives often lack the necessary expertise to interpret complex financial and economic information, the law made it compulsory in 1985 to designate one or more accountants in enterprises with a works council in order to:

- provide the works council with a complete run-down of the annual accounts and business reports;
- certify that the information given is complete and correct. If this cannot be guaranteed or if gaps or shortcomings are established the works council has to be informed; and
- analyse and explain figures about the financial structure and future development to the members of the works council.

The auditor may attend works council meetings where economic and financial information is given. He/she has to be present if requested by the majority of the personnel delegation.

2. Advisory competence

Granting advisory opinions is, without a doubt, one of the works council's most important tasks. These may concern issues clearly defined by law or matters where the central management seeks its opinion. Collective Labour Convention No. 9 lays down the scope of its advisory competence.

The works council can grant advisory opinions on vocational training and retraining, personnel management, the organisation of work, structural changes of the enterprise potentially affecting employment, etc.

3. Power to decide

The works council has decisive competence in a number of cases clearly defined by law:

- drafting and changing the work rules;
- setting up the general criteria for collective dismissal or recruitment on economic or technical grounds;
- setting the dates of annual holidays and a roster, where necessary;
- selecting the working language and, if necessary, taking measures relating to linguistic matters to improve relations between management and personnel;
- supervising compliance with social legislation;
- setting the dates of official paid holidays if they fall on a Sunday when the joint committee fails to do so in time;
- jointly establishing with the employer how to use the proceeds of disciplinary fines; and
- monitoring compliance of legislation pertaining to the social rehabilitation of disabled personnel in the enterprise.

4. Miscellaneous

If not specifically left to the control of the employees themselves, the works council has to oversee the implementation of the social programmes set up by the enterprise for the well-being of its personnel; e.g. if employees contribute to a pension fund that is entrusted to a non-profit organisation, half of the managing board of this organisation has to consist of members of the works council.

E. Functioning of the works council

The main principles are as follows:

- the works council meets at the enterprise's place of business. It is chaired by the head of the enterprise or his representative and a member of the workers' delegation acts as secretary. If there is no agreement about the secretary's appointment or if there are no special provisions in the work rules, he/she is designated by the representative union or representative managerial union whose list had the largest number of votes;
- the works council meets at least once a month at the request of the head of the enterprise or at least one third of its members;
- meetings including those held outside working hours are regarded as working time and paid accordingly. The employees' representatives' travelling expenses are paid by the employer;

- the meetings' venue and materials are provided for by the head of the enterprise;
- the joint committees lay down work rules that can be used by the works councils in the various companies. These must contain a number of items, such as time limits for convening meetings and the roles of the president and secretary; and
- prior to the social elections of 1995, a non-elected candidate could never succeed a deputy representative. As a result of the modification of Article 21(3) of the Organisation of the Economy Act this is now possible.

If there are no longer any deputy members available to occupy a vacant seat, they can be replaced by non-elected candidates. They complete the mandate and are granted a special protected status.

§ 2. THE COMMITTEE FOR PREVENTION AND PROTECTION AT WORK (CPPW)

A. *Situation*

The basis for safety policy is rooted in the Law of 1899 governing the health and safety of workers employed in industry and commercial enterprises. Health and Safety Committees became obligatory by the Regent's Decrees of 11 February and 3 December 1946 and later in the ARAB/RGPT[346] of 1947. A new law on health and safety was adopted in 1952, which in its turn was replaced by the Workers' Health and Safety Act.[347, 348] The latter seeks to improve the workers' well-being by taking measures with regard to:

1. safety at work;
2. protecting employees' health at work;
3. psychosocial stress caused by work: a.o. protection against violence, bullying and sexual harassment;
4. ergonomics;
5. occupational hygiene;
6. improvement of the workplace; and
7. measures taken to improve the work environment as regards their influence on items 1. to 6.

---

346 ARAB / RGPT Algemeen reglement voor de arbeidsbescherming / Règlement général pour la protection du travail (General rules on employment safety).

347 Workers' Health and Safety Act, 4 August 1996, *BS/MB* 18 September 1996.

348 As a result of the revision the Health and Safety Committee was renamed Committee for Prevention and Protection at Work.

B. *Composition*

Just like the works council, the Committee for Prevention and Protection at Work has a bipartite composition. The employers' delegation is composed of one or more acting or deputy members designated by management and chaired by the head of the enterprise.

The workers' delegation is composed of a number of active and deputy members, elected at the same time as the employees' representatives on the works council, following the same procedure and formalities. However, managerial staff are not represented separately.

A health and safety adviser and industrial medical officer sit on the committee and attend its meetings but do not form part of either the employers' or workers' delegation in order to ensure impartiality.

C. *Establishment*

Committees for Prevention and Protection at Work are obligatory both in the private and public sector. In the private sector this obligation applies not only to commercial enterprises, but also to non-profit organisations, such as schools, nursing homes, etc. However, in the public sector the tasks of the Health and Safety Committee are usually performed by a specific advisory committee.

Committees have to be set up in enterprises (i.e. technical operating units) normally employing more than 50 workers, or 20 workers in mines and underground quarries. A committee also has to be set up when the legal entity employs at least 50 workers, regardless of the number of workers employed in the various branches. Some enterprises employing less than 50 workers may also be obliged to set up a committee by way of a Royal Decree.

If no committee has been established, its tasks are carried out by the union delegation. This applies both to enterprises that are exempt from holding social elections for threshold reasons or because there were no candidates. The workers themselves are consulted in enterprises that have neither a committee nor union.

D. *Tasks*

The Committee for Prevention and Protection has an advisory role and is also closely involved in the recruitment of prevention officers.

E. *Functioning of the committee*

1. Meetings

The committee meets monthly and at the request of at least one third of the workers' delegation. If there is a medical supervision department, the committee has to meet at least twice a year with a maximum interval of six months to discuss matters relating to medical supervision.

The committee meets at the headquarters of the technical operating unit.

2. Chairperson – secretariat

The employer or his representative acts as chairperson. He/she determines the items on the agenda and approves the minutes of the previous meeting.

The secretariat is taken care of by the Internal Service for Workplace Health and Safety (*infra*).

F. *Safety policy when there is no Committee for Prevention and Protection*

If an enterprise does not have a CPPW, its tasks are carried out by the union delegation.

In the absence of both a Committee for Prevention and Protection and a union delegation, the employer shall consult workers directly on all matters relating to health and well-being at work which require their direct participation.

G. *Economic and social competences*

By linking the formation of works councils, Committees for Prevention and Protection at Work and, in most cases, the union delegation as well (*infra*) to minimum thresholds, a lot of employees in small and medium-sized businesses are excluded from the social dialogue. However, Directive 2002/14/EG of 11 March 2002 forced Belgium to reconsider this, but the social partners were not able to see eye to eye on the matter. As a result of this dawdling, Belgium was sanctioned by the European Court of Justice on 29 March 2007 for not transposing the Directive on time.[349] The inertia even jeopardised the social elections. At the last moment, an agreement was reached, which was made into a law.[350] A number of additional tasks were assigned to the Committee for Prevention and Protection at Work. In the absence of a works council, economic and financial information should be

---

[349] Case C-320/06 *Commission v. Belgium* [2007].

[350] Law of 23 April 2008, *BS/MB* 16 May 2008.

delivered to the committee. If there is no works council and no union delegation has been set up, the Committee for Prevention and Protection takes the place of these bodies with regard to the right to consultation. However, it is still doubtful whether this constitutes a sufficient implementation of the Directive. Indeed, without an active works council, Committee for Prevention and Protection at Work or union delegation, employees remain deprived of information and consultation.

H. Addendum

In addition to setting up a committee, employers who engage a certain number of workers have to establish an Internal Service for Workplace Health and Safety. This service:

- assists the employer, members of the hierarchy and employees in applying all legal or regulatory provisions relating to the workers' well-being and other preventive measures and activities;
- carries out health monitoring assignments;
- works together with the external service when requested; and
- assists the employer, members of the hierarchy and employees in developing, programming, executing and assessing dynamic risk management policies.

In some cases, the employer may or must appeal to the External Service for Workplace Health and Safety. This service operates as a non-profit organisation officially recognised by the government. It has two divisions. One is multidisciplinary and carries out risk management and the other performs medical surveillance.

§ 3. PROTECTION AGAINST DISMISSAL FOR EMPLOYEE REPRESENTATIVES AND NON-ELECTED CANDIDATES[351]

The law provides for the protection against dismissal of employee representatives who sit on the works council and the Committee for Prevention and Protection at Work, and for non-elected candidates who participated in the social elections.[352]

---

351 Deckers, H. and Dear, L., *La protection des représentants du personnel. Colloque de la Conférence libre du jeune barreau de Liège*, Limal, Anthemis, 2011, 388 pp.

352 Law of 19 March 1991 on special provisions relating to the dismissal of workers' delegates in works councils, workplace Health and Safety Committees, and candidate workers' delegates, *BS/MB* 29 March 1991.

A. *General rule: protection against dismissal*[353]

Employee representatives and candidates can only be dismissed for just cause subject to prior approval by the labour courts or for economic or technical reasons recognised by the competent joint committee or the National Labour Council.

It is important to note that an employment contract *can* be terminated when the term expires; the work has been completed; the employee ends the contract unilaterally; both parties end the agreement; due to *force majeure* or on the employee's death. Other forms of termination under civil law cannot be invoked.

(Candidate) employee representatives can only be transferred from one technical operating unit to another within the same legal entity if they give their consent in writing or on the grounds of economic or technical reasons recognised by the joint committee.

Protection against dismissal no longer applies when:

- the employee representative resigns from the works council;
- he/she is no longer a member of the organisation that nominated him/her;
- his/her mandate has been withdrawn by the labour tribunal for serious misconduct, at the request of the representative union or representative organisation of managerial staff who nominated him/her;
- he/she is given a managerial position; or
- he/she changes category, for example from blue-collar to white-collar worker, unless the union asks the employer to extend the mandate.

B. *Protection*

Acting and deputy employee representatives, but also non-elected candidates who participated in the elections for the first time or the non-elected candidates who sit on the committee, are protected against dismissal from the 30th day prior to the election's notification until the date candidates are nominated for the next elections.

[353] Dismissal means:
- any termination of the employment contract by the employer with or without indemnification, with or without advance notice;
- any termination of the employment contract by the employer for particular reasons constituting just cause; or
- failure of the employer to respect an order of the labour courts ruling that the employment contract continues to apply during court proceedings.

When the minimum number of persons required for the works council has not been met and a works council no longer has to be set up or renewed, candidates are protected for a period of six months starting on the first day of the elections.

Persons aged 65 and over no longer have a protected status unless the enterprise where they work habitually employs such older workers.

Non-elected candidates are protected from the 30th day prior to notification of the electoral date until two years after notification of electoral results.

C. *Dismissal for economic or technical reasons*

Employers are sometimes obliged to dismiss workers. Employers wishing to dismiss an employee representative for economic or technical reasons have to inform the competent joint committee (or the National Labour Council when there is no acting joint committee) by registered letter. This body has two months to respond to the employer's request.

Disputes can be settled in two ways:

1. The joint committee takes a decision within this term:
   - the joint committee recognises the economic or technical reason and the employer can dismiss the worker. If the employer failed to respect the prescribed period and dismissed the worker anyway, the dismissal is unlawful;
   - the joint committee does not recognise the economic or technical reasons. The employee then remains in service.

   Until 1993, appeals against the joint committee's decisions were not granted. However, further to a request for a preliminary ruling, the Constitutional Court held that this is in breach of Articles 10 and 11 of the Constitution.[354] As a result, the Labour Tribunal of Brussels declared it was competent to accept appeals against such decisions taken by Joint Committee No. 140.[355] In principle, therefore, the Law of 19 March 1991 should be amended.
2. The joint committee does not take a decision within this period:
   employers can dismiss workers legally only in the event of a closure of enterprise, a division of enterprise or if they belong to a certain category of workers.

[354] Judgment M. 57/93, 8 July 1993, *BS/MB* 28 August 1993.

[355] Labour Tribunal Brussels 16 November 1993, *JTT* 1994, p. 294.

If the dismissal is the result of a closure of (a division of) the enterprise:

- the employer submits the recognition of the economic and technical grounds to the labour tribunal. The employment contract continues to exist during court proceedings; or
- the employer dismisses immediately. The worker or his/her union seeks the worker's reintegration. If this is refused or reintegration is not requested, the worker or his/her union may petition the labour tribunal to establish the absence of economic or technical reasons *a posteriori* and claim compensation.

The dismissal affects a specific category of workers:

- the employer applies for a court order to have the economic or technical grounds recognised. The subsequent proceedings are the same as those in the case of dismissal for just cause.

If the tribunal recognises the economic or technical reasons, the employer may only inform the worker of the dismissal after the term for appeal has expired, or if an appeal has been lodged, the third working day after notification of the judgment. The worker continues to be employed during the course of court proceedings.

The burden of proof for justifying economic or technical grounds and the facts that the dismissal may not be discriminatory lies with the employer.

D. *Dismissal for just cause*

1. Procedure

An employer seeking to dismiss a protected employee for just cause must inform the employee and his/her union within three working days following the day he/she was informed of the fact justifying his/her dismissal. He/she also has to send a petition to the president of the labour tribunal within this time frame.

A negotiation period of five days commences on the third working day after the day the registered letters were sent. The employee and his/her union contact the employer to inform him of their viewpoint and present their version of the facts. During this period of negotiation, the parties involved (employer, union and employee) are invited to appear individually, without legal counsel, before the president of the labour tribunal.

The president sets a new date for a court hearing immediately after the negotiation period to try to reconcile the two parties. If he succeeds, the terms are officially recorded and sealed. If not, the president rules on the possible suspension of the employment contract (and consequently the mandate) during the court procedure.

The court's decision has to be communicated to the parties within three working days after the ruling. As regards candidate employee representatives, the employer decides whether or not to suspend the contract. If the employer still wishes to dismiss the employee after the negotiation period has ended he can start summary proceedings within three working days of the negotiation period in the case of candidate employee representatives and within three days of the president's decision in the case of an employee representative.

The matter is dealt with during the next session to reconcile the parties. If this fails the president refers the matter to a court chamber. Although the hearing usually has to take place within thirty working days, the president can extend this period to 45 days with the parties' approval. He also decides the terms for submitting documents and conclusions.

Appeal against the tribunal's final decision is possible by sending a registered petition within ten working days. The president of the labour court sets a date for the court hearing and refers the matter to a chamber. The case has to be heard within thirty working days (and in exceptional circumstances 45 days) after the president's decision. All procedural details are set out in the law. The court's decision is communicated within eight days.

In the case of dismissal for just cause pursuant to Article 35 of the Employment Contract Act, the term of three working days starts on the third working day after the term for appeal has ended. If an appeal has been lodged, it starts on the third working day after notification of the decision.

2. Termination of the employment contract

If the contract of employment has been suspended, the employee can terminate it without a period of notice. If it has not been suspended, statutory notice periods have to be respected. A reduced period of notice is applicable for white-collar workers.

If the employer terminates the agreement and fails to respect the statutory procedures referred to above, the employee or the union that nominated the employee will request to have him/her reintegrated within the enterprise by sending a registered letter within thirty days after notification of the dismissal, the termination of the contract or the nomination, if this occurred after the dismissal or termination. If the employer's reaction is positive, the employee's salary and social contributions have to be paid.

If reintegration has *not* been requested, the employer has to pay an amount equal to at least the employee's current salary for a duration of:

- two years if he/she has less than 10 years seniority;
- three years if he/she has between 10 and 20 years seniority; or
- four years if he/she has more than 20 years seniority.

If the requested reintegration is refused, the employer will have to pay an amount equal to the salary for the remaining mandate in addition to the flat-rate amount of 2, 3 or 4 years' salary.

Such compensation is also due when the contract is terminated for just cause or if the employer prevents the employee from working during the procedure despite the authorisation granted by the labour tribunal.

3. Financial consequences of suspending an employment contract

If the contract of employment is suspended during the procedure, the employer has to pay an indemnity to supplement the employee's unemployment benefit to ensure his/her earnings equal his/her net reference wage. This reference wage consists of:

- the average amount of net wage and advantages acquired by virtue of the employment contract; and
- where necessary the average net amount of advantages in kind.

The net amount is obtained by deducting personal social security contributions and tax from the gross amount.

The additional amount has to be paid regardless of the tribunal's decision concerning the employer's motive.

CHAPTER 3
THE UNION DELEGATION[356]

SECTION 1. CONCEPT AND SITUATION

The union delegation is a body representing union members at enterprise level.

Before the Second World War, unions already had representatives in large companies, albeit only informally. After the War, when the establishment of a works council became obligatory, the legislature also sought to give legal status to the union delegation. The National Labour Conference of 6 July 1946 charged the General Joint Council with establishing general principles on the rights and obligations of the union delegation. The General Joint Council's efforts resulted in the agreement of 16 - 17 June 1947, concluded between representative employees' and employers' organisations. Although it did not have force in law, it resulted in collective labour agreements in almost all sectors. These collective labour agreements worked out a status for union delegations.

In 1963, the then Minister of Employment, Servais, tried unsuccessfully to award legal status to union delegations.

When in 1968, the Collective Labour Agreements Act authorised the National Labour Council to conclude collective labour agreements at national level, the social partners used this opportunity to grant full legal status to the union delegation. Thus, on 24 May 1971, fifty years after the Freedom of Association Act, Collective Agreement No. 5 was concluded in the National Labour Council.

SECTION 2. FRAMEWORK AGREEMENT

Collective Labour Agreement No. 5 is a framework agreement, i.e. its provisions contain generally formulated minimum rules. These provisions have to be developed more specifically in collective labour agreements concluded in joint (sub-)committees or at enterprise level. The only restriction is that they have to be developed in accordance with basic provisions.

[356] Lagasse, F., 'La délégation syndicale: son institution, sa composition, ses attributions, le statut de ses membres', *JTT* 1998, pp. 345–356.

Collective Labour Agreement No. 5 contains a number of concrete obligations and general principles.

§ 1. CONCRETE OBLIGATIONS

a. the obligation to set up a union delegation, when this has been requested by one or more unions (Art. 7);
b. the right of the unions to appoint candidates (Art. 7, 10, 16);
c. the status of members of the union delegation (Art. 18–20);
d. the competence of the union delegation (Art. 11–14);
e. the facilities awarded to the delegation to carry out its tasks (Art. 22);
f. the obligation for the members of the union delegation to provide information and the right to communicate information (Art. 23);
g. if there is no works council, the right to carry out some of its tasks (Art. 24);
h. the right to seek the intervention of permanent delegates (Art. 25).

§ 2. GENERAL PRINCIPLES

The general principles apply to the fundamental employee-employer relationship:

- employees must respect the authority of their employer; and
- employees must perform their tasks conscientiously.

In turn, employers:

- must respect the dignity of their workers; and
- may not hinder or infringe, directly or indirectly, trade union freedom.

The parties' rights and obligations can be summarised as follows:

- employers' organisations undertake to encourage their members to respect trade union freedom;
- employees' organisations undertake to choose the members of the trade union delegation judiciously, to enable them to speak with the necessary authority;
- multi-industry employee organisations undertake to encourage their members to adopt a practice of social dialogue in accordance with the spirit of the collective labour agreement;
- employees' and employers' organisations undertake to ensure that the heads of enterprise and the union delegates respectively pursue justice, fairness and conciliation.

SECTION 3. ESTABLISHMENT

§ 1. WHO CAN APPOINT UNION DELEGATES?

Representative employee organisations that have signed Collective Labour Agreement No. 5 can ask the employer to set up a trade union delegation. He cannot refuse this if a minimum threshold of workers is employed. This varies from one sector to another and is set out in collective labour agreements.

Only organisations represented in the competent joint committee are allowed to appoint members. A union that has signed the agreement, but is *not* represented in the joint committee, has the right to participate in the election if it can prove its representativeness, for example, by obtaining at least one mandate during the previous social elections. Alternately, it has to prove it represents at least 10% of personnel.

§ 2. WHICH EMPLOYEES ARE REPRESENTED BY THE UNION DELEGATION?

The terms of Article 6 of Collective Labour Agreement No. 5 are somewhat unclear: 'Employers recognise that their unionised personnel is represented by a trade union delegation whose members are appointed or elected from amongst the employees of the enterprise.' This text raises a number of questions:

- *Does Article 6 mean that the union delegation also represents non-union employees?*
  It is generally accepted that the union delegation represents only unionised members. However, this does not prevent the union delegation from organising information meetings for all employees.
- *Which employees does Article 6 refer to: blue-collar workers, white-collar workers, or also executive and managerial staff?*
  In principle, employers' and employees' organisations can freely choose who falls under their scope. In this context, it is also important to consult the multi-industry collective labour agreement. If nothing has been stipulated, the concept 'employees' has to be interpreted in a broad sense, i.e. blue-collar and white-collar workers, including executive and managerial staff, domestic workers, apprentices, foreign workers, and all persons working under the authority of someone else in a relationship other than a contract of employment.
- *Does the union delegation also represent the union vis-à-vis the employer?*
  Article 6 could suggest that the trade union delegation represents employees but not the representative employee organisation *vis-à-vis* the employer.

However, this is not the case. The trade union delegation represents both the union and unionised personnel.

§ 3. COMPETENCE OF THE UNION DELEGATION

Article 11 gives a non-exhaustive list of the union delegation's competence. It refers, among others, to:

- industrial relations;
- negotiations for concluding collective labour agreements without affecting existing collective labour agreements or other agreements concluded at other levels;
- application in the enterprise of social legislation, collective labour agreements, employment regulations and individual employment contracts; and
- respecting the general principles set out in Articles 2–5 of Collective Labour Agreement No. 5.

The union delegation often has authority in other matters. This is usually provided for in special laws or separate collective labour agreements.

§ 4. THE FUNCTIONING OF THE UNION DELEGATION

A. The right to be heard

The union delegation has certain procedural rights, i.e. the right to be heard by the employer or his representative in the case of impending or existing disputes or strikes. It also has the right to assist employees who have submitted individual complaints.

To prevent individual or industrial disputes, the union delegation always has to be informed beforehand about any planned changes to wages and working conditions.

B. The right to provide information

The union delegation has the right to provide oral or written information of a professional or union nature without disrupting work activities. Subject to approval by the employer it can also hold information meetings at the workplace.

C. *The right to assistance*

In the event of an industrial dispute, the union delegation can seek help from full-time union officials if negotiations between the employer and the union delegation break down. It can also ask the competent joint committee's conciliation bureau to intervene.

§ 5. PROTECTION OF MEMBERS OF THE UNION DELEGATION

Union delegates have a renewable four-year mandate. In addition to being entitled to a number of facilities for practising their mandate, they enjoy protection against dismissal.

A. *Who is protected?*

Only official union members have a special protected status. Persons performing union duties without being elected or appointed are not protected.

B. *To what extent are they covered?*

Article 17 of Collective Labour Agreement No. 5 prohibits all forms of discrimination against union delegates. Their mandate may not give rise to any disadvantages or special advantages. They are entitled to normal promotion prospects and cannot be dismissed for reasons specifically connected to the execution of their office. However, dismissal for personal, economic or technical reasons is still possible.

C. *Dismissal: procedure*

With the exception of dismissal for just cause, employers seeking to dismiss a member of the union delegation have to follow the procedure set out in the sectoral or enterprise collective labour agreement. In contrast to the procedure for members of the works council or the Committee for Prevention and Protection, they do not need prior authorisation by the court. However, they do have to inform the union immediately, although failure to do so is not penalised.

The procedure for dismissal must comply with the provisions of Article 18 of Collective Labour Agreement No. 5. The employer has to inform the union and union delegation beforehand by means of a registered letter.

The union concerned has seven days to respond by registered letter whether or not the dismissal is acceptable.

If the validity of the envisaged dismissal is not recognised, the employer can submit the case to the conciliation bureau of the competent joint committee. The contract cannot be terminated in the course of this procedure.

The following scenarios are possible:

- the conciliation bureau reaches a unanimous decision after thirty days;
- the employer's reason for dismissal is regarded as valid and the employer terminates the employment contract;
- the worker can go to court if he/she feels the notice of dismissal is too short or the severance pay is too low;
- the employer's reason for dismissal is not accepted and the employer either has to retain the union delegate or terminate his/her contract and award severance pay; or
- the conciliation bureau is unable to reach a unanimous decision and the employer has two options: either to keep on the employee pending the court's ruling or to dismiss him/her and award severance pay if the dismissal is not upheld in court.

The employer has to pay a flat-rate compensation in the following cases:

- when the procedure was not followed;
- when the employer dismissed the employee and the validity of the reason for dismissal was not recognised by the conciliation bureau or the court;
- when the employer dismissed a delegate for just cause and the court rules that the dismissal was unfounded; or
- when the contract of employment was terminated due to serious misconduct by the employer and the employee is entitled to terminate the agreement immediately. For example, an employer sexually harasses a union delegate.

The amount of compensation due equals one year's gross pay unless otherwise provided for in a collective labour agreement. Furthermore, it cannot be cumulated.

D. More favourable provisions

Some multi-industry or enterprise collective labour agreements deviate from the provisions of Collective Labour Agreement No. 5 concerning protection against dismissal. The main derogations are as follows:

a) the period of protection is explicitly defined and starts before the mandate begins. In other words, protection comprises more than four years;
b) the monetary penalty exceeds one year's gross pay;

c) the procedure is specified in more detail. For example, compensation is paid in the case of just cause when neither the conciliation bureau nor the representative union is notified;
d) stricter anti-discrimination rules are in place.

E. Union delegates entrusted with assignments of the Committee for Prevention and Protection at Work

Union delegates performing tasks belonging to the Committee for Prevention and Protection are protected against dismissal pursuant to the Law of 19 March 1991.

CHAPTER 4
SUPRANATIONAL CONSULTATION

The European Works Council[357]
The provisions of Directive 94/45/EC[358] to promote the right to information and consultation of workers in undertakings and groups of undertakings in the European Union and the European Economic Area were transposed into Belgian law by Collective Labour Agreement No. 62 of 6 February 1996.[359] Two additional laws of 23 April 1998 dealt with the protection against dismissal of employee representatives and the confidential nature of information communicated by the enterprise.[360] The new Directive 2009/38/EC was transposed into Belgian labour law by Collective Agreement No. 101 of 21 December 2010.[361] This collective agreement is largely similar to the Directive.

Employees' representatives in the European Company
Council Directive 2001/86/EC of 8 October 2001, which regulates the cooperation between companies and employees' organisations in the *Societas Europaea*,[362] was transposed by the Royal Decree on Labour Relations of 1 September 2004.[363] The Directive was transposed by the National Labour Council on 6 October 2005[364] by way of Collective Labour Agreement No. 84. Simultaneously, Collective Labour Agreement No. 62*ter* incorporated Article 3*bis* into Collective Labour Agreement No. 62 on the establishment of a European Works Council. When a company complies with the conditions of Collective Labour Agreement No. 84, a European Works Council no longer has to be set up separately.

357 Humblet, P. and Rigaux, M., 'La transposition en droit belge de la directive 94/45 concernant l'institution d'un comité d'entreprise européen ou d'une procédure dans les entreprises de dimension communautaire en vue d'informer et de consulter les travailleurs' in M. Rigaux and F. Dorssemont (eds.), *Comités d'entreprise européens / European Works Councils*, Antwerp, Intersentia, 1999, pp. 89–134.
358 OJ L 254, 30 September 1994.
359 Made generally binding by way of the Royal Decree of 22 March 1996, *BS/MB* 11 April 1996.
360 *BS/MB* 21 May 1998.
361 Declared generally binding by the Royal Decree of 24 March 2011, *BS/MB* 8 April 2011.
362 OJ L 294, 10 November 2001.
363 *BS/MB* 9 September 2004.
364 Transposition into Belgium law has not been fully completed.

The role of employees in a European Cooperative Society (SCE)

Directive 2003/72/EC of 22 July 2003 supplementing the statute of a European Cooperative Society with regard to the role of employees was implemented by Collective Agreement No. 88 of 30 January 2007.[365] Basically, the regulation is nearly analogous to that of Collective Labour Agreement No. 84.

365 Declared generally binding by the Royal Decree of 16 March 2007, *BS/MB* 10 April 2007.

CHAPTER 5
COLLECTIVE LABOUR AGREEMENTS[366]

Belgium uses legally binding collective labour agreements. In this regard it is important to note that the representative unions have a monopoly for concluding such agreements. They also conclude collective labour agreements at enterprise level. Limiting representativeness to the three major unions has been very important in terms of social stability as there is little or no competition between the various unions.

SECTION 1. ORIGIN OF THE COLLECTIVE LABOUR AGREEMENTS ACT

The oldest collective labour agreement can be traced back to the agreement on pay and working conditions concluded by employers and workers in the cloth industry of Verviers in September 1789.

However, the Le Chapelier Act complicated all further experiments of this nature so that only 19 agreements of this kind were concluded between the fall of the *Ancien Régime* and the First World War.

In 1919, the country was rocked by a significant outbreak of collective conflicts despite the government's commitment to new social policy. Thousands of blue- and white-collar workers went out on strike. In order to stabilise the country the government tried arbitration to force workers to reach a solution. As the situation did not improve, the authorities set up joint committees in the mines and the metallurgical industry where strikes were the most vehement, to examine the possibility of cutting working time. This process of institutionalised consultation was applied many times in the years to come. In 1939, roughly 47 committees of this kind were active. Their consultative structure was ideal for concluding collective labour agreements.

[366] Cordier, J.P., *Les 40 ans de la loi du 5 décembre 1968 sur les conventions collectives de travail*, Brussels, Bruylant, 2008, 200 p.

During the period between the two World Wars, a lot of attempts were made to grant legal status to collective labour agreements, but for various reasons these failed.

The biggest problem relating to collective labour agreements was the question as to what extent these conferred rights to workers. This problem was partly solved by Articles 12 and 13 of the Decree Law of 9 June 1945. These enabled joint committees or unions to request, by way of Royal Decree, that the individual standard provisions of a collective labour agreement be granted binding effect *erga omnes*.

In the case law after 1945 there was no unanimity on the status of collective labour agreements that were not legally binding.

This permanent confusion increased the need for a coherent codification. In 1963, the Minister of Employment, Servais, introduced a bill and presented it to the National Labour Council. It contained not only provisions on collective labour agreements, but also on the union delegation, strikes and lock-outs.

The National Labour Council presented its views on this matter in Opinion No. 196 of 30 April 1964. No objections were raised by either employers' organisations or the Christian and liberal unions. However, the social-democratic union rejected the proposal outright and considered the provisions on strikes unacceptable. Taking into account the social-democratic veto, the Minister only kept the relevant provisions on collective labour agreements and submitted an amended law proposal on 23 February 1967. Parliament adopted the proposal without much discussion and approved a text that deviated very little from the original draft.[367]

SECTION 2. CONCEPT AND CONTENT

A collective labour agreement is an agreement concluded between one or more employees' organisations and one or more employers, governing individual and collective relations between employers and employees within the enterprise or in an industry, and regulating the rights and obligations of the contracting parties.

A collective labour agreement consists of two parts: a normative and an obligatory part. The normative part is subdivided into the individual and collective, and the obligatory part into explicitly obligatory and implicitly obligatory provisions.

---

367 Collective Agreements and Joint Committees Act of 5 December 1968, *BS/MB* 15 January 1969.

The normative part contains standard provisions for employers and workers. They set out collective and individual relations between employers and workers within a particular branch of industry or enterprise.

As a general rule, the following are regarded as individual, normative provisions:

- the creation, existence, duration and termination of the convention;
- annual holidays and paid leave;
- professional classifications;
- pay and bonuses;
- working hours;
- etc.

These individual standard provisions are included in the worker's individual contract of employment falling under the scope of the collective labour agreement.

Individual standard provisions are converted automatically in two steps.

Firstly, provisions of the individual contract of employment breaching the collective labour agreement are automatically null and void. Secondly, they are replaced by individual provisions of the applicable collective labour agreement.

The collective normative part groups the provisions relating to the collective labour relations in the enterprise or sector of activity, such as:

- the legal status and functioning of the union delegation;
- social funds, such as funds for social security; and
- privileges awarded to certain categories of workers.

The obligatory part concerns agreements concluded by organisations with a view to being executed by their members.

The relevant provisions only apply between the contracting parties, i.e. unions and employers' organisations or individual workers.

The obligatory part contains express and implied provisions.

Express provisions are:

- obligations relating to the execution of the normative provisions;
- the obligation to set up councils or social services;
- requests to make the agreement legally binding;

- provisions relating to the term during which the collective labour agreement is in force; and
- sanctions for failing to comply with contractual obligations.

Implied provisions are regarded by doctrine and case law as inherent to all collective labour agreements. Social peace and abiding by the principle of good faith, for example, do not have to be explicitly mentioned in a collective labour agreement.

The obligation of social peace does not constitute an absolute ban on all forms of industrial action:

- unions are allowed to resort to industrial action to formulate new demands;
- industrial action can be taken in order to force the other party to respect the collective labour agreement;
- resorting to industrial action is allowed for obtaining an interpretation in accordance with the spirit of the agreement;
- action is also allowed for solving a conflict that has arisen during the discussion preceding the conclusion of a collective labour agreement (in such cases it is not a new demand); and
- action can be taken in defensive response to action by the other party.

The contracting parties can also agree that:

- the obligation of social peace is absolute: the parties undertake not to resort to any forms of pressure for the duration of the collective labour agreement;
- the parties are free to amend the collective labour agreement at all times;
- the unions guarantee that their members will respect the collective labour agreement's application;
- the unions will pay damages if the social peace obligation is not respected; and
- the social peace obligation has to be respected after expiry of the collective agreement.

'Full performance', or abiding by the principle of good faith, means that the parties must use their influence to ensure that members will respect the agreement.

The unions are also under the obligation to inform. Individual employers or workers cannot be expected to respect a collective labour agreement if they have not been informed of its existence.

The mutual duty for the contracting parties to abide by the principle of good faith means that unions and employers' associations will do the utmost to ensure that peace is maintained as regards the matters agreed on. However, this does not guarantee that the collective labour agreement will be respected. Members breaching the agreement will be held personally liable.

SECTION 3. LEGAL NATURE OF THE COLLECTIVE LABOUR AGREEMENT

The legal nature of the collective labour agreement has led to discussion in legal doctrine. There are two opposing views in this respect.

The first holds that collective labour agreements are regulations, creating rights and obligations, not only for the contracting parties, but also for employers and workers who are not parties to the agreement.

The second advocates that collective labour agreements are basically contracts.

The legislature opted for a dualist solution in the Law of 5 December 1968, which provides that a collective labour agreement is essentially a contract, but that its normative provisions contain standards relating to pay, and terms and conditions regulating the individual employment relationship and collective labour relations between the employer(s) and employees covered by it.

This legislative option of regarding collective labour agreements as contracts has a number of consequences at the legal level.

Only a Royal Decree can form the object of an annulment following a ruling of the Administrative Division of the Council of State. The validity of a collective labour agreement as such is examined by ordinary courts.

A collective labour agreement declared generally binding has the same binding force as a Royal Decree.

SECTION 4. SCOPE OF THE COLLECTIVE LABOUR AGREEMENTS ACT

The Collective Labour Agreements Act applies to all workers and employers in the private sector and their organisations.

In order to apply, persons without a contract of employment who perform work under the authority of a person are considered to be workers.

The Crown, acting through a Ministerial Decree, can extend the application of the Collective Labour Agreements Act partly or wholly to public sector employees.

However, the Constitution would have to be changed for the Collective Labour Agreements Act to apply to the public sector. By virtue of Article 107 of the Constitution, the public authorities are empowered to establish, unilaterally, the working conditions of civil servants. This would be compromised by the Collective Labour Agreements Act.

SECTION 5. WHO CAN CONCLUDE A COLLECTIVE LABOUR AGREEMENT?

A collective labour agreement can be concluded between:

- one employer and one or more representative unions (collective agreement concluded at enterprise or company level);
- various employers and one or more representative unions; or
- representative employers' associations and one or more representative unions.

The following are regarded as representative unions and employers' associations:[368]

- national multi-industry unions represented in the National Labour Council and the National Economic Council with at least 50,000 members;
- unions belonging or affiliated to one of the multi-industry employee organisations referred to above;
- employers' associations recognised as representative of a certain branch of industry by the Crown on the recommendation of the National Labour Council; and
- national organisations representing small and medium-sized businesses recognised as representative pursuant to the criteria of the Law of 6 March 1964.

Only collective labour agreements concluded between the persons referred to above (employers) or representative employers' associations and unions fall under the scope of the law on collective labour agreements.

However, this law does not prohibit other groups from concluding collective agreements. An employer is free to conclude a collective agreement with a non-representative group of workers, but it will not be a collective labour agreement in a legal sense. Parties cannot enforce such agreements by invoking the provisions

[368] Article 3 of the Collective Labour Agreements Act.

of the Collective Labour Agreements Act, but will have to resort to civil law. Legal recourse is only possible if the non-representative employee organisation or union has legal personality. If this group is merely a *de facto* association, for example a strike committee, the accord is regarded as a gentlemen's agreement only and is not legally binding.

SECTION 6. TYPES OF COLLECTIVE LABOUR AGREEMENT

Various types can be distinguished:

- collective labour agreements concluded within or without a joint body;
- collective labour agreements with multi-industry scope and collective labour agreements applicable to a certain industry;
- national and regional collective labour agreements;
- collective labour agreements concluded at branch level and collective labour agreements concluded at enterprise level;
- collective labour agreements concluded for a fixed or indefinite period;
- generally binding and non-generally binding collective labour agreements;
- etc.

SECTION 7. HIERARCHY OF THE DIFFERENT TYPES OF COLLECTIVE LABOUR AGREEMENTS

Where several collective labour agreements have contradictory provisions, Article 51 of the Collective Agreements Act establishes the hierarchy of these sources of law:

1. (collective labour) agreements concluded within the National Labour Council and declared generally binding;
2. (collective labour) agreements concluded within a joint committee and declared generally binding;
3. collective labour agreements concluded within a joint sub-committee and declared generally binding;
4. collective labour agreements concluded within the National Labour Council and *not* declared generally binding;
5. collective labour agreements concluded within a joint committee and *not* declared generally binding;
6. collective labour agreements concluded within a joint sub-committee and *not* declared generally binding; and
7. collective labour agreements concluded outside any joint body.

This hierarchy does not regulate the possibility to derogate from a higher level to a lower level agreement in favour of the worker.

A collective labour agreement concluded at a higher level usually sets out minimum regulations rather than maximum ones.

If a collective labour agreement concluded at a higher level does not regulate certain matters or standards, then a lower level agreement with more favourable terms and conditions will prevail. For example, with regard to the legal status of the union delegation, several sectoral collective labour agreements provide longer redundancy compensation than one year as set out in Article 20 of Collective Labour Agreement No. 5. However, if a collective labour agreement concluded at a higher level establishes maximum standards, it will prevail over a lower one, even if it is more favourable to the workers. Article 16 of Collective Labour Agreement No. 5, for example, fixes the maximum duration for union delegate mandates at four years. Longer periods of protection are not possible.

Articles 9, 10 and 11 of the Collective Agreements Act also establish a similar hierarchy to the one contained in Article 51, but it is not identical. This often leads to different interpretations in case law and doctrine.

SECTION 8. COLLECTIVE LABOUR AGREEMENTS: FORMAL REQUIREMENTS

Concluding a collective labour agreement is subject to certain formal validity requirements. For example, the parties must have legal capacity.

§ 1. DOCUMENT IN WRITING[369]

Agreements must be drawn up in writing on pain of nullity. Union delegates are always presumed to be competent to conclude agreements on the union's behalf. This presumption is *juris et de jure*.[370]

The agreement has to be signed by the contracting parties or their designated representatives.[371] These signatures can be replaced by:

369 Article 13 of the Collective Labour Agreements Act.
370 Article 12 of the Collective Labour Agreements Act.
371 Article 14 of the Collective Labour Agreements Act.

- a statement to the effect that the chairperson and the secretary of the joint body have signed the minutes of the meeting approved by the members;
- the signature of a member of each organisation represented on the joint body in which the agreement was concluded; or
- the signature of the person who reconciled the parties in the case of a labour dispute and who testifies that the parties have confirmed their agreement in the written record of conciliation.

A collective labour agreement can be drawn up by correspondence or exchange of telegrams.

§ 2. LANGUAGE[372]

The agreement has to be drafted in in Dutch and in French. However, it can be drafted in the language of the region concerned, provided it refers exclusively to the Dutch language region, the French language region or the German language region.

§ 3. COMPULSORY INFORMATION[373]

The agreement should provide the following information:

- the name of the organisations concluding the agreement;
- the name of the joint body, if the agreement is concluded in such a body;
- the identity of the persons concluding the agreement, and, if the agreement is concluded outside a joint body, the capacity in which such persons act and, where applicable, their functions in the organisation;
- the person, the branch of industry/activity or the undertakings and the territory to which the agreement applies, unless the agreement is binding on all the employers and workers covered by the joint body in which it is concluded;
- the duration of validity of a fixed-term contract, or the manner and period of prior notice to terminate an agreement of unspecified duration or an agreement of specified duration containing a renewal clause;
- the effective date if the agreement does not enter into force on the date of its conclusion;
- the date on which the agreement was concluded; and
- the signature of the persons with signing authority.

372 Article 13 of the Collective Labour Agreements Act.
373 Article 16 of the Collective Labour Agreements Act.

§ 4. REGISTRATION[374]

The agreement must be registered with the Federal Public Service Employment, Labour and Social Dialogue. Registrations can be refused if the agreement fails to fulfil the conditions laid down above.

The following documents also have to be registered:

- the adhesion of an organisation or employer to the agreement; and
- notice of intention to terminate an agreement of unspecified duration or an agreement of specified duration containing a renewal clause.

An agreement is legally binding on the signatories even if it has not been officially registered.

A copy of the registered agreement can be obtained on payment of a fee.

§ 5. PUBLICATION[375]

The objective, the date, the duration and the scope of the agreement concluded in a joint body are published in the Official Belgian Journal.

§ 6. FORMAL REQUIREMENTS FOR AGREEMENTS CONCLUDED BY A JOINT BODY

To have binding force, individual normative parts of collective labour agreements not declared generally binding should satisfy the following requirements:

- the agreement must be concluded by all the organisations represented in the joint body (Article 24);
- the objective, date, duration, scope and place of registration must be published in the Belgian Official Journal (Article 25); and
- the collective bargaining agreement must be published fully in the Belgian Official Journal.

[374] Article 18 of the Collective Labour Agreements Act.
[375] Article 25 of the Collective Labour Agreements Act.

SECTION 9. PERSONS AND ORGANISATIONS BOUND BY THE AGREEMENT

Even when a collective labour agreement has been concluded in accordance with the legislative requirements, the question of its obligatory binding force remains, that is, the extent to which the provisions of the agreement have to be respected by the employers and workers concerned.

§ 1. COLLECTIVE LABOUR AGREEMENTS NOT DECLARED GENERALLY BINDING

A. *Persons bound by the agreement*

Article 19 of the Collective Labour Agreements Act details the persons and organisations bound by the agreement:

- the organisations that have concluded it and employers who are members of such organisations or have concluded such an agreement themselves, starting on the date it becomes effective;
- the organisations and employers adhering to the agreement and employers who are members of such organisations, starting on the date of adhesion;
- the employers who become affiliated to an organisation bound by the agreement, starting on the date of their affiliation; and
- all workers in the service of employers bound by the agreement.

In the case of a total or partial transfer of an undertaking, the new employer must respect the terms of the agreement that bound the former employer, until the agreement ceases to apply.[376]

An employer whose affiliation to an organisation bound by the agreement ends, remains bound by said agreement until the terms of said agreement are amended and significantly change the obligations arising out of the agreement.[377]

In the case of dissolution of an organisation bound by an agreement, the rules governing the individual relations between employers and workers (drawn up by virtue of the agreement) will continue to apply to the organisation's members until the terms of said agreement are amended and significantly change the obligations arising out of the agreement.[378]

376 Article 20 of the Collective Labour Agreements Act.
377 Article 21 of the Collective Labour Agreements Act.
378 Article 22 of the Collective Labour Agreements Act.

An individual contract of employment modified implicitly by a collective labour agreement remains unchanged if the agreement ceases to apply, save when otherwise provided for in the said agreement.[379]

In the case of modification of the scope of a joint committee or joint sub-committee, the agreements concluded within the latter will remain binding for the employers and workers to whom it applied before such modification, until such time as the joint committee or joint sub-committee under whose jurisdiction they fall has settled the application of the agreement on said employers and workers.[380]

B. *Binding force of normative and obligatory provisions*

The following distinction has to be made as regards the normative part of the agreement:

- *The collective labour agreement is binding on the employer*:
  He is either a party to the agreement or a member of an organisation that signed the agreement. Employers and their workers are bound by the normative individual and normative collective provisions;
- *The collective labour agreement is not directly binding on the employer, but his enterprise falls under the jurisdiction of the joint body in which the collective labour agreement was concluded*:
  the normative individual provisions can be enforced.[381] Said provisions are binding, save when otherwise provided in the individual labour agreement.

The obligatory part of the collective labour agreement is subject to difficulties in terms of enforceability.

Article 4, paragraph 2 provides that damages arising from failure to respect the obligations set out in the agreement are due only if this is explicitly provided for in the agreement. Furthermore, if a damage clause was included in the agreement and the court were to condemn the organisation concerned, the problem of execution would still remain. However, as unions generally do not have legal personality, execution is impossible.

379 Article 23 of the Collective Labour Agreements Act.
380 Article 27 of the Collective Labour Agreements Act.
381 Article 26 of the Collective Labour Agreements Act.

§ 2. GENERALLY BINDING COLLECTIVE LABOUR AGREEMENTS

A collective labour agreement is made legally binding when the Crown declares the individual and collective normative provisions of said agreement applicable by way of Royal Decree to all employers and employees falling under the scope of the joint body in which the collective labour agreement was concluded.

Agreements concluded in a joint body can be declared binding at the request of the joint body or at the request of one or more representative employers' associations or unions.

Only collective labour agreements concluded in a joint body can be declared generally binding.

Moreover, only the individual and collective normative provisions can be made generally binding. Obligatory provisions are excluded.

A Royal Decree declaring a collective labour agreement generally binding must be published in the Belgian Official Journal. It becomes effective when the agreement enters into effect. Where the agreement is for a fixed term, the Royal Decree ceases to apply when the collective agreement expires. If the agreement is for an indefinite period or for a fixed term and is renewable, the Crown can repeal the Royal Decree on the date the collective labour agreement ends.

The Crown can also refuse to declare a collective labour agreement generally binding if formal and validity requirements have not been fulfilled, but never for economic or political reasons. However, on the approval of the joint body concerned, it can wholly or partly repeal the Royal Decree declaring the agreement generally binding if said agreement no longer reflects the situation or fulfils the conditions justifying its establishment. The Crown can never repeal a collective agreement on its own initiative.

Extension of a collective labour agreement is indivisible. Therefore, the Crown cannot select certain provisions and declare generally binding only those meeting its approval.

The practice of extending general binding effect differs from sector to sector and is directly linked to the unions' representativeness. It is rarely used in sectors with high degrees of unionism because the unions are strong enough to have the agreement enforced by their members.

SECTION 10. INTERPRETATION OF COLLECTIVE LABOUR AGREEMENTS

Disputes on the interpretation of one or more provisions can be solved by the parties in two ways.

Firstly, they can refer the matter to the labour tribunal. The tribunal's interpretation of the contested clause is binding on the parties. Secondly, they can hold additional, interpretative negotiations leading to the conclusion of a complementary collective labour agreement. The latter does not confer any new advantages; it only seeks to clarify the original agreement.

A collective labour agreement not declared generally binding should be regarded as an agreement, whereas a collective labour agreement declared generally binding should rather be seen as a regulation.

SECTION 11. COLLECTIVE LABOUR AGREEMENTS AT ENTREPRISE LEVEL

§ 1. CIRCUMSTANCES LEADING TO THE CONCLUSION OF A COLLECTIVE LABOUR AGREEMENT AT ENTERPRISE LEVEL

There are two possibilities:

- the matter set out in the collective labour agreement at enterprise level is also dealt with in a collective labour agreement at branch or national multi-industry level. The agreement at enterprise level must be either complementary or contain more favourable regulations for workers; or
- the matter has not been dealt with in a collective labour agreement. In such cases the parties are totally free to conclude an agreement, insofar as the provisions are not contrary to public policy or morality and the law's mandatory provisions.

The agreement's provisions cease to apply and are replaced by new provisions when a collective labour agreement more favourable to the workers is concluded at sectoral or multi-industry level.

§ 2. PERSONS COMPETENT TO CONCLUDE A COLLECTIVE LABOUR AGREEMENT AT ENTERPRISE LEVEL

A. *Employers*

An individual employer – not necessarily belonging to a representative employers' association – can conclude a collective agreement for his enterprise. He is not obliged to conclude it himself and can mandate other persons to act on his behalf.

B. *Workers*

The union delegation as such is not authorised to conclude a collective agreement autonomously. Only the mandator of the representative union (usually the regional union secretary) can bind his organisation.

The union delegation may participate in negotiations and co-sign the agreement.

A collective labour agreement concluded by an employer and a union delegation not mandated by the organisation has the legal force of custom or a unilateral employer's engagement at the most.

§ 3. NEGOTIATORS

Given that negotiations held with a view to concluding a collective labour agreement do not take place in a joint body, the number of members does not play a part in this respect. The employer can be assisted by persons he considers useful in the negotiations: experts, representatives of an employers' federation, etc. The same applies to the members of the union delegation. In principle, therefore, the negotiation group is free to choose its composition, unless the agreement's provisions state otherwise.

§ 4. VALIDITY CONDITIONS

See above.

§ 5. CAN AN EMPLOYER HOLD VALID NEGOTIATIONS WITH ONLY ONE REPRESENTATIVE UNION?

The definition given in Article 5 of the Collective Labour Agreements Act does not oblige employers to involve all representative unions in the conclusion of a collective labour agreement. On the contrary, the wording reveals that one sole trade union can conclude a valid agreement with an employer.

SECTION 12. CONTROL AND PENAL PROVISIONS

The Collective Labour Agreements Act is enforced by the officers of the judicial police and officials appointed by the Crown. These officials can carry out inspections, investigations and surveys deemed necessary for the exercise of their duties.

Any employer found guilty of obstructing inspections or failing to comply with a collective labour agreement will be punished by a fine and/or prison sentence. Only failure to respect collective labour agreements declared generally binding is punishable.

IV
FUNDS FOR SOCIAL SECURITY[382]

Employers and employees can set up a fund for social security at sectoral level. On the basis of a collective labour agreement, agreements are concluded concerning payments to this fund. The money in question can be used for various purposes:

- financing, granting and paying social benefits (e.g. trade union bonuses);
- financing and organising vocational training for employees and youngsters; or
- financing and ensuring the health and safety of the employees.

The funds have legal personality; they are jointly managed by representatives of both the employers and the employees.

In certain sectors (such as the building sector) the financial obligations of the fund are quite demanding. This is a consequence of, amongst others, the fact that (re)training, for instance, is fully organised via the fund. These costs (in addition to the social security contributions) lead to an increase in the labour costs, thus encouraging moonlighting. Another problem concerns the benefits for union members. Some sectors provide supplements to the unemployment benefits in the event of economic unemployment, although these are limited to members of the representative trade unions. Sooner or later, this practice may very well clash with the prohibition of discrimination.

382 Law of 7 January 1958 concerning the social security funds, *BS/MB* 7 February 1958.

V

INDUSTRIAL ACTION[383]

Belgian law does not have a legal definition of industrial disputes. Whilst recognising the existence and need to prevent such conflicts, the legislature has not specified the characteristics that would distinguish them from individual conflicts.

CHAPTER 1

STRIKES, LOCK-OUTS AND FACTORY OCCUPATION

SECTION 1. STRIKES

Article 1 of the Essential Services Act describes a 'strike' as a 'collective and temporary decision of workers to stop working'. This implies that:

- employees temporarily cease to fulfil their contractual obligation to work. A partial or alternative resumption does not suffice;
- strikes are collective. A one-man strike does not constitute a strike (unless the enterprise has only one employee);
- the cessation of work is only temporary. Strikers go back to work when the strike has ended; and
- a striker is a person who has ceased his/her contractual obligations. Members on a picket line are therefore not necessarily strikers.

Case law and doctrine often refer to the definition given in the Dictionary of Social Legislation: 'A voluntary and un-coerced decision taken by all or a group of workers to deliberately stop working temporarily as a means of achieving a specific objective.' As this text never became legally binding, its definition is indicative only.

---

383 Vannes, V., *Le droit de grève*, Brussels, Larcier, 2013, 864 pp.; Van Gehuchten, P.P. and others, *Actualités du dialogue social et droit de grève*, Waterloo, Wolters Kluwer, 2009, 388 pp.

Strikes can be subdivided according to their:

- objective: professional strikes, solidarity strikes and political strikes;
- origin: regular strikes, spontaneous strikes and wildcat strikes; and
- the methods used: 'ordinary' strikes, work-to-rule strikes, lightning strikes, selective strikes, plant occupations, boycotts, go-slow strikes, etc.

In the past, the type of strike used affected the courts' view of collective action. However, the Court of Cassation ended this situation with its principle ruling of 21 December 1981.[384, 385]

§ 1. LEGAL POSITION

Before the Act of 24 May 1921, it was considered a criminal offence to organise and participate in a strike.[386] Although the sanction under public law was repealed by the 1921 Act, striking remained an offence under civil law.

Initially, participating in a strike was considered to be a breach of contract, but not serious enough to warrant a unilateral termination of the contract of employment. Strikers were often dismissed for just cause. The answer to the question of whether or not all forms of professional collaboration had become impossible depended on the nature of the work stoppage. Regular strikes (i.e. recognised by the representative unions and respecting the obligation of social peace and the conciliation procedure) were considered legal. Taking part in such actions did not justify dismissal for just cause. Spontaneous strikes (i.e. recognised by the representative unions, but not respecting the social peace obligation and conciliation procedure) were often regarded as unlawful. Wild-cat strikes started by officials not recognised by the union and not respecting conciliation procedures were regarded as unlawful by the courts, as were political and solidarity strikes. However, some case law upheld the legitimacy principle of strikes and rejected all distinctions between lawful and unlawful strike as lacking a legal basis.

In its rulings of 21 December 1981, the Court of Cassation concluded the following on the basis of Article 3 of the Essential Services Act:

[384] Cass. 21 December 1981, *Pas.* 1982, I, p. 531.
[385] See below.
[386] See below.

- by virtue of Article 3 of the Essential Supplies and Services Act in Peacetime of 19 August 1948,[387, 388] workers have the right to derogate from Article 1134 of the Civil Code and not perform their work due to a strike;
- taking part in a strike does not constitute an illegal act as such; and
- there is no legal provision forbidding workers from participating in a strike that has not been organised or recognised by an official union.

A strike usually signals the beginning of industrial action. Workers not only stop working; they also hand out pamphlets, block access to the company, harass non-strikers, etc. Such acts can constitute grounds for dismissal when violence is used. Although the Court of Cassation has not ruled on such matters, they can constitute grounds for dismissal for just cause. However, the courts may take into account exceptional circumstances of a particular case.

Certain authors defend the viewpoint that dismissal for just cause is justified when participation in a strike violates penal law and/or the striker abuses his/her right to strike. The latter hypothesis is particularly controversial.

A worker taking part in a strike is in breach of his/her employment contract and therefore is not entitled to pay during the period he/she is on strike. If the strike is officially recognised by the union, an indemnity is paid from a strike fund. These indemnities are not benefits or replacement income.

§ 2. EFFECTS OF STRIKES ON THE CONTRACT OF EMPLOYMENT OF NON-STRIKERS

The contract of employment of the non-striker is suspended because the employer has failed in his obligation to employ the worker. However, the question is whether the non-striker is entitled to wages for the days he/she wanted to work but was prevented from doing so owing to the strike. A distinction is made according to the nature of the strike.

Article 27 of the Employment Contract Act provides that workers who are unable to get to work due to circumstances beyond their control are entitled to guaranteed daily wages if they can prove that the circumstances preventing them from working were beyond their control. Full wages are therefore due when an employee is late for work or not able to turn up at all due to a public transport workers' strike.

387 *BS/MB* 21 August 1948.
388 Hereinafter Essential Services Act.

Article 27, paragraph 2 of the Employment Contract Act states that a worker who is capable of work and arrives at the workplace, but is unable to work due to circumstances beyond his/her control is entitled to his full daily wage. However, the law adds that a full daily wage is not due if the circumstances preventing that person from working are caused by industrial action. This covers both strikes within and outside the enterprise.

However, the Employment Contract Act does not provide a solution for the days following the first strike day. The question of whether or not a non-striker willing to work is entitled to compensation is a civil law issue.

Employers are under a contractual obligation to employ their workers. Failure to meet this obligation constitutes a fault and is subject to the payment of compensation to the worker. He/she can claim the earnings and the additional advantages lost as a result of the strike. The employer can only be exempted if he can prove that for him the strike constituted a *force majeure*.

In practice, employers sometimes pay non-strikers – even if they cannot put them to work – to compromise the strike.

SECTION 2. LOCK-OUT[389]

In 1984,[390] the Court of Cassation confined lock-out to two cases. It can only be used if industrial action coincides with *force majeure* or if it fits in the framework of *exceptio non adimpleti contractus*. We believe this ruling has been superseded by the ratification of the Revised European Social Charter.

Indeed, despite the fact that the exclusion is not explicitly mentioned in Article 6 of the Revised European Social Charter, employers are generally held to have this right to collective action. With the exception of Article 31, no conditions are imposed on lock-outs. This suggests that a limitation is only possible through the intervention of the legislator, something which has not yet happened.

389 Humblet, P., 'Lockout: A Dadaist Study of a Relic(t)' in F. Pennings, Y. Konijn and A. Veldman, *Social Responsibility in Labour Relations*, Alphen aan den Rijn, Kluwer Law International, 2008, pp. 479–493.

390 Cass. 7 May 1984, *JTT* 1984, p. 292.

SECTION 3. FACTORY OCCUPATION[391]

The concept of factory occupation covers all forms of industrial action occurring in the workplace. Four types of occupation can be distinguished:

1. occupation of the enterprise without a take-over when there is still a contract of employment. This is a strike at the workplace;
2. occupation of the enterprise with a production take-over when the contract of employment still applies;
3. occupation of the enterprise without a production take-over after termination of the contract of employment; and
4. occupation of the enterprise with production take-over after termination of the contract of employment.

It is extremely difficult and complex to assess whether an occupation is lawful or not. First of all, the issue of liability is involved. Only the first two types of occupation fall under the scope of labour law. When assessing the lawfulness of these forms of occupation it is important to consider not only property law. Article 6(4) of the Revised European Social Charter does not only recognise strikes at work but also other forms of collective industrial action provided they respect earlier concluded collective labour agreements.

Employers usually react to such forms of industrial action by going to court[392] and getting an eviction order.

[391] Lagasse, F. and Vannes, V., 'Occupation d'entreprise, voie de fait et pouvoir judiciaire', *JTT* 1988, pp. 105–114; Magrez, M., 'L'occupation d'usine: une voie de fait répréhensible ou l'exercice d'un droit', *RCJB* 1968, pp. 403–418; Martens, P., 'A propos des occupations d'entreprise', *Jur. Liège* 1986, pp. 593–594; Taquet, M. and Wantiez, C., 'De la licéité de l'occupation d'usine', *JTT* 1977, pp. 189–196.

[392] See below.

CHAPTER 2

SETTLEMENT OF INDUSTRIAL CONFLICTS BY MEDIATION AND CONCILIATION[393]

SECTION 1. CONCILIATION AND MEDIATION

Mediation means settling a dispute with the help of an objective third party. It usually covers dispute resolution procedures such as arbitration and reconciliation.

In arbitration, a third person is asked to issue an opinion on the grievances of the conflicting parties on the basis of the information given to him. His opinion is legally binding on the two parties.

In the case of conciliation, the intervention of the third party or mediator goes much further: he is expected to reconcile the conflicting parties.

Arbitration is almost never used as a dispute resolution mechanism in Belgian industrial relations. The legislator and the social partners have clearly opted for conciliation.

SECTION 2. CONCILIATION PROCEDURES

As in most other Western European legal systems, Belgium has no legal conciliation framework for the uniform settlement of industrial disputes.

However, in most sectors the social partners have developed dispute resolution procedures. These are outlined in collective labour agreements or the rules of the joint committees and their conciliation and mediation services.

---

393 Rigaux, M. and Humblet, P., *Conciliation, médiation et arbitrage. Vers une régulation européenne des modes alternatifs du règlement des conflits (collectifs) du travail?*, Brussels, Bruylant, 2011, 268 pp.

Conciliation procedures may figure in purely procedural collective labour agreements or in collective agreements establishing the legal status of the union delegation. In certain branches of industry the procedures are linked to the social peace obligation clause included in the collective labour agreement establishing the setting up and financing of a sectoral social security fund. If workers fail to respect the procedure in the case of an industrial dispute, employers stop their contributions to the said fund.

Most of the of conciliation procedures are similar. As a general rule, they consist of the following elements:

1. meeting between the union delegation and the head of the enterprise;
2. full-time union officials and employer representatives are informed of the negotiations at enterprise level;
3. intervention of the joint committee's conciliation bureau;
4. negotiation in the joint committee;
5. a second attempt at conciliation;
6. notice of strike or lock-out; and
7. intervention by the official (social) conciliator.

SECTION 3. CONCILIATION BODIES

§ 1. VOLUNTARY OR COMPULSORY CONCILIATION

The conflicting parties are free to accept or reject the conciliation.

Although in principle any person or body can act as conciliator provided they are accepted by both parties, the State and the social partners have set up a special procedure for conciliation purposes. This includes both bodies with a conciliatory mission and (government) officials entrusted with the task of conciliation.

§ 2. INFORMAL CONCILIATION: CONCILIATORY BODIES

A certain number of bodies governed by public law are mandated with the task of conciliation, i.e. the National Labour Council, joint committees and joint sub-committees. However, the National Labour Council only uses its conciliatory competence in exceptional circumstances.

Article 10 of the Decree Law of 9 June 1945 granted joint committees a conciliatory mission. In addition to adopting the principles of this Decree Law, the Collective

Labour Agreements Act extended the joint committees' competence. In practice these committees were not always sufficiently armed to complete their mission successfully.

Current legislation has also granted them a conciliatory mission. They are moreover legally obliged to set up a conciliation bureau, i.e. a place where employers and employees can meet and confer at any time. The internal regulations of the board often set out the conciliation procedure.

In addition to governmental bodies we need to mention conciliation bodies set up by the social partners.

§ 3. LABOUR CONCILIATORS

The State appoints officials to mediate between conflicting parties.

Although labour inspectors have jurisdiction to conciliate in industrial disputes, they rarely do so in practice. Labour conciliators are *the* specialists in terms of conciliation. Article 2 of the Royal Decree of 27 July 1964[394] defines the tasks of these officials as follows:

> 'The labour conciliator should:
> - inform the Minister of Employment of industrial conflicts;
> - monitor and help to prevent industrial disputes and follow the outbreak, course and ending of such disputes;
> - start a conciliation procedure, either on their own initiative or at the request of either party;
> - keep up permanent contact with employers' associations and trade unions and with the labour and employment inspectors of the Ministry of Employment;
> - compile all reports on labour relations in an industry, a branch of industry or a particular enterprise.'

Labour conciliators can therefore intervene in all industrial disputes at any time. In practice, however, they usually intervene only when negotiations have stalled or if there is no conciliation procedure.

Labour conciliators can intervene on their own initiative, at the request of the Minister, employers, employers' organisations, or unions. They cannot refuse requests for conciliation.

394 *BS/MB* 12 August 1964.

CHAPTER 3

REGULATIONS FOR SETTLING INDUSTRIAL DISPUTES

SECTION 1. THE ESSENTIAL SUPPLIES AND SERVICES IN PEACETIME ACT OF 19 AUGUST 1948[395]

After the Second World War, the Decree Law of 12 April 1945 prohibited strikes to facilitate the rebuilding of Belgium's war-ravaged economy.

As this law limited a number of civil liberties it soon provoked considerable dissatisfaction amongst workers. It was repealed following union pressure and replaced by the Essential Services Act.

The law sought to find a formula respecting the general interest whilst safeguarding individual liberties and freedom of association.

However, it is important to note that the Essential Services Act is not truly a requisitioning law, but a conflict management model for the social partners. Joint committees play a very important role because they essentially decide which needs and services are vital and how they should be assured. The State only intervenes when the parties are unable to agree.

SECTION 2. SCOPE OF THE ACT

This act only applies to the private sector, provided the parties fall under the jurisdiction of a joint committee.

The public sector and all the enterprises not governed by a joint committee therefore do not fall under its scope. In the past, however, the State used this act a number of times (*contra legem)* to requisition public servants.

---

[395] Defalque, M., 'Les prestations d'intérêt public en temps de paix', *Rev.Trav.* 1960, pp. 1744–1755; Magrez, M., 'Le régime des prestations d'intérêt public en temps de paix', *JT* 1963, pp. 685-689.

SECTION 3. THE CONCEPT 'VITAL GOODS AND ESSENTIAL SERVICES'

Parliamentary documents on the Act of 19 August 1948 defines essential services as follows: 'private activities leading to the production of vital goods, necessary for the population, or activities forming a vital part of production or distribution, or relating to the distribution of these services meeting the population's fundamental needs'.[396]

Rather than defining the concept, the legislator chose instead to enumerate the characteristics of vital goods and essential services.

SECTION 4. LEGISLATIVE MECHANISMS

§ 1. DEFINITION OF VITAL GOODS AND ESSENTIAL SERVICES

The law provides three ways of determining vital goods and essential services.

A. *Joint committees identify vital goods and essential services*

As regards those enterprises falling under their jurisdiction, joint committees have a duty to identify and define the arrangements, supplies and services that must be maintained in the event of collective and voluntary stoppage of work or collective lay-off of employees (lock-out), in order to meet certain vital needs, to carry out urgent work on machinery or material (plant) and to perform certain tasks as a result of *force majeure* or an unforeseen necessity. Joint committees shall also be responsible for identifying these vital goods.[397]

Coordinated decisions of a joint committee can be made legally binding by Royal Decree at the request of the Minister of Employment.[398]

To facilitate decision-making within the joint bodies the legislator abandoned the rule of unanimity. Decisions are now valid provided they receive 75% of the votes of each side.[399]

396 *Documents parlementaires* Chamber 1947–48, No 414.
397 Article 1 of the Essential Services Act.
398 Article 2 of the Essential Services Act.
399 *Ibid.*

B. The Minister requests the joint committee to identify vital supplies and services

If the joint committee has not decided what supplies and services are vital, the Minister can submit a request to this end. The former has six months to perform this task.

C. Definition of vital needs and services by the Minister of Employment

If the joint committee fails to take a decision within the six-month term or does not obtain the required majority, the Crown (i.e. the Minister of Employment) will establish what needs are vital and the arrangements, tasks or services that have to be guaranteed.[400] The same procedure has to be followed for sectors that do not have a joint committee. The Minister of Employment therefore plays a supplementary role and only intervenes when the joint committee is unable to fulfil its task. Moreover, he/she has seek prior advice from the National Labour Council. In addition, the said decision will have to be discussed by the council of ministers.

§ 2. IMPLEMENTATION OF DECISIONS

Workers and employers decide after mutual consultation which workers will have to assure vital goods and services.

Joint committees can agree to appoint members by a select committee to oversee the implementation of binding decisions in the industry concerned, in a group of enterprises or in a single enterprise. This committee is composed of an equal number of employers' and employees' representatives.

If there is disagreement between the employer(s) and employees on the matter, this select committee can be authorised to designate the individuals needed to guarantee the vital needs.

If no select committee was set up, or if it failed to implement the decisions, the Minister of Employment or the Minister of Economic Affairs can intervene and appoint persons to requisition employees and assure the implementation thereof.

In order to prevent strike-breaking by employers, only workers employed in the enterprise concerned may be designated.

[400] Article 2*bis* of the Essential Services Act.

SECTION 5. THE LEGAL POSITION OF REQUISITIONED WORKERS

When workers have been requisitioned, they are not subject to the provisions of an employment contract. However, Article 6, paragraphs 1 and 2 of the Essential Services Act nevertheless stipulates that the assurance of vital needs and services does not modify the nature or the conditions of the employment contract. In other words, the worker has been forced to execute the contract of employment. He/she cannot be regarded as a striker and, therefore, is entitled to pay if he/she carries out his/her normal duties.

SECTION 6. PROHIBITION TO DISMISS WORKERS REQUISITIONED TO ASSURE VITAL GOODS AND SERVICES

Notice cannot be served on workers requisitioned to assure goods and services unless the employer has been granted permission by the Minister or the select committee referred to above.

CHAPTER 4
SETTLEMENT OF INDUSTRIAL DISPUTES BY THE COURTS[401]

SECTION 1. GENERAL OVERVIEW

Since the mid-1980s, employers have occasionally turned to the courts to seek judicial intervention in industrial disputes. For example, when a plant is blocked by a picket line, the court is asked to forbid this on the grounds of, among other things, the right to work.

The majority of legal scholars believe that it is not incumbent on the judiciary to settle industrial disputes. Such conflicts should be solved through the appropriate channels, for example conciliation bureaus.

As a rule, employers never ask the courts to end an industrial dispute, but to stop certain forms of strike action which are held to violate subjective rights – qualified by some as 'acts of violence'. Refusal to intervene would constitute a breach of Article 6(1) of the Convention for the Protection of Human Rights and Fundamental Freedoms, and Article 14 of the International Covenant on Civil and Political Rights. Nowadays the courts' intervention is no longer contested.

SECTION 2. PROCEDURE

The question arises as to which court has jurisdiction. Although labour tribunals would seem the most appropriate, employers usually appeal to courts of first instance. Employers generally apply for a summary procedure by means of *ex-parte* proceedings. They resort to such action because, unlike in the Netherlands, for example, they cannot prosecute the unions involved in collective action because these have no legal personality and because the identity of the members of the striking pickets is often unknown.

401 Demez, G., 'La judiciarisation des conflits collectifs', in Arcq, E., Capron, M., Leonard, E. and Reman, P. (eds.), *Dynamiques de la concertation sociale*, Brussels, CRISP, 2010, pp. 487–511.

Employers claim damages to ensure that striking pickets follow the opponent's instructions. Amounts vary.

If the court follows the employer's reasoning, the former will order the picketers to end their action.

This order is remitted to a bailiff. The latter takes the writ to the enterprise where the industrial dispute is taking place and serves it on the persons guilty of the alleged offence.

To ensure compliance with the court order, the plaintiff will usually request the police to check the picketers' identities. Refusal to comply with this request may result in the payment of damages.

The procedure described here is very effective and is contested for various reasons. In the past, some courts did not verify the facts, and employers were taken on their word. Heavily criticised in doctrine, this practice seems to have been relegated to the past.

In its report of 11 July 2002, the European Committee of Social Rights, a committee of experts operating within the framework of the Revised European Social Charter, censured the Belgian legislature because Belgian courts had issued a number of rulings preventing workers from striking. It was particularly critical of the fact that the courts' rulings were based on abuse of the law, and/or the principle of proportionality. It is not up to the courts to decide on the desirability of a strike.

In 2009, the three representative trade unions and the European Trade Union Confederation filed a complaint against Belgium, stating that court interference in collective disputes is in conflict with Article 6, para. 4 ESC.[402, 403]

On 4 April 2012, the Committee of Ministers of the Council of Europe partly followed the trade unions' reasoning.[404] The Belgian government passed this matter on to the social partners. To date, however, no solution has been found.

402 Complaint No 59/2009, www.coe.int/t/dghl/monitoring/socialcharter/Complaints/Complaints_en.asp.

403 Dejonghe, D. and Raepsaet, F., 'L'intervention du juge des référes sur requête unilatérale en cas de conflit collectif : contraire à la Charte sociale européenne ?', *RDS* 2013, pp. 75–169; Neven, J.F., 'Les piquets de grève, la procédure sur requête unilatérale et les pouvoirs du juge des référés après la décision du Comité européen des droits sociaux du 13 septembre 2011', *RDS* 2012, pp. 389–428.
Neven, J.F., 'Les interventions judiciaires en cas de grève après la décision du Comité Européen des droits sociaux du 13 septembre 2011' in E. Plasschaert and O. Rijckaert (dir.), *Le droit social en chantier(s)*, Brussels, Larcier, Conférence du jeune barreau de Bruxelles, 2012, pp. 233–310.

404 Https://wcd.coe.int/ViewDoc.jsp?Ref=CM/ResChS(2012)3&Language=lanEnglish&Site=CM&BackColorInternet=C3C3C3&BackColorIntranet=EDB021&BackColorLogged=F5D383.

IN CAUDA

When this book was written in the spring of 2016, it became known that within the government there were plans to reform labour law thoroughly. In this reform the emphasis would be on more flexibility on the part of the employee (especially) with regard to working hours, a change of the rules and regulations with regard to telework and dismissal law. The termination pay will probably be replaced by a transition pay which is meant to support the employee in finding a new job. However, it is still unclear how these principles will/can be transposed into legislation.

GENERAL BIBLIOGRAPHY

This bibliography only contains references to books that give a general introduction to (certain aspects) Belgian labour law and/or give an overview of Belgian industrial relations.

IN DUTCH

HUMBLET, P., JANVIER, R., RAUWS, W. and RIGAUX, M., *Synopsis van het Belgisch arbeidsrecht*, Antwerp, Intersentia, 2014, 410 p. (triennial update).

LENAERTS, H., *Inleiding tot het sociaal recht*, Antwerp, Kluwer, 1995, 662 pp.

VAN EECKHOUTTE, W., *Sociaal Compendium Arbeidsrecht*, Mechelen, Wolters Kluwer (updated annually).

VAN EECKHOUTTE, W., *Sociaal Zakboekje*, Mechelen, Wolters Kluwer (updated twice a year).

IN FRENCH

ARCQ, E., *La concertation sociale*, Brussels, Dossier du CRISP, 2008, 134 pp.

ARCQ, E., CAPRON, M., LEONARD, E. and REMAN, P. (red.), *Dynamiques de la concertation sociale*, Brussels, CRISP, 2010, 609 pp.

CHLEPNER, B.S., *Cent ans d'Histoire Sociale en Belgique*, Brussels, Institut de sociologie Solvay, 1956, 429 pp.

CLESSE, J. and KEFER, F., *Manuel de droit du travail*, Brussels, Larcier, 2014, 544 pp.

FRANÇOIS, L., *Introduction au droit social*, Liège, Faculté de droit, 1974, 190 pp.

FRANÇOIS, L., *Théorie des relations collectives du travail en droit belge*, Brussels, Bruylant, 1980, 388 pp.

HUMBLET, P., JANVIER, R., RAUWS, W., RIGAUX, M. and LAUVAUX, V., *Aperçu du droit du travail belge*, Brussels, Bruylant, 2004, 460 pp.

MAGREZ-SONG, G., 'Un siècle de relations collectives de travail', in P. VAN DER VORST (ed.), *Cent ans de droit social belge*, Brussels, Bruylant, 1986, pp. 279–318.

PIRON, J. and DENIS, P., *Le droit des relations collectives du travail en Belgique*, Brussels, Larcier, 1970, 301 pp.

VAN DER VORST, P. (ed.), *A l'enseigne du droit social belge*, Brussels, Ed. de l'ULB, 1978, 392 pp.

VANNES, V., *Le droit de grève*, Brussels, Larcier, 2013, 840 pp.

IN ENGLISH

Blanpain, R., 'Belgium', in *International Encyclopedia for Labour Law and Industrial Relations*, Deventer, Kluwer Law International, loose-leaf.

Blanpain, R., *European Employment and Industrial Relations Glossary Belgium*, European Foundation for the Improvement of Living and Working Conditions, London, Sweet and Maxwell - Luxembourg, Office for Official Publications of the European Communities, 1992, 238 pp.

J. Rombouts, 'Belgium: Promoted within a Coordinated Industrial Relations System', in Y. Ghellab and D. Vaughan-Whitehead (eds.), *Sectoral Social Dialogue in Future EU Member States: The Weakest Link*, Budapest, International Labour Office, 2003, pp. 43–76.

IN GERMAN

Humblet, P., 'Neuerungen im belgischen Arbeitsrecht in den Jahren 2006 bis 2009', *Europäische Zeitschrift für Arbeitsrecht*, 2010/2, pp. 266–276.

Humblet, P. and Plets, I., 'Neuerungen im belgischen Arbeitsrecht in den Jahren 2010 bis 2013', *Europäische Zeitschrift für Arbeitsrecht*, 2014/2, pp. 405–412.

E-ADDRESSES

NATIONAL AND INTERNATIONAL TRADE UNION ORGANISATIONS

ABVV-FGTB	www.abvv.be
ACLVB-CGSLB	www.aclvb.be
ACOD-CGSP	www.acod.be
ACV-CSC	www.acv-online.be
BBTK-CETCA	http://bbtk.org
CCOD-CCSP	www.acv-online.be
ICFTU	www.icftu.org
LBC-CNE	http://lbc-nvk.acv-online.be
VSOA-SLFP	www.vsoa.be and www.slfp.be
WCL	www.cmt-wcl.org

NATIONAL AND INTERNATIONAL EMPLOYERS' ORGANISATIONS

IOE	www.ioe-emp.org
UNICE	www.unice.org
UWE	www.uwe.be
VBO-FEB	www.vbo-feb.be
VEV	www.voka.be
VKW	www.vkw.be

ORGANS OF THE PBO-OED (PUBLIC LAW INDUSTRIAL REGULATORY BODY)

CESRW	www.cesrw.be
CRB-CCE	www.ccerb.fgov.be
NAR-CNT	www.nar-cnt.be
SERV	www.serv.be

GOVERNMENT SITES

General site	www.fgov.be
Federal Public Service Employment, Labour and Social Dialogue	www.meta.fgov.be
National Office for Social Security	www.socialsecurity.fgov.be

LEGISLATION AND JURISPRUDENCE

www.belgielex.be

www.ingramcontent.com/pod-product-compliance
Ingram Content Group UK Ltd.
Pitfield, Milton Keynes, MK11 3LW, UK
UKHW051921100926
8556IPUK00021B/1300

9 781780 684